❦

The Secret Diary of
Elisabeth Leseur

Elisabeth Leseur

The Secret Diary of Elisabeth Leseur

The Woman Whose Goodness
Changed Her Husband
from Atheist to Priest

SOPHIA INSTITUTE PRESS®
Manchester, New Hampshire

The Secret Diary of Elisabeth Leseur is a combined edition of *My Spirit Rejoices* (Manchester, New Hampshire: Sophia Institute Press, 1996) and *Light in the Darkness* (Manchester, New Hampshire: Sophia Institute Press, 1998).

Sophia Institute Press®
Box 5284, Manchester, NH 03108
1-800-888-9344
www.sophiainstitute.com

Library of Congress Cataloging-in-Publication Data

Leseur, Elisabeth, 1866-1914.
  [Journal et pensées de chaque jour. English]
  The secret diary of Elisabeth Leseur : the woman whose goodness
    changed her husband from atheist to priest.
      p. cm.
  First work originally published: My spirit rejoices. c1996. 2nd work
    originally published: Light in the darkness. c1998.
  Includes bibliographical references.
  ISBN 1-928832-48-2 (pbk. : alk. paper)
  1. Leseur, Elisabeth, 1866-1914 — Diaries. 2. Catholics — France
    Diaries. 3. Wives — France — Diaries. 4. Catholic Church
    Apologetic works. I. Leseur, Elisabeth, 1866-1914. Vie spirituelle.
    English. II. Title.
  BX4705.L6117 A3 2002
  282'.092 — dc21   2001008051

06 07 08 09 10 9 8 7 6 5 4

Contents

⚛

Chronology

Elisabeth Leseur

Felix Leseur

— *At home in Paris, 1910* —

❧

The lives of
Elisabeth and Felix Leseur

1861
March 22: The birth of Felix Leseur.

1866
October 16: The birth of Pauline Elisabeth Arrighi.

1879
May 15: Elisabeth receives her first Holy Communion,
followed the next day by Confirmation.

1887
Elisabeth meets Felix at the home of mutual friends.

1889
May 23: Elisabeth and Felix are officially engaged.
July 31: Elisabeth and Felix are married.
September: Elisabeth falls ill with an intestinal
abscess, which never fully heals.

1893
Elisabeth and Felix travel to Italy.

1896
April-May: Elisabeth and Felix travel
to Tunisia and Algeria. Elisabeth experiences
a crisis of faith and abandons religion.

1897

Elisabeth and Felix tour the Austro-Hungarian Empire.

1898

Elisabeth returns to the practice of the Faith.

1899

Summer: Elisabeth and Felix visit Russia, Turkey, and Greece.

1899

Spring-Summer: Elisabeth and Felix travel to
Spain, Morocco, and Germany.

1901

Summer: Elisabeth and Felix visit Holland;
Elisabeth's liver problems begin.

1902

Elisabeth and Felix construct a summer house at Jougne.

1903

March: Elisabeth meets Fr. R. P. Hébert, O.P.,
her future spiritual director.

1903

April: Elisabeth and Felix travel to Rome for Holy Week;
she has an audience with Pope Leo XIII and formally
consecrates her life to God in St. Peter's.

1905

April 13: Elisabeth's sister Juliette dies of tuberculosis.

1907

Autumn: Elisabeth suffers renewed liver troubles; her
doctors require her to adopt a regimen of rest and quiet.

1911

April 10: Surgeons remove a cancerous
tumor from Elisabeth's breast.

1912

June: Accompanied by Felix, Elisabeth
makes a pilgrimage to Lourdes.

1913

February-March: Symptoms of Elisabeth's cancer recur.
July: Elisabeth's final decline begins.

1914

May 3: Elisabeth Leseur dies in the arms of Felix.

1915

Felix reconciles to the Catholic Church.

1917

Spring: Felix publishes Elisabeth's
Journal et pensées de chaque jour.

1919

Felix enters the novitiate of the Dominican order.

1923

March 23: Felix takes final monastic vows.

1923

July 8: Felix is ordained to the priesthood.

1924-1942

Felix travels throughout Europe giving talks about Elisabeth's
doctrine and her apostolate and publishes more of her writings.
At the urging of Felix and others, the Church initiates the
process for Elisabeth's canonization. World War II and
Felix's declining health soon interrupt these efforts.

1950

February 27: Felix Leseur dies.

1990

The Church reopens the cause for Elisabeth's canonization.

The cause for the
canonization of Elisabeth Leseur
is being handled in Rome by:

Fr. Innocenzo Venchi, O.P.
Postulator Generalis
Curia Generalizia dei Padri Domenicani
Convento Santa Sabina (Aventino)
Piazza Pietro d'Illiria, 1
00153 Roma (Italia)
Telephone: (39) 6 57 941
Fax: (39) 6 57 50 675
e-mail: postulatio@dominicans.it

✑

In Memoriam

by Felix Leseur

"My God, have pity on us, on me!"
(Elisabeth's prayer during her suffering)

By the time this volume appears, I shall have left the world, and entered the novitiate of the Order of Friars Preachers. The evolution of my soul and of my whole existence since the age of four and a half years will then have reached its logical termination.

It is always wonderful and impressive to contemplate the action of God's grace, and to see how sweet and strong — and at the same time how simple and human — are the means He employs to guide a man to the path designed for him from the beginning. God alone acts, utilizing and rewarding the prayers sent up, the sacrifices and sufferings accepted and sometimes voluntarily sought and offered up for the conversion of a soul. He alone takes possession of the soul and claims it for His service.

My beloved wife, Elisabeth, prayed incessantly for my return to the Faith and to the practice of religion; day by day for this intention did she accept and offer up all her privations, sacrifices, trials, sufferings, and at the end, even her death.[1]

---

[1] Elisabeth Leseur died of cancer on May 3, 1914.

But she did this secretly, for she never argued with me and never spoke to me of the supernatural side of her life, save by her example. She carried out herself the advice that she gave in her *Journal*: "Let us not think that by our personal action we can hasten the coming of God's Kingdom in souls. As soon as the divine hour has come, our efforts will be useless, or rather they will only be an active prayer, an appeal to Him who transforms and saves. Nevertheless, let us make this appeal to Him with the humble conviction that He alone will do what must be done, and will bring life to the souls for which we act and pray."

I have, since her death, learned to appreciate the eloquence and persuasive power of her silence. God heard the constant prayer that it concealed and, when the sacrifice was fully accomplished, answered it abundantly. In His infinite goodness, He allowed the silence to be broken after Elisabeth's death, so that she spoke to and instructed me in my innermost thoughts, as she would never have done in life, and very often I might have exclaimed, "Being dead, she speaketh." But above all, her intercession, when it became more direct and more powerful, called forth our divine Lord's grace and mercy, so that He let my poor soul hear His voice.

God has completed the conversion which was begun in me by the shining influence of my holy companion, Elisabeth, and which was determined by reading her writings, particularly her *Journal* and *Thoughts*, which I found after her death and which are presented in this volume, along with a number of her other writings.

⚭

The genesis of these pages

These pages were not written day by day, but, rather, when their author, impelled by an inner compulsion, felt the need to pour out in secret the thoughts and emotions that filled her heart.

And although she gave one of her manuscripts the name of *Journal*, it is not a journal in the true sense of the word. She wrote irregularly, often at long intervals; little is related of the events of her life.

Strictly speaking, Elisabeth's *Journal* is the history of a soul, noting the principal stages of its evolution, a kind of examination of conscience set down by hand at odd moments. And as the author wrote for herself alone, this conscience disclosed itself to God in all simplicity, truth, and freedom, without a thought of style or of composition. It will be seen how absent is literary artifice from these pages, so perfect in form, so sublime in inspiration, so devoid of effort and affectation. Just as her thoughts came to her she put them down, as fast as her pen would write, in a flowing hand, with nothing added later and hardly a word crossed out, showing no sign of effort, but only the impulse of the spirit.

I did not suspect the existence of this journal; it was revealed to me only after the writer's death, by her sister to whom she had given some passages from it in confidence — a single, happy, and providential act of trust by which the manuscript was saved. The author, in her humble modesty, considering that it had given her all the spiritual benefits she had expected from it, wished to burn it. Her sister intervened again and again to dissuade her, and her affectionate insistence prevented the destruction. "You are right," she said to her sister one day. "When I am dead my dear husband will read this, and it will explain many things to him!"

⁂

The parts of this book

I found the manuscript of the *Journal* and saw that there was a long interval or gap in it. Begun on September 11, 1899, it ended for the first time on August 11, 1906, filling one school copybook bound in black. In a similar copybook it was suddenly resumed on October 19, 1911, to be continued until January 9, 1914, when, in the writer's last illness, and a few months before her death, she could write no more. Therefore, from August 1906 to October 1911 there was a gap of more than five years, all the more regrettable because those years were among the most interesting of Elisabeth Leseur's religious development. It was the period when her soul firmly and definitely began to walk in the narrow way of sanctification where divine predestination was leading it.

However, Providence has permitted this gap to be filled in. In making further search, I came upon a copybook called *Book of Resolutions*, which filled up this gap and slightly overlapped the second part of the *Journal*, since it began in October, 1906, to end on July 18, 1912. And this was indeed, as I had supposed, the decisive time in an exceptionally edifying life; this copybook is one of the most moving parts of the whole work, differing slightly from the *Journal* in arrangement, but thoroughly in keeping with it; and its dates provide helpful points of reference.

The *Daily Thoughts* are entirely distinct from the *Journal*, although contained in one of the same copybooks, preceding the *Journal's* second part. They are detached fragments, written down from day to day, when daily meditation or prayer might prompt them, and when the writer judged them worth preserving.

Some of them are more developed, even taking on a certain hymn-like character, such as that which follows the unhappy date of April 13, 1905. But most of the time they take the usual form of such thoughts: they are sometimes very short, often more detailed, composed in a style that is forceful and concise. They send a ray of living and unforgettable light into the recesses of the soul and spirit. Written during the same years as the *Journal*, or, more exactly, during the first seven years, from 1899 to 1906, they underline, develop, and complete it, and are its best commentary.

I have added as an epilogue to Elisabeth's private writings the *Spiritual Testament*, which left me the last thoughts and final advice of her whom I had just lost. I greatly hesitated before making public a document of so intimate a nature, but I was strongly encouraged to do so, and I submitted to the arguments that were put before me. And the *Spiritual Testament* is in fact the natural conclusion to her spiritual diary; it shows what exquisite charity and surprising tenderness this holy soul carried to the threshold of the tomb, and what were her constant spiritual preoccupations even to her death.

Thus, the *Journal*, the *Book of Resolutions*, the *Daily Thoughts*, and the *Spiritual Testament* succeed each other in chronological order, and enlighten, explain, and complete each other. The loftiness of inspiration grows, the approach to God is continuous, and certain passages, such as those that end the *Journal* (July 16, 1913 and January 9, 1914), have a sound that is already not of this earth.

Finally, included here are a number of prayers and works of spiritual guidance that Elisabeth wrote for friends and relatives who asked her for spiritual help. These writings further reveal the secret of her goodness and how her holy example won souls for Christ.

Such is the manuscript; let us now see what its author was.

Elisabeth sought holiness while living in the world

Renunciation, detachment, voluntary poverty, dislike of the world, sacrifice and forgetfulness of self, acceptance of suffering, and utmost charity toward God and neighbor are the theme of each one of these pages.

A reader might well suppose them to be written by a religious, or at least by a woman living apart in some voluntary retreat or exceptional circumstances. The reader might indeed say, "This is certainly very beautiful and very admirable, but almost too much for me. I could never find myself in a similar state of interior life; I could not therefore follow so steep a way, nor profit by such an example. In the incidents and worries of daily life how could one realize so lofty an ideal?"

And in this the reader would be entirely mistaken; for the writer was a woman of the world, living in the world and fulfilling superbly the obligations of her state.

Elisabeth Leseur was born on October 16, 1866 and was thirty-three when she began to write her *Journal* in September, 1899; she was therefore still in the full bloom of her youth. We liked at this time to have guests and to pay visits; we had made for ourselves a very comfortable home; we led a varied existence, enriched by wonderful travels from which we both derived great satisfaction.

With a mind open to everything, remarkably quick and penetrating, she rejoiced in everything beautiful in nature or in the genius of man. A very cultivated woman, she had learned Latin, knew English, spoke and wrote Russian fluently, and had begun to master Italian when illness struck her down in the last months of 1913. She knew how to understand and appreciate art in every form — painting, sculpture, music, and literature; and her travels in Spain, Italy, northern Africa, Greece, the East, Russia, and Germany had made her taste very fine and true.

Her conversation was lively, interesting, attractive, and spirited, but always simple and modest, without ever making a show of her intellectual superiority.

She was thoroughly gay and took care to be so always; she even considered gaiety a virtue. In her final years, she remembered gladly that St. Teresa of Avila[2] (who, along with St. Catherine of Siena,[3] was among her favorite saints and whose works were among her bedside books) recommended her sisters to be always

REJOICE!

---

[2] St. Teresa of Avila (1515-1582), Spanish Carmelite nun and mystic.

[3] St. Catherine of Siena (1347-1380), Dominican tertiary.

gay. Her lovely laughter rang out at every opportunity, with its fresh, frank sound.

Elisabeth was a warm friend to all

Physically she was very attractive, with ways and manners full of distinction, and a kindness that made her always welcoming, smiling, and amiable, a perfect hostess — in short, the accomplished mistress of her house. Being greatly drawn to young people, who repaid her affection fully, she had made her home a center of warmth and gentility, as eagerly frequented as she was herself sought out.

But she put family affection before everything. The *Journal* and the *Spiritual Testament* show sufficiently her intense affection for and devotion to those who belonged to her. If God had willed her to have children — this was her great desire, and the privation was an inconsolable grief — she would have proved herself a true Christian mother, as she showed in the maternal love she bore her niece and nephews. These dear children loved her well in return, even while unable to realize the full extent of their loss when she died.

But she was also a rare friend, in whom might be found a singular power of affection. This was very apparent in her last years. Her state of health then necessitated great care. We went out hardly at all and entertained very little; she paid no more visits and frequently spent the day stretched out in her invalid's chair; yet visitors flocked to her, and never perhaps was her company more sought out. I sometimes even dreaded the fatigue that might result from all these long talks. She had become more and more a center of attraction, and there is nothing more touching and consoling to me than to think of the anxious sympathy that surrounded her in the last months of her life, and the vivid, tender remembrance — a veritable cult — in which she is held by all those who knew her.

Elisabeth hid her self-mortifications

When, in 1900, detachment from the world began to work little by little in her, and when in 1906 the renunciation was complete, so that the practice of voluntary poverty was her rule and worldly company a pain and mortification to her soul, she knew how to hide this so well beneath her cheerfulness and smiles that no one was aware of it. Even I, who had been told, did not always perceive or understand it, and I sometimes, even often, helped to make the mortification more painful still.

Elisabeth, therefore, living in the world, fulfilled every duty of her state, and her example shows how it is possible, when one has the will and calls upon divine grace, to live an intense spiritual life and to practice the highest evangelical virtues in the midst of outward activity.

Her religious upbringing was not exceptional

But to reach that degree of perfection,[4] it is essential to have a profound faith and ardent charity, to be imbued with our Lord's teaching, and to realize fully the celebrated words of St. Paul: "It is not I that live, but Christ who liveth in me."[5] Elisabeth had attained all these virtues. She was inspired by real religious feeling, which she lived out concretely. All her moral being was rooted in God; and she applied to the letter the apostolic precept "to re-establish all things in Christ"[6] to the point that by the time she died, her soul had already attained the divine courts of Heaven.

[4] Let me say here that in using in this introduction such expressions as *holiness*, *perfection*, *Christian heroism*, and so forth, I do not wish to prejudge in any way the decisions of the Church, to which I have submitted in filial devotion.

[5] Gal. 2:20.

[6] Eph. 1:10.

From what source had she derived a religious feeling so wonderfully rich?

From her family or her education? Not especially. She belonged to a bourgeois family like so many others. Her father, a good and distinguished man, who had made himself eminent as a lawyer at the Paris bar, occupied himself little with supernatural things. Her mother, a model of maternal devotion, performed her religious duties without any exceptional fervor. Her sisters were thoroughly pious, without approaching what Elisabeth herself became when her spiritual evolution had taken place; her brother still less. Elisabeth received the Christian education of most young people of her social class, learned her catechism and made her first Communion at the parish church, and received an excellent course of instruction. Her childhood friends, in whom she met with most precious affection, were in the same circumstances as her, with the same education, the same inclinations. Nothing of this could explain what happened in her soul toward her thirtieth year.

I sought to destroy her Faith

Can her marriage then explain it? Alas! I now come to a subject that is very grievous to me, and full of pain and remorse.

When I married, I was profoundly anti-religious. I had been brought up in a thoroughly Catholic family by a father and mother who both practiced their religion, and I had been instructed by distinguished priests. Leaving college, I became a medical student, and I quickly lost my Christian belief. The materialistic influences around me, assisted by my own passions, carried me on to paganism and atheism. The history of religion always interested me, and I searched polemics for weapons against this Catholicism, this Christianity even, that I had learned to detest. I therefore primed myself exclusively with the works of the Church's adversaries and of the modernists: Strauss,[7] Havet,[8] Renan,[9] Réville,[10] Harnack,[11] and Loisy,[12] among others. I collected for myself an extensive library of Protestant and rationalist writings.

I have since been able to judge of the poverty of their arguments, their profound ignorance of Catholicism, the misery and emptiness of their so-called histories and decadent philosophies; but at that time I was infatuated with their systems.

In marrying, I undertook to respect my wife's Faith and to let her practice it freely. But I rapidly grew to tolerate only with impatience convictions that were other than my negations; and as religious neutrality is as much of an illusion in private relationships as in public institutions, I made Elisabeth the object of my retrogressive proselytizing.

I set myself to attack her Faith, to deprive her of it, and — may God pardon me! — I nearly succeeded. During 1897 I managed, by a course of reading and much pressure brought to bear on her, to dissuade her from the practice of her religious duties, seriously to upset her faith, and to lead her in the direction of liberal

---

[7] David Friedrich Strauss (1808-1874), German theologian, author of a controversial *Life of Jesus* (1835), which tried to prove the Gospels to be a collection of myths.

[8] Ernest Auguste Havet (1813-1889), French educator. He was the editor of Pascal's *Pensées* and author of *Christianity and Its Origins* (1872-1884).

[9] Ernest Renan (1823-1892), French Orientalist and historian. Like Strauss, Renan was author of a controversial *Life of Jesus*, in which he denied Christ's divinity.

[10] Albert Réville (1826-1906), French Protestant clergyman, author of *History of Religions* (1889).

[11] Adolf von Harnack (1851-1930), German Lutheran theologian. He was suspected of heresy from the 1890s because of his criticism of the Apostles' Creed.

[12] Alfred Firmin Loisy (1857-1940), French Catholic theologian and biblical scholar, regarded as the founder of the Modernist movement; he was excommunicated in 1908.

Protestantism — which to my mind was only a stage on the way to radical agnosticism. I therefore put into her hands Ernest Renan's *History of the Origins of Christianity;*[13] but, thanks to Divine Providence, the very work that I thought would accomplish my hateful object brought about its ruin. Elisabeth with her unusual intelligence possessed the even rarer gifts of a sane and steady judgment and uncommon good sense. She was not deceived by the glamour of the form of this book, but was struck by the poverty of its substance. The perpetual shifting, the doubtful and frequently contradictory hypotheses, and the lack of sincerity that abound in this work deeply troubled her. She felt herself approach the abyss, and sprang backward, and from then on she devoted herself to her own religious instruction.

Elisabeth's studies reinforced her Faith

She had always been a great reader and loved books as much as I did; I possessed many, even too many, and now she wished to have her own. To counterbalance my anti-Christian library, she gathered together one composed of the works of the great masters of Catholic thought: Fathers, Doctors, mystics, St. Jerome,[14] St. Thomas Aquinas,[15] St. Francis de Sales,[16] St. Teresa of Avila, and many more. Above all she read and reread the New Testament, the Gospels, the Acts, the Epistles; she never passed a day without meditating upon some passage from it. She thus acquired a reasoned and substantial faith. Knowing the opposing arguments,

---

[13] Renan's seven-volume work (1863-1881), of which the *Life of Jesus* was the first volume.

[14] St. Jerome (c. 342-420), Doctor who translated the Bible into Latin.

[15] St. Thomas Aquinas (c. 1225-1274), Dominican philospher, theologian, and Doctor.

[16] St. Francis de Sales (1567-1622), Bishop of Geneva.

possessing her own replies to them, and strengthening perpetually the foundations of her belief, by the grace of God she established her faith indestructibly, made it impervious to attack, and was soon able to direct well-aimed thrusts at anyone who might seek to assail it again.

⚸

Elisabeth's <u>spiritual isolation</u>
caused her great suffering

All this labor, which lasted for many years, she performed alone — *entirely alone*. Her surroundings provided nothing but opposition. My most intimate friends, however good and devoted, were either indifferent or frankly hostile to religion. At that time I was engaged in foreign and colonial politics; I was writing; and I was contributing to important daily papers of the Left or anti-clerical party. We ordinarily socialized with politicians, publicists, journalists, physicians, university men, scholars, men of letters, musicians, playwrights, and artists; and it is not among these, as a rule, that the Church finds her defenders.

For my part I felt a smothered irritation at seeing my effort collapse on the verge of accomplishment, and I redoubled my use of criticism, polemics, and raillery. It was I who did so much to enclose my unfortunate Elisabeth in that spiritual solitude of which she so often complains in her *Journal* and which caused her so much pain; and this is now the great regret of my existence.

This was how things stood until 1903, when she was asked to be the godmother of a grown-up friend who had been converted and sought the grace of Baptism. Elisabeth agreed, and by Divine Providence it was at this ceremony that she met the Dominican who was to become her director and spiritual guide, a priest of wise counsel who greatly helped her with his knowledge and experience. She repaid him in the end, for he has told me since her death that it was often the penitent who edified the confessor. He had tremendous admiration for her. "She was truly a saint," he used to say to me with great feeling.

Elisabeth has noted briefly, but vividly, in her *Journal* (October 19, 1911) the history of this crisis in her soul. At the end of it her faith was a new thing, unassailable, unshakable, and radiant, opening henceforth to her the way to the sanctification in which she was so marvelously to progress. Her ascension to God had begun.

⚹

Elisabeth endured great bodily sufferings

And this faith "that could move mountains"[17] had been set by God upon the firmest rock of all — that is, upon suffering.

First there was the suffering of her body. Elisabeth's life was one long illness. Ever since her infancy, she had suffered from a liver complaint, which became her perpetual and increasing affliction. During her adolescence, an attack of typhoid fever endangered her life.

Later, in 1889, barely a month after our marriage, she nearly succumbed to a very grave complaint.[18] We were in the country, and it needed all the enlightened and devoted care that she received to save her. Since she was obliged to stay in bed for eight months, she was brought back in an ambulance to Paris, and lying on a stretcher, she made her first entry into the home we had furnished with so much pleasure during our engagement.

From this complaint she never entirely recovered. For some years, she could come and go without any apparent discomfort, and she could take without too much difficulty the long journeys of which I have spoken; but her illness followed her always and everywhere, although known only to her immediate family and to

[17] Cf. 1 Cor. 13:2.

[18] An intestinal abscess.

me. Providence lightened her burden to allow her those expeditions in the country or abroad, some of which, as will be seen in her *Journal,* had a determining influence on her interior life. But this infirmity was inevitably telling upon her health and was partly responsible for the illnesses that developed in the last years of her life.

Up until 1908 she was able to lead an apparently normal existence — without, however, being entirely spared, for in 1895 a serious carriage accident again put her life in peril for two months. But on the whole, she lived more or less like everyone else, and the friends whom she received or who received her, seeing her so active, alive, and spirited, never suspected how heavy a cross she carried in secret.

From April, 1908, attacks of liver trouble, violent and disquieting, compelled her to modify her way of life, to reorganize it on lines of repose and to spend long hours in an invalid's chair. In 1911 a grave operation was performed,[19] to which she refers in her *Book of Resolutions* (March 17, April 9, and June 8, 1911) and from which her recovery was hampered by painful complications. In 1912 and the beginning of 1913 she suffered frequently from exhaustion, and her life became more and more sedentary. Apart from regular visits to her mother, summer excursions to our corner of Jougne, in the Doubs country, and some fine expeditions by motor car that she owed to the devoted affection of one of our best friends, she remained mostly at home in bed, obliged to take every possible precaution. Finally, at the beginning of July 1913, she was struck down by her last illness,[20] a terrible malady with its alternations of alleviation and atrocious suffering, which for ten months was her Calvary, until the end came, when she was forty-eight years old, on May 3, 1914.

[19] To remove a cancerous tumor on her breast.

[20] Widespread cancer.

Her *Journal* shows throughout how Elisabeth endured these terrible afflictions — with the most admirable resignation, sweetness, and patience imaginable. She gave wonderful testimony of a strong soul, the absolute mistress of its body; she showed the power of complete abandonment to God's will, what strength a human being can draw from Him, and what a fine example the practice of the highest of Christian virtues can give to others. She never complained, remained smiling in the midst of the worst torments, comforted those around her, and looked to the Eucharist, and to prayer and self-sacrifice, for the support she needed.

During the last months, when she sometimes suffered a martyrdom of pain, she contented herself, while the crisis lasted, with repeating in a gentle plaintive voice, which went to the bottom of one's heart and which I can only recall with the most poignant emotion, "My God, have pity on us, on me!" — even now naming herself last. And then, when the crisis had passed, she would become once more smiling and valiant.

All who came marveled at her, and — a significant fact — it was from 1908, when exterior activity became more and more impossible for her, that she exercised the greatest influence on those around her, that her room was most frequented by people who came to her for moral guidance. It was from her invalid's chair that she directed the greatest number of souls, and became the source of the extraordinary spiritual radiance that shone from her in her last years. When I think that I was foolish and criminal enough to attempt to destroy the lever that was to carry her so high and uphold her so powerfully! To what a Hell would I have reduced her and condemned myself at the same stroke!

Elisabeth experienced great mental sufferings
Besides the sufferings of her body, Elisabeth had great grief of heart. Quite early Elisabeth had known the sorrow of losing those

she loved. In 1887 her youngest sister, who also was an exceptionally gifted child, died quite suddenly at the age of twelve. Elisabeth was twenty-one, and this blow — which was her first encounter with irrevocable loss — affected her cruelly and left an ineffaceable impression.

Two years later, at the end of December, 1889, her father died after only three days' illness of the influenza that was then claiming many victims, and his death occurred in circumstances particularly cruel for poor Elisabeth. She had just been brought to Paris, as I have already described, condemned to her bed for many more months. She could not go and kiss for the last time her unfortunate father, whom she had seen full of life but a few days before. One can imagine what this separation must have cost her.

The only consolation — and of what a kind! — that could be afforded her was to arrange for the funeral procession to alter its course between the church and the cemetery and pass beneath the windows of our apartment. Thus Elisabeth, carried on an invalid's chair into the drawing room, saw her father's coffin pass, and saluted it with her tears and prayers.

In May 1901, her brother Pierre's eldest son, Roger, a very lovable and intelligent child of seven, was fatally struck down by a violent illness. Elisabeth, who loved him very much, was deeply grieved, and suffered, too, for the pain of the unhappy parents.

Finally, on April 13, 1905, she lost her second sister, aged thirty-two, after a long and terrible illness.[21] She was a woman of exquisite character, for whom Elisabeth had a half-maternal affection, and who was the confidant of her soul. The *Journal* will show how deeply this blow struck her. Elisabeth commemorated the life and death of this dearly beloved sister in a volume written for her mother and her family, and distributed outside to none but a few friends and religious communities. It is called *A Soul: Memories*

---

[21] Tuberculosis.

Recalled by a Sister and appeared in 1906.[22] It betrays intense feeling, and certain pages, such as that in which her sister's death is described, are extremely poignant, and their beauty presages that of the *Journal* I now publish.

After this heartrending event, of which the wound never healed, Elisabeth had more to undergo: the loss of very dear friends, the serious illness of her last sister, an accident in 1912 to her youngest nephew's hand, which nearly resulted in the amputation of his arm, and her mother's increasingly precarious health. All these added their pain to that which already weighed so heavily on her stricken heart.

Elisabeth experienced profound spiritual suffering

And finally, after these sufferings of body and mind, there were those of her soul. Elisabeth lived in an isolation of thought that was very painful to her. The *Journal* will show how the atmosphere of hostility to her Faith that surrounded her, and the necessity of hiding all the riches of her religious development, lacerated her spirit. Alas, for that I am principally responsible, and since I have understood this, it has been my constant grief. I suffer in my turn, and I can only implore my dear Elisabeth to pardon me and to prove her pardon by asking God to inspire me with her ardent faith, some of her great Christian virtues, and the self-giving and self-sacrifice she practiced.

We can see, therefore, that Elisabeth led a life of suffering. She knew it in all its aspects, better than anyone else, and she knew how to accept it, to offer it to God, and to transform it so that she might apply its merits for the good of the souls she loved and of every soul. This higher use of suffering is the chief thing her life

---

[22] *Une Âme (souvenirs recueillis par une soeur)* (Paris-Auteuil: Imprimeries des Orphelins-apprentis, 1906).

teaches. How she understood and practiced it is shown in the following admirable letter, the owner of which has kindly sent it to me. It is written to the wife of one of our friends, a man of great intelligence and high character, active and Christian, who devoted any spare time allowed him by his profession to the defense of Catholicism and to charitable works. He was on the verge of the worst misfortune that could befall him, the loss of his sight.[23] Elisabeth was much moved to learn to what danger this friend was exposed, and she wrote thus to his wife:

October 27, 1911

Dear Friend,

I learn from my sister that your husband has been troubled with bad health this summer, which has perhaps been an even greater trial for you than for him, for the sufferings of those we love are harder to endure than our own. I want to send you all my sympathy and my most affectionate wishes for his complete and quick recovery.

I know what illness is and can guess what sacrifice it must entail for an active man accustomed to spend his energy freely; but I know also all that suffering means, the fine and mysterious power it possesses, what it obtains and what it accomplishes. After all, our activity (a duty we owe to God and to others) is of little importance and is exercised only when Providence wishes to make use of it.

---

[23] I was then divided from him, at the opposite pole of ideas; but he inspired me with sympathetic respect. Since then, the threat that was averted has reappeared; I have become more intimately acquainted with him and have found that it is impossible to approach him without feeling oneself improved by the nobility of his soul and his abnegation. How true it is that suffering, when accepted in a Christian manner, is a great agent of perfection.

And so when Providence prefers to work by means of suffering I think we should not complain too much, for we can then be sure that the work will be well done and not mixed up with all the misery of egotism and pride that sometimes spoils so much of our outward activity.

I know by experience that in hours of trial certain graces are obtained for others, which all our efforts had not hitherto obtained. I have thus come to the conclusion that suffering is the higher form of action, the highest expression of the wonderful Communion of Saints, and that in suffering one is sure not to make mistakes (as in action sometimes) — sure, too, to be useful to others and to the great causes that one longs to serve.

All this does not mean that I would not be very happy to see your husband resume his active career; it only means that I am persuaded of the good he now performs in the active and truly fruitful passivity of illness. You will permit and he will pardon this friendly "sermon" from one who has experienced what she speaks of, who has seen Providence gradually withdraw from her every form of activity, leaving her nothing but apparent inertia, and who feels that she never did more for God than on the day when to ignorant eyes she did nothing.

If someday I can get about again, I will do so; but tell your dear husband again and again that neither of us are now wasting our time.

This winter I shall still be condemned to all kinds of precautions. After my grave operation in April, I had in September serious trouble with an arm, which has much shaken me. You will therefore excuse my illegible writing. Since writing is a form of activity, God has wished it to be a little difficult for me. I am, you see, destined to be a spiritual idler.

Once more, dear friend, forgive me for this letter, on account of our friendship. Our best remembrances to you and your husband, and my heartfelt embrace for you.

My warmest thanks are due to the owners of this letter for allowing me to reproduce the whole of it. Apart from its beauty, it contains the ruling thought that the whole *Journal* so finely develops.

⁂

Elisabeth grew in <u>charity</u>

Elisabeth's faith was then confirmed and deepened by suffering, and she increased in charity.

Charity was the chief force of her religious life. First, there was the love of God, and this love streams and overflows in her writings, as it filled her daily life. And then there was the love of her neighbor. Elisabeth never thought of herself; she sacrificed herself incessantly for others, as I saw and admired without understanding, for the motive escaped me, and I even often charged her with exaggeration.

The good she did in lavishing her money, time, and energy on those around her is unimaginable. She took naturally to good works; she even tried to institute a place where solitary girl-workers, exposed to all the dangerous chances of life in Paris, might obtain food, lodging, and companionship in the best and most economical conditions. She took a house in a nearby suburb, fitted it up, and received boarders. She exacted a small monthly payment from them, rightly holding that their cooperation was desirable. Religion was the foundation of the work, but all the opinions of the boarders were scrupulously respected; and religion was to be preached only by example and by the atmosphere of the house. Unfortunately, Elisabeth was badly supported; she failed in her attempt and, after some years, was obliged to bring the work to an end with heavy monetary loss, which was, however, largely allowed for in her original calculations.

She then resolved to devote all her zeal and efforts to some existing work that had given proof of its vitality and usefulness. After a number of experiments, her choice fell on the popular Catholic

Union, which is concerned chiefly with poverty-stricken families of the St.-Denis plain — an admirable work, superintended very competently by an excellent woman who has given to it her whole heart, mind, time, and considerable fortune, under the higher direction, if I am not mistaken, of Monsignor Gibergues. She and Elisabeth were in quick and close sympathy. Elisabeth recognized the extreme usefulness of the work; she gave herself entirely to it. And when her ill-health prevented her from visiting, she assumed the duties of secretary, which she performed with her habitual exactitude and care until the end of 1913, when her last illness confined her to her bed.

But these works were only a slight manifestation of her overflowing charity. It was over certain hidden troubles and especially over souls, that she showered the greatest part of her charity. Misfortunes she alleviated to her utmost, both materially and morally; toward souls she inclined with the most ardent desire to bring them fraternal help in Jesus Christ.

This exquisite charity was in a way even physically perceptible. It brightened and transfigured her frank, kind welcome, through which one could see, as through a sheer veil, the beauty of her interior being, and whose surprising charm was so strongly felt by all who approached her that one of her friends once cried, "Elisabeth! One can see her soul in her face!" There was no sadness she did not share, no wound she did not tend, no wish she failed to understand, no call to which she did not respond. The words of St. Vincent de Paul might be perfectly applied to her: "You bring souls to God by your sweetness, by your compassion for their errors, and by the feeling that makes you share their misfortunes."

Elisabeth cultivated tender respect for others
She had the most delicate understanding of souls, and, as she says herself, was called to apostolic work, which she practiced by

example, by the confidence she inspired, and by the disinterested gift of herself. She had the greatest respect for the views of others, and would not on any account allow herself to criticize them.

This was the experience of her most intimate friend who came often to keep her company. Elisabeth and she were completely divided as to belief and practice; but their loyalty to one another, their mutual reliance, their high characters, and their affinity of mind and tastes had united them like sisters. And this friend said to me of her after her death, "Elisabeth had in recent years a profound influence on me and my ideas; and this was unknown to herself, for she never attempted to convert me or even to approach the question of religion. But what I saw of her was so beautiful!"

And I can give another example of this tolerance (apart from the *Journal*, where such examples abound) in a passage from a letter written in June 1904, in which she showed me her affection in the most touching words, and added:

> *Thank you for everything, and above all for being yourself.*
> *And forgive me for being myself — that is, someone who*
> *of herself is not worth much and who is a little improved only*
> *by the influence of accepted suffering — accepted, thanks to*
> *a help and a force greater than her own. You must therefore*
> *be indulgent to convictions that time and God have made very*
> *profound, thanks to which I have been saved from becoming*
> *an irritable and egotistical being. You may be sure that these*
> *convictions will never trouble you or others — and it is so*
> *good to introduce a little infinity and eternity into a love such*
> *as I bear you, and into a life that has been darkened and de-*
> *prived of so many things by the trials you know of!*

❧

She practiced kindness

Besides having this respect for others, Elisabeth was extremely kind. She never allowed herself to pass harsh judgment on others.

She had a horror of malevolent criticism, slander, talebearers, and drawing-room gossip. Someone once spoke in Elisabeth's presence about a woman of whom it was alleged that her good conduct could not be relied upon. "Why do you say so?" she asked. "You cannot know; one is never certain of those things." "Oh, but the facts are notorious and utterly proven!" she was told. "In that case, we still should not speak of them," she said. In this exchange one has the perfect portrait of her.

People came to her with confidence, appreciating her delicacy, her refined sympathy, the sweetness of her devotion, knowing that she loved them for their souls and for God without a single personal motive; and she, who merited so well their attachment, applied herself with infinite pains to direct them to the higher life. One day her youngest sister, passing Elisabeth her daybook, asked her to write a motto in it. Elisabeth meditated, took the book, and wrote on the endpaper: "Every soul that uplifts itself uplifts the world." In that profound thought she defined herself.

⚘

She influenced many souls

She did indeed uplift all who surrounded or approached her, and it was a strange thing to see this woman, so modest, so humble of heart, condemned to practical immobility, shedding around her far and wide the light of her great influence. As regards her relations and friends, this could be understood, but her influence spread itself to people she did not know, who had merely heard of her and of what she was, who came to confide in her and to solicit her comfort. During the unhappy days after her death, before her burial, while she still lay on her bed with a calm expression and a truly supernatural beauty, the last reflection of the soul that had animated and transfigured that body, there was an uninterrupted procession at her bedside. People came to pray near her, to bring her a last token of affection, and I thus saw in my home numbers of people whom I did not know, whom I had never seen before and have never seen since, and who gave free vent to their sincere and touching grief. A great many people attended her funeral. They expressed such real and unanimous emotion and gave witness to such an uncommon distress that the clergy assisting at the service were utterly astonished. They made inquiries, and their questions were at once reported to me: "But who was this woman? We have never seen such a funeral before!"

I have since come to understand the radiance shed by this soul so full of God, in reading letters of hers written to many people, most of whom have been willing to confide them to me. They can be counted by the hundreds and are admirable both in form and substance. They are addressed to correspondents of widely different circumstances, outlooks, and natures: provincial nuns, Jewish friends, atheist university men, and many others, most often to those of weak and unsteady will, bruised and broken hearts, or tormented and scrupulous souls. To all she spoke in appropriate language, lofty and precise. Often they are veritable letters of direction, for that was the role that, almost in spite of herself, she had been led to play by her faith, her charity, her Christian virtue, her dearly bought experience, and her surprising rectitude of judgment.

She had become a director of souls. Her correspondence with the nun who was the friend and confidant of her heart is full of enlightened and prudent counsel; and it was Elisabeth, living in the world, who guided the nun in spiritual ways.

Elisabeth wrote a great deal; she has left numerous manuscripts, small works, meditations, and correspondence, some of which are included in this volume, whose singular beauty and elevation perpetuate her loving apostolic work.

God had thus granted to her struggles and suffering their significance and their recompense. He had made of Elisabeth an elect being who spread divine light all about her and made it loved. Even those whose beliefs were opposed to hers came under this gentle influence. My friends who were indifferent or even irreligious nevertheless had a special respect for her and her convictions. In their affectionate sympathy, they abstained with great care from anything that could cause her the least pain, and gradually, moved by the beauty of her soul, came to admire her sincerely.

I received proof of this. One of Elisabeth's friends, whom she loved deeply, although this friend shared none of her religious or philosophical ideas, but who is a noble-hearted woman of rare intellectual and moral powers, and the directress of one of the large Paris schools, wrote me a letter from which I extract the following passage: "Since these grave events that have beset our land, I have often thought what she would have done and what she would have been in such circumstances to all who loved her. Living — in spite of our very different lives — and dead, Elisabeth was one of my friends toward whom my thoughts turned and still turn most often. Some beings are a light toward which all turn who need light to live by!"

What a testimony! And it is confirmed, among so many like it, by a testimony from one of our friends whom we considered, and whom I still consider, as a brother, whose faith was as opposed as possible to Elisabeth's.

He is one of the leaders of higher education, a celebrated biologist, and one of the foremost atheist philosophers; but he is also goodness itself and the personification of affection and devotion. He married a charming woman, brought up with Elisabeth and her sisters, whom Elisabeth regarded as one of themselves. This woman had solid religious convictions that her husband — thereby giving me, without knowing it, the most direct example — scrupulously respected, to the point of saying to her, at certain times when Elisabeth's influence seemed to him desirable, "Well, go and see Elisabeth; go and take your bath of serenity!"

He often came to talk to Elisabeth for hours; he knew her soul and admired and loved it. Her death was for him and his wife a great grief, and he said to me at that unhappy time these words, which struck me: "Elisabeth was at the summit of humanity." That was the rationalist version of her director's phrase: "She was truly a saint."

⚭

Her holy example slowly won my admiration

The priest is right: she is a saint. Since God has taken her to Himself, I am not alone in praying to her, and it has been told to me in confidence that special graces are believed to have been obtained by her intercession. I know of happy events that may be said to have been brought about by her intervention; and indeed the evolution in my own mind and life bears witness to her supernatural influence.

I have already told how irritated I had been by the failure of my campaign against her faith, and how obstinately I was bent upon controverting all her religious opinions. But from 1908 my attitude was modified. When I saw how ill she was, and how she endured with equanimity of temper a complaint that generally provokes much hypochondria, impatience, and ill-humor,[24] I was struck to see how her soul had so great a command of itself and of her body; and knowing that she drew this tremendous strength from her convictions, I ceased to attack them. In 1911, after her operation, my surprise was changed to respect and, in 1912, on the occasion of a journey to Lourdes, to admiration. She had vowed to thank the Blessed Virgin both for the success of her operation and for the cure of her sister and of her young nephew.

In June she went to fulfill this vow, accompanied by her sister and her sister's little son, and as I could not let Elisabeth in her state of health travel without me, I went too. I went to Lourdes with the preconceived intention of bringing back from there

[24] Liver problems.

nothing but confirmation of Zola's unhappy book.[25] An expedition I had made there thirty years before had produced a detestable impression upon me: I had seen only the hucksters in the Temple. I thought this was a final judgment; and yet here I was unconsciously reconsidering it.

I did not find faith at Lourdes, but I acquired sympathy for the pious manifestations that I beheld. I was especially moved by the Benediction of the Blessed Sacrament given to the invalids of a Spanish pilgrimage in front of the Church of the Rosary. But my most unforgettable impression was of Elisabeth praying at the grotto. In the lives of the saints, it is often told that the blessed were lifted up from the ground by the ardor of their devotion to God, in the ecstasy of prayer. I saw something of this, when, concealing myself in order not to disturb her in her fervor, I watched her. I had before my eyes the spectacle of something that evaded me, that I did not understand, but which I recognized clearly as being "the supernatural," and I could not withdraw my eyes from so moving a sight.

I returned from Lourdes troubled by what I had seen and felt in that land of miracles. Oh, I was certainly still a rationalist, on the surface at any rate — deeper down, Elisabeth acted upon me without my perceiving it; and this action grew stronger during her last illness. I could never weary of admiring her moral force in the midst of a real martyrdom. It was she, and not I, who was the comforter in the intervals between one crisis and another. When, having left her in the afternoon, I returned home in the evening, I was aware, as I approached her bed, of a calmness in her welcoming smile that would have been impossible in myself. For my own part, I knew well what kind of an invalid — intolerable to myself and to

---

[25] Émile Zola (1840-1902), anticlerical French novelist. The book in question is part of his trilogy *Trois Villes* ("Three Cities"): *Lourdes, Rome, and Paris*.

others — I would have been, instead of the source of serenity that she was to all around her; and I bowed down before the grandeur of the spirit that sustained and uplifted her. And when she received Holy Communion in her room, it made me happy to make the preparations myself and thus show her my sympathy and respect for all she felt.

And then I have said what a look of immortal beauty she wore upon her deathbed, which produced in me the deepest emotion. Her face, peaceful now after the last suffering, had the calm of another world. One could read beatitude in it, and I sensed — obscurely, because I was still an unbeliever — but in some way with certainty, the truth of the passage in the beautiful Preface to the Mass for the Dead: "Life is changed, not taken away."[26]

⚜

She gave her life for me

After Elisabeth's death, when everything seemed to collapse around me, I came upon the *Spiritual Testament* she had written out for me, and, guided by my sister-in-law, I found her *Journal* too. I threw myself into the reading of them; I read and reread them, and a revolution took place in my whole moral being. I understood the celestial beauty of her soul and that she had accepted all her suffering and offered it — and even offered her very self in sacrifice — chiefly for my conversion. As soon as her operation was decided on, she had concluded with God a kind of pact (see the *Book of Resolutions*, March 17 and April 9, 1911, and the second part of the *Journal*, March 6 and October 17, 1912), vowing to exchange her life for my return to the Faith.

Her sacrifice was absolute, and she was convinced that God would accept it and would take her early to Himself. She was equally persuaded that He would ensure my conversion. She

[26] *Vita mutatur, non tollitur.*

opened her heart to her spiritual director about this, and he has told me that she had not a single doubt on this subject, that she had the certainty of receiving this consolation either here or in Heaven.

One day, she declared with absolute assurance, "I shall die before you. And when I am dead, you will be converted; and when you are converted, you will become a religious. You will be Father Leseur." During the latter part of her life, she made the same statement more than once. Elisabeth was sure that she would die soon, sure that my conversion would follow her death, which she had accepted and offered up to God for that end, and sure also of my religious vocation, which, I plainly see, was a second intention for which she prayed. Some weeks before her death, we were speaking, one night, of her belief in a future life and the Communion of Saints, and she ended with this pronouncement, spoken with almost solemn authority: "You will come and find me again — I know it."

❧

Her love and example called me back to God

And so I perceived clearly the inner meaning of her existence, so grand in its humility, and I began to appreciate the splendor of the faith of which I had seen such wonderful effects. The eyes of my soul were opening little by little. Although Elisabeth had apparently disappeared, I felt her come to me, to direct me. All that I found of hers, all the manuscripts I gathered together, brought me her inspiration, and my former hostility quickly gave way to the wish to know Catholicism. Her library was opened to my inquiries, and that exegesis upon which I had so eagerly fed in the past now appeared to me in all its poverty. How indeed can such sterile negations weigh against the positive force of truth and of life that abounds in the Catholic Faith when it is accepted, understood, and practiced? I was cured of those negations once and for all, and I turned toward God, who called to me.

In the spring of 1915, the change was complete; it only remained for me to perform the outward act, to become reconciled to the Church in confessing my errors and faults to a priest. But before this last step, I stood hesitating and anxious. Elisabeth intervened once more. On the occasion of a party at the house of a friend, I chanced to be thrown together with a man whom Providence had sent to be my friend and brother, who was to remove my last doubts and lead me (for which I bless him each day) to the priest who welcomed me with so much goodness. I had at last found the harbor, the peace of soul that allows grief to remain but assuages bitterness. Elisabeth had led me to the truth, and in my inmost being, I continue to feel her guiding my steps to a more perfect union with God.

⸎

I decided to publish Elisabeth's writings

I soon had the idea of publishing Elisabeth's writings, particularly the *Journal*, which, with divine grace, had so powerfully led me. It had become my daily reading; I drew from it so much support, sweetness, and certainty that I told myself it might well be of the same great benefit to other souls as it had been to mine. The more I read it, the more I was persuaded that it was a book of rare beauty both in religious inspiration and in literary form.

The designs of God's Providence are shown plainly in Elisabeth's life and work. I am convinced that in reading these pages where the acceptance of suffering is so perfectly practiced, where it is shown how it may be offered to God for the relief of others' pain and the sanctification of souls, many torn hearts will find the means both of using for supernatural ends and of enduring with courage the cruel sacrifices which have been imposed on them.

I now, therefore, give to my family, my friends, and to all, these precious pages. I pray that the Holy Spirit will spread them far and wide and that they may help to work in as many souls as possible the renewal that they have accomplished in my own soul. Thus will be realized and perpetuated the apostolic work to which God had called my holy and dear Elisabeth, and I end by placing this book in the special protection of St. Dominic[27] and St. Catherine of Siena.

---

[27] St. Dominic (c. 1170-1221), founder of the Dominican Order.

✢

The Secret Diary
of Elisabeth Leseur

❧

The Journal, Part 1
1899-1906

A new commandment
I give unto you:
that you love one another,
as I have loved you.

John 13:34

⚜

September 11, 1899

For a year I have been thinking and praying a great deal; I have tried unceasingly to enlighten myself, and in this perpetual labor my mind has matured, my convictions have become more profound, and my love of souls has increased, too. What is there greater than the human soul, or finer than conviction? We must create in ourselves a "new spirit,"[28] the spirit of intelligence and strength; we must renew ourselves and live our interior life with intensity. We must pray and act. Every day of our life must carry us nearer to the supreme Good and Intelligence — that is, nearer to God.

⚜

September 19, 1899

I want to love with a special love those whose birth or religion or ideas separate them from me; it is those especially whom I must try to understand and who need me to give them a little of what God has placed within me.

⚜

September 20, 1899

I set myself to study philosophy, and it interests me greatly. It throws light on many things and puts the mind in order. I

[28] Cf. Ps. 50:12 (RSV = Ps. 51:10).

cannot understand why it is not made the crown of all feminine education. What a woman so often lacks is true judgment, the habit of reasoning, the steady, individual working of the mind. Philosophy could give her all that, and strip from her so many prejudices and narrow ideas that she transmits religiously to her sons, to the great detriment of our country.

⸕

September 21, 1899

How fine was the beginning of the Christian Church, recorded in the Acts of the Apostles! "And all they that believed were together, and had all things in common. Their possessions and goods they sold, and divided them to all, according as every one had need. And continuing daily with one accord in the Temple, and breaking bread from house to house, they took their meat with gladness and simplicity of heart; praising God, and having favor with all the people."[29]

"Having favor with all the people," that is, with the little ones, the humble, those who believed as they did, and those who did not yet partake of their divine Faith. The despised and hated men had soon found a way of "having favor with all the people."

How many Christians nowadays could give themselves the same testimony? How many have in their hearts the evangelical flame that purifies and enlightens all that comes near it? Let us go back to the holy source, to the Gospel, the word of God. Let us draw from it lessons of moral strength, heroic patience, tenderness for all creatures and for souls. Let us Christians be sure never to "break the bruised reed" nor to "quench the smoking flax."[30] That reed is perhaps the mournful suffering soul of a brother;

---

[29] Acts 2:44-47.
[30] Isa. 42:3.

and the humble flax extinguished by our icy breath may be some noble spirit that we could have restored and uplifted. Let us beware: nothing is so delicate and so sacred as the human soul; nothing is so quickly bruised. Let each one of our words and deeds contain a principle of life that, penetrating other spirits, will communicate light and strength and will reveal God to them.

⚭

September 25, 1899

No one knows what passes in the profound depths of our soul. To feel God near, to meditate, to pray, to gather all our deepest thoughts so as to reflect on them more deeply: that is to live the inner life, and this inner life is the supreme joy of life. But so many moving thoughts and ardent desires and generous resolutions should be translated into deeds, for we are in the midst of human life and a great task lies before us.

It is the time for painful effort: one must tear oneself asunder, forsake the realm of thought for that of reality, face action, know that one will either not be understood or be understood wrongly, and that one will perhaps suffer at the hands of humanity for having willed the good of humanity. We must already have drawn from God an incomparable strength and armed our hearts with patience and love, in order to undertake day by day and hour by hour the work that should belong to every Christian: the moral and material salvation of his brothers.

⚭

February 14, 1900

The moral improvement, the transformation and education of souls, the task that the world at present offers us, is so immense that it may well confound our feeble wills. What can be done against evil and indifference by such an obscure creature as I? Nothing of myself, no doubt; but all by and with God.

I believe that in good there is a great expansive force; I believe that no humble, unknown act or thought, seen by God alone, is lost, and that all, in fact, serve souls. I believe, according to a saying I love, that "when we do good, we know not how much good we do." What we have to do is to work on ourselves, to accomplish our own inner transformation, to do each day and each hour our duty and all the good that we can do.

Above all we must ask God to fill us with an intense charity. Charity is love: the love of God that renews and transforms the soul and life and becomes the secret cause of our acts, the love of all creatures, the powerful and living love of souls, the love of all that suffers and laments.

Such love could save the world. Why groan, when with such a love one might act? Why hate, since hate destroys, when that divine love can bring life and transformation to hearts?

⚘

March 28, 1900

This winter's exhausting activity, which in spite of everything is so empty, begins to pass away. During that time, the only good moments are those given to God, to the poor, and to work. I am going to give myself to these with more ardor than ever. In certain ways my ideas have changed: I believe much more in individual effort, and in the good that may be done by addressing oneself not to the masses but to particular souls. The effect one can exert is thereby much deeper and more durable. Did not He who remains the Eternal Model in all spiritual things do the same? And it did not hinder Him from transforming the world.

Following Him, let us turn with tenderness to every person, however poor or sinful, and let us endeavor to be "all things to all men."[31] Let us think less of humanity and more of men; or rather

---

[31] 1 Cor. 9:22.

let us remember that humanity is only made of human beings and that each one of them needs the light and strength that God gives, and it belongs to us to spread this light as far as we can. What a mission for weak and sinful creatures such as we! I tell myself again and again that the Apostles were hardly greater than we when they began their divine labor, and that the strength of the Holy Spirit was necessary to transform them and make them into new men. Let us beseech God ardently for this coming of the Holy Spirit, who is at once strength and sweetness, love and peace; let us ask of Him that complete transformation of our inner being and our life that will enable us to labor for our brothers.

⚸

March 29, 1900

A great talk last night with P—, D—, and the O—s. So many people of this generation lack a guiding principle, and yet we have an absolute need of being led by an idea greater than ourselves.

What a fine thing is harmony in a human life, when every act, whether great or small, springs from one fundamental thought, when everything — heart, mind, and will — has but one end, when the love of God has possession of the soul and transforms it, when that harmony is the result of long interior travail, sometimes painful but always fertile, making of the soul "something achieved," and something divinely beautiful.

I read the Gospel, and by that sweet light I discover in myself many a nook of egotism and vanity. Unique book, perpetually read and perpetually new, supremely beautiful, resplendent with truth, of exquisite grace and charm, from which one can draw unendingly and never exhaust it!

O blessed gift of God, why do men forget you when by you alone can they learn charity afresh?

❧

May 29, 1900

After five weeks of travel in Spain, I resume my customary life, but I resume it, I think, under different conditions. During this journey I have thought and prayed a great deal, and I have seen clearly into myself and into my life. That life I have consecrated to God; I have given myself to Him with my whole heart; I have prayed ardently for those whom I love, for him whom I love more than all. And now I want to be no longer a useless creature; I have seen plainly what are my greatest duties, and I want to fulfill them.

To do each day, humbly, and so that God alone may see it, all the good that one can do; always to seek out all the misery and grief within reach in order to relieve them; to cultivate in oneself a lively sympathy for everyone; and to do all this for God alone — that is the goal of all human existence.

My own life, which until now has been often so empty and useless, will be transformed, I hope, by the strength of God and by close union with Him.

Around me are many souls that I love deeply, and I have a great task to fulfill with regard to them. Many of them do not know God or know Him only imperfectly. It is not in arguing or in lecturing that I can make them know what God is to the human soul. But in struggling with myself, in becoming, with His help, more Christian and more valiant, I will bear witness to Him whose humble disciple I am. By the serenity and strength that I mean to acquire, I will prove that the Christian life is great and beautiful and full of joy. By cultivating all the best faculties of my mind, I will proclaim that God is the highest Intelligence and that those who serve Him can draw without end from that blessed source of intellectual and moral light.

In order to give, one must acquire; and to serve my brethren before God for one day, or for even a small part of every day,

I must first have purified and strengthened my soul for many days.

⚬

July 30, 1900

We have been spending a week with our friends the H—s on the banks of the Meuse in complete repose. We came back by the banks of the Rhine and saw Aachen, Bonn, Frankfurt, and Mainz. From Mainz we went by boat to Koblenz, from there to Luxembourg, and returned by Metz. This last town left a painful impression on us; it is both French and German: French in appearance and population, German in its innumerable soldiers and barracks.

After thirty years there still rises *un parfum français* from this soil of Lorraine. We saw with emotion the battlefield planted with crosses. During all that expedition in Germany, one thought never left me: that we are still a great people from a moral and intellectual standpoint, *"le grand peuple,"* and that it rests with us to remain so always.

The genuine union of all is necessary for that, and in everyone a profound sense of duty; we must set ourselves to perform all the tasks Providence has appointed us, to banish egotism and hatred from our lives, and make the name of Frenchman synonymous with justice, light, and moral force.

We must become a people truly strong, not only by force of arms — that is too little — but by the valiant nobility of character of all of us, from the humblest to the greatest. Chastity, determination, and the dignity of life should be perpetually taught and developed in all. Woman, whose immense role and influence the French do not yet fully grasp, and who does not always grasp it herself, should from now on realize her task and consecrate her life to it.

To recoil from duty and sacrifice is cowardly. Today, there is a duty to bear children (and it is often a sacrifice); it is a duty to have a care for those in less fortunate circumstances than our own in the matter of wealth or education; it is a duty to develop unceasingly one's intelligence, to strengthen one's character, to become a creature of thought and will; it is a duty to view life with joy and to face it with energy. Finally, it is a duty to be able to understand one's time and not despair of the future.

All this a woman can do. As much as man, she is a being who thinks, acts, and loves; she can proudly reclaim her right to duty. But for that she must come and draw her strength from the source of all strength, and to increase her intelligence she must bring it into contact with the supreme Intelligence. But this also is true of man. He also is powerless without God; and the great and strong nations are those who have taken God as the foundation of their social and national organization — only it must be truly God and a true religious feeling, not merely the exploitation of this greatest of all feelings. God must live in our hearts and lives, and there must be complete religious liberty. The expression *to believe* implies the adherence of one's whole being and is not compatible with religious intolerance.

My duty as a "Frenchwoman" will always be as sacred to me as my duty as a Christian, or, rather, one duty includes and implies the other. I only trust that each will be always understood by me in its broadest and noblest sense.

⚓

September 12, 1900

After going to and fro between Paris and the country, and entertaining strangers, here we are restored to calm. I am reading Latin authors: after Horace, Juvenal; and I shall continue at this. It interests me greatly to delve into a time and a society that I know so imperfectly. For two days I have been able to read and meditate quietly, and that has soothed my agitation and done good to my soul. I do not forsake the New Testament, and the farther I read into the Gospels and Epistles, the more do I find a charm, a strength, a life that is incomparable. God is indeed there; from this reading I come each day calmed and strengthened; my will is reinforced there and my heart warmed. God, the Supreme Teacher, through this book of books, educates my inmost being. It helps me to understand life, to smile at duty, and to will strongly.

⚘

November 28, 1900

Nearly three months without writing anything. Illness of my little niece,[32] occupations of all kinds, calm of spirit in the midst of apparent tumult, and a will more resolute than ever to be devoted to God and to duty. Inasmuch as I advance, upheld by God, in the way that He has traced for me, that which stands for me for "duty" becomes more and more clear to me. The great thing is not to lose oneself in unrealizable plans and projects, not to live in tomorrow, but patiently to turn thought into action, good will into determination.

Spoke and discussed a great deal with some dear friends who do not believe. More than others I love these beings whom divine light does not illuminate, or rather whom it illuminates in a manner unknown to us with our restricted minds. There is a veil between such souls and God, a veil through which only a few rays of love and beauty may pass. Only God, with a divine gesture, may throw aside this veil; then the true life shall begin for these souls.

And I, who am of so little worth, yet believe in the power of the prayers that I never cease to say for these dear souls. I believe in them because God exists, and because He is the Father. I

---

[32] Marie Duron (b. 1893), daughter of her eldest sister, Amélie, and her only niece, whom she loved as her own child.

believe in them because I believe in this divine and mysterious law that we call the Communion of Saints. I know that no cry, no desire, no appeal proceeding from the depths of our soul is lost, but all go to God and through Him to those who moved us to pray. I know that only God performs the intimate transformation of the human soul and that we can but point out to Him those we love, saying, "Lord, make them live."

Reflected a good deal on social questions, which even the most humble of us might help to solve. Social questions are essentially the questions of Christianity, since they are concerned with the place of each man in the world and his material, intellectual, and moral improvement. These questions, which will last as long as the world, can advance only through Christianity; that is my absolute conviction. Christianity alone addresses itself to the individual, to that which is most intimate in him; it alone penetrates to the depths of being, and is able to renew it.

It is the duty of every Christian to interest himself in the crisis through which the people are passing, one which perhaps will change them profoundly. For new needs there should arise new apostles. The people — the masses that form the majority of the country, those workmen, peasants, and humble laborers of every kind — need to be shown the True Source of all liberty, justice, and real transformation. If we do not make God known to them we shall have failed in the most important and pressing duty of all. But this is a work that demands a forgetfulness of self, a disinterestedness, a persevering will for which we need God and for which we must transform ourselves absolutely.

⚜

January 17, 1901

The new year, the new century, have begun for me in the midst of so many different occupations that if I have found time to reflect and pray I have certainly not found time to write.

What serious thoughts came with the beginning of this century, the close of which I shall not see — gratitude for God's gifts, a stronger turning to Him, an ardent desire to increase His Kingdom within me!

And how many prayers, spoken or implied, have gone out from those depths of the soul that He alone knows, asking for light and for true life, the inner life of the soul for all those I love, for him whom I love more than all. Perhaps neither my dear Felix nor my family nor those other souls for whom I can do so little, know to what an extent I love them. In that dear eternity, in the very center of love, we will take our full joy in these affections. But O my God, how can one love if one does not love through Thee?

⁂

March 11, 1901

Some joyful days, because of a present from Felix, and more because of the words that accompanied it — words so full of love that I am moved to great happiness. I do not deserve to be so loved, but I rejoice fully in it. Apart from that love that is the very foundation of my life, I am always meeting with fine affection on my way, for thus has God blessed me.

Now I must make sure that it is not an egotistical happiness that I draw from all these affections, but that they are transformed into devotion and charity, that they push me to act with God for others.

Have read with interest Father Gratry's *Sources*,[33] and now another of his books where I often find my own thoughts. These thoughts rise from the depths of myself to the surface and then return to that place, from which they must soon burst forth again, transformed by God into acts and living words.

[33] Auguste Gratry (1805-1872), *Les sources*.

⤲

April 22, 1901

"These things I have spoken to you, that my joy
may be in you, and your joy may be filled."[34]

"This is my commandment, that you love
one another, as I have loved you."[35]

O Jesus, after the Last Supper, in the peace and melancholy
of the evening, from Thy soul and Thy lips were spoken ineffable words that have come to us through the centuries. The world
has often forgotten them, and forgets them still, but the least of
Thy children can sense them pulsing in her ear and in her heart.
After the Supper, there resounded like a blessed refrain the last
words of Christ, an appeal for love between men and for love of
men for God: "Love one another."

This is the Law, the supreme Testament of Him who is Love.
He who has ceased to love is not a Christian, is not a disciple of
Christ. There is no exception to this rule. Those who are separated from us by birth, education, belief, the poor savage whom
we never see, those who are most abject and most guilty — all
are entitled to our love, all should be brothers to us. Do they not
all stand before God, beloved by Him? Has not each a soul like
our own, which should be only the more dear to us for being far
from the one Light?

Let us open our hearts to admit all humanity. At the touch
of the divine, let us resound with every generous thought, every
human affection; let us learn to find in each soul the point at
which it is still in touch with the Infinite, with God.

[34] John 15:11.
[35] John 13:34.

❧

June 10, 1901

On April 8, Mamma and Juliette left for Italy. On May 9, Pierre L—[36] made his first Communion. The day before, Roger[37] became violently feverish and shortly thereafter became very ill. His parents and I nursed him. On Sunday, May 12, Mamma returned, and on Monday, May 13, at eight in the evening, our little dear passed from us. Those hours spent beside him, at times so heartrending, were also sometimes very sweet. He left us quietly for eternity, and the veil between the two worlds seemed light indeed. Dear little one, who art in the midst of Light and of Love, pray for us.

Renewal of effort and work on myself, and prayer with stronger will and more serenity, which I pray God may sustain in me.

For several days I have longed for calm and seclusion and felt an ardent wish to get close to nature, to be like the sweet St. Francis in the midst of flowers and birds, and there to pray, work, and meditate in solitude, or at least (for Felix belongs always to my solitude) with a few loved ones who would sometimes leave me alone with God. My God, wilt Thou give me one day the joy of this solitude for two, united in the same prayer, the same faith, and the same love? But for the present I must banish these thoughts. God wants other things from me, and when I wish to meditate I have no solitude but what is within me.

❧

August 28, 1901

A stay in Savoy from July 14 to 31, in a charming and soothing landscape. An exquisite calm life, full and rich interiorly. Beautiful mountains, carpets of green, great fields of corn and

[36] Her nephew, the second son of her husband's brother Paul.

[37] The eldest son of her brother Pierre, seven years old.

oats, churches nestling in every corner — these made up our lovely sojourn. What a wonderful life one could lead there with those one loves!

Religious discussions with the S—s. O my God, it is indeed true that Thou alone canst make certain things understood; all the arguments in the world are nothing to Thy sovereign voice in the depths of the soul. Thou alone canst penetrate the depths and reach that mysterious place in the soul where great transformations occur. That thought is reassuring: without it I would sometimes suffer cruelly from being unable to express what I feel, from being unable to open wide my soul and show what God, and He alone, has made of it — all the love and joy that He has showered upon it. May His Spirit act in these souls that are so dear to me, in this soul that is dearer to me than all others; and may the light shine upon them, bringing with it life, the true life.

A few days in Holland, from which I came back ill. Interesting country, full of fine things. A rather melancholy landscape. I love the countries of light, of those beautiful, gentle colors, where all looks so harmonious: Greece, Italy, the East.

Now to resume daily life. I want to study Latin this winter, to be usefully but obscurely employed, and to live from one day to another doing the task of the moment — which is the best way, I believe, to perform each task well.

❧

September 10, 1901

Sweet and joyous meditation on those words of Christ "I am come to cast fire on the earth; and what will I but that it be kindled?"[38] That fire is charity, the absolute, exclusive, and ardent love of God and, through Him, of all humanity. But what souls

[38] Luke 12:49.

will be sufficiently holy to make men understand what this charity is, and how shall this fire be kindled?

Each one of us can be a humble worker at this great task, and I have seen clearly what I can do in my own corner of life. Above all, to work on myself, to try to develop in myself all the instincts God has given me; to strengthen my will by regular work; to elevate my soul unceasingly by sacrifice and the acceptance of my usual sufferings, and by a constant and tender sympathy for all who approach me. To do the humblest things in the conviction that they always bring to me the beauty and truth for which I long. To love exclusively and to seek duty in everything, however obscure or painful it may be, whether intellectual or purely material; to miss no opportunity to act or to perform some devotion, especially if it will not be noticed. Never willingly to give up any act of devotion or sacrifice unless it brings me praise or flatters that subtle pride that so quickly prevails.

To go always to the little ones, the suffering, those for whom life is hard; but to have no scorn for those lighthearted ones who live for themselves. They more than the others, perhaps, need to be loved, need a little charity to show God to them. Resolutely to devote my intelligence, my will, my heart, all my soul and my being to God, to the advancement of God's Kingdom in the world and in souls. To raise, strengthen, and spread a little of the warmth that He has put into my heart, the "fire" that kindles me, which I grieve to be unable to kindle in other souls.

When I have done this, God will do the rest. We pray, suffer, and labor in ignorance of the consequence of our acts and prayers. God makes them serve His supreme plan; gradually they take their effect, winning one soul, then another. They hasten the coming of the Kingdom of God and by the other beings, acts, and desires they give birth to, they will exert an influence that will endure until the end of time.

One resolution that I have taken and begun to put into practice, notwithstanding physical and moral weakness, is to be "joyful" in the Christian sense of the word, as joyful as I can be toward life, toward others, and even toward myself. My God, help me, and "Thy Kingdom come!"

❧

October 9, 1901

Days of great interior happiness, rich in firm resolutions. I am going to fill my life with work and charity and the accomplishment of duty, all my duty.

❧

November 20, 1901

I love interior solitude with God alone; it strengthens my soul, and gives it light and fervor again. But sometimes isolation, which is a different thing entirely from solitude, weighs it down.

I thirst for sympathy, to bare my soul to the souls that are dear to me, to speak of God and immortality and the interior life and charity.

But the human soul is so subtle and delicate that it must feel the same notes resonating in another of those divine instruments before it can sound its own. The perfect union of two souls — how beautiful a harmony that would make! With him I love best in the world, let me one day make this harmony, O my God!

I have ordered all my days so that as much as possible they may represent, as it were, the whole of my life in miniature. Prayer, my precious morning meditation, work seriously performed, some work or care for the poor, and my family and home duties. Just at present, visits to Juliette take the place of visits to the poor. As soon as I can, I want to devote myself to some fine and useful work.

❧

November 28, 1901

Talked to A— and his wife yesterday about the unjust and un-Christian ostracism to which Jews are subjected in certain circles. My God, wilt Thou not give to poor human beings a spirit of intelligence and wisdom, which is the gift of Thy eternal Spirit? Wilt Thou not awaken soon in souls the spirit of charity that Thou camest to bring to the world, and of which Thou hast said that it contained the Law and the prophets?[39]

I wish I could organize a holy crusade against hate and to promote justice and love among men. At any rate, in this spiritual plot that God has given me to cultivate, I want to plead by my attitude, my words, and my acts before everyone I meet the great cause of charity. Will I not thus be defending the cause of God Himself? My God, help us; send a ray of light and of love into our midst.

❧

December 18, 1901

The study of Latin interests me and opens out a whole horizon of reading and intellectual pleasure for the future.

In the eyes of many people, a woman's life is virtually contained between her twentieth and her fiftieth year. And yet what wasted force lies in the twenty or thirty years that, in first youth or still more in maturity and old age, are for too many women but an empty time in their existence! Serious work, activity of mind, action all the more productive in that it is based on a strengthened will and on judgment developed by life — these should fill the later time of life, and give it a special serenity and beauty.

But that needs a long preparation. One must have acquired in youth the habit of work, organized one's life, and assumed the

[39] Cf. Matt. 22:40.

interior government of oneself, so that on the surface at the very least, no physical suffering, none of the lacerations of old age can trouble one's being. One must have lit in oneself so bright a flame of sympathy and tenderness that all who are beginning as we are ending can come to find there light and fire.

It is a suffering sent from God, which I offer to Him, that among all the beloved friends surrounding me, I should have no one to whom I might open my heart in saying to him or her, "Look," and who might understand and help me. But perhaps to hear one's ideas and beliefs perpetually criticized, to know them misunderstood, to have prejudice and ignorance against one, is to some extent to suffer persecution for justice's sake.

Could I on this account deserve some pity from God? Because it is a deep and secret suffering, one of those that God alone sees, for which He makes sometimes the most sweet compensation. When I want to pour out my soul I go to Him and, whether at church or in the silence of my room, He brings me increased strength and fills me with joy greater than any words can say. After all, perhaps He alone can penetrate to the infinite depth and sensitivity of the human soul.

⁂

February 3, 1902

A bad spell for more than a month: bodily fatigue, domestic troubles, and, worse than that, a kind of sadness and moral apathy, a lack of the fervor and inner joy that God has sometimes given me so abundantly. And yet not for one moment has my will ceased to belong to Him; duty has cost me dearly, but it has not ceased to be duty.

A new year has begun. I want to make it fuller than preceding ones. Many things to reform: pride; the tendency to delay in getting to work, to let days slip away; to allow myself to be invaded by outward excitements. And yet I have an immense need of calm and of interior life. God alone knows what difficulty I sometimes have in overcoming certain physical and moral miseries in order to arrive at that complete possession of myself, at that Christian serenity that nothing can disturb.

To try more and more, by example and tenderness and by developing and elevating my intelligence, to spread more life and light among the minds and souls I encounter along my way. To show that what good I have is from God, and that the rest is — alas! — from me. To examine and decide, after reflection and prayer, to what work I shall consecrate my life this year, apart from my immediate duties.

⚬⚬

Holy Saturday, March 29, 1902

A week of meditation and prayer and union with God.

My God, help me to fulfill the task, to break the last bonds, to complete that interior evolution that Thou alone hast accomplished in me, in whom the mysterious working of Thy Providence is forever visible, for which I will never cease to bless Thee and love Thee.

I have a great task before me, and nothing human to help me to fulfill it. Perhaps one day I shall have the great joy of seeing my faith, which is my whole life, understood and shared by those and by him whom I love so much. As it is, all that my soul holds of desires, fervor, and tenderness must remain enclosed within itself and poured out only before God. Whatever suffering this entails, I offer for the souls who are so dear to me. Nothing is lost, not one grief or one tear.

I am reading Father Gratry's *Knowledge of God;*[40] it has strength and beauty. The eternal Word, which "enlighteneth

[40] Auguste Gratry, *De la connaissance de Dieu* (Paris: Gervaise, 1881).

every man that cometh into the world,"[41] lifted for Plato a corner of the veil that conceals the one true Light. He knew the only way in which the soul may know God, and describes wonderfully that place in the soul where man can make contact with God. This is an inspiring book; it truly reaches that "root" of the soul of which Plato speaks.

⚭

September 3, 1902

More than five months without writing, but much has happened in those five months. Our stay at Jougne[42] was a very sweet time of happy family life, enlivened by the shouts and laughter of children; then came the short journey to Vienna, completed by me in a state of physical and moral malaise that was very painful; then the return, to hear the startling news of poor Adolphe's death; and then another two weeks of sweet and calm days.

In coming back to Paris I have felt such emptiness, sadness, and suffering inside that nothing but prayer and divine aid can help me to change these into joy for others and strength for myself. At the same time I have never for an instant ceased to feel the active presence of God in me. When I look back and see the wonderful work that God has accomplished in me, the veritable creation of a soul, which only He can perform, I realize what duties this grace imposes on me; and I hope, yes, I hope with all my heart, that some day soon He will grant the same grace to the dear soul that is so close to mine and that I love so deeply.

I want to live an entirely new life. No one must know the struggles, regrets, and griefs that, like every other human being,

---

[41] John 1:9.

[42] A village in the department of Doubs, near the Swiss frontier, where from 1902 she spent each summer with her family. She went there for the last time in 1912.

I endure; I must organize my existence in such a way that all its various and sometimes complicated duties take their place.

Since I may not have a consistent life on broad, clear lines, but must partly veil my inmost being in order to consort with ideas and feelings that are opposed to mine, I want at least to unite with this first duty my wish to work for God and for souls. It is a delicate task, for which I need the help of a greater strength than mine.

Help me, my God, and, without my knowing it, use me for a little good. According to a comparison I like, let me be the rough vessel giving forth light and warmth. Thou art that light; come and enlighten, through me, the souls that are infinitely dear to me. What a joyful day it will be when those souls shall know and love all that Thou hast made me know and love, I who am poor, insignificant, and weak — that day when I shall be able to reveal to them the soul Thou hast truly recreated in me, and when I shall live with them — with him — O my God, this deep, intimate, and blessed life that makes new creatures of us and that transforms everything in us and about us!

⚜

October 18, 1902

Cowardice, weakness, awkwardness in my demeanor with others — things that can harm the ideas I cherish; acute physical suffering and deep moral suffering; and in the midst of this a will unshakably turned to God, a plenitude of confidence in Him and love for Him; daily duties performed at whatever cost by great effort, without fervor, but still performed; then, little by little, calm returning to me, and divine strength penetrating me again; new and energetic resolutions, the hope that God will help me to do my duty, all my duty — that is the tale of these last weeks and of my soul during this time.

I feel that all of my knowledge, assisted by that inner light and grace of which the trace is so apparent in my life, must be a knowledge of reconciliations. I must profess simply and strongly a faith that divine labor has at length created in me, but I must do this in a way that never wounds or offends conviction or its absence in others. I must sacrifice, unknown to anyone, my tastes and inclinations, everything but the principles by which I live. I must do what seems to me my duty — works of charity, devotion to others and to the poor — in a way that can offend no one nor interfere with my immediate duties. I must never sacrifice intellectual work and must perform it regularly. I must become even a little worldly, in spite of my love of home and of simplicity and solitude, in order to please Felix and those about me.

This, in fact, is my task: to do my different duties without anyone's suspecting what trouble I have in reconciling them, to forget myself, to develop what God has given me of reason and intelligence, to banish pride even in the most subtle forms I know so well, to love strongly without self-seeking, to accept by divine grace the duty of every day and hour and never to neglect it, however small it may be. I shall often fall, but that help from above for which I shall humbly petition daily will not fail me. Besides, to live is to fight, to suffer, and to love.

❧

December 10, 1902

A painful event: the separation from our friends, the S——s. Many miserable thoughts and feelings. I hoped for much from that woman's soul, and yet how should one expect much of a poor soul that no divine strength upholds? How should there be sacrifice without God, without immortality, without infinite love?

A sad feeling of separation from this person whom I love; I can do nothing for her but pray. Nothing but that! But that is everything! What souls are needed now to combat hatred, prejudice, egotism, and pride! What intelligence, perception, generosity, and total selflessness! A part in this great work is offered to me, but how little worthy I am! And yet God will help me if I call Him to me by sacrifice and prayer.

I have felt strongly, during this time, that I am at a turning point in my life, that I have come to a time when I must make a more noble, lofty work of it, and make it serve better the holy cause of God and of souls. During Advent I want to consider this and the means to bring it about.

↭

March 25, 1903

A fine morning, sweet and blessed.[43]

May God be praised for all the graces He has accorded me and for this great supreme grace, for all that He has ordained, and for leading my soul to a life wholly new and full of Him.

↭

March 31, 1903

The day before yesterday, Sunday, profound joy — full and complete communion with Jesus Christ, the giving of myself, of the future, and of my whole soul.

↭

May 12, 1903

What events in a few months in the life of my soul! What a gentle, smooth achievement of this long transformation, willed by God, arranged by Him in such an admirable way that only

---

[43] It was the occasion of the baptism of an adult convert to whom Elisabeth was godmother. It took place in the Dominican convent chapel in the Faubourg St.-Honoré. At this touching ceremony Elisabeth met Rev. R. P. Hébert, O.P., who became her spiritual director.

now, in looking back from the heights where Christ Jesus has led me, I can contemplate the stages, and bless the work He has done.

At Rome, where we stayed three weeks, I had some precious hours. At St. Peter's one morning, in close and joyful communion with Him who desires my whole soul, I made a solemn consecration of my soul and my life to God and to the task of charity and light that must be mine from this time forward.

On our return, Maurice's[44] illness, with terrible pain; many miserable hours. The dear boy is better. May God be forever blessed!

In regard to these little ones I have a mission to fulfill: to be their friend and guide, to employ all the intelligence and devotion I can in order to instill character into them and make valiant Christians of them.

&

July 9, 1903

I smile in rereading the first pages of this book and in reviewing all my illusions and errors of youth. How well I see now my mistake in thinking that certain virtues and greatness could exist outside Christianity, and how different in fact were certain things that seemed so pure and generous to me. But even out of my error God has fashioned truth, and He has taken me to Himself by unlooked-for ways. And now by His grace my faith is so rooted, conscious, and profound that it cannot be disturbed by any suffering because of it inflicted on me by people or circumstances.

&

July 23, 1903

I must go back a little and review these blessed memories and fix the deep impressions of these last months: first, the continual

[44] The second son of her younger sister Amélie Duron, then three years old, who was very ill with diphtheria.

life-giving action of God in me during these last years, and then the *dénouement*, both natural and marvelous, which He has ordained. The unforgettable hours in March, in the chapel that is now closed; then at St. Augustine's, in complete union with God, and the solemn feeling that a new existence was beginning; then that touching baptism, prepared also by God, mingled with all those cherished memories. Then the journey to Rome, which seemed willed by God for the crowning of His work; and two mornings there that I will never forget.

The first, Sunday, April 19, when, before going to Mass, I got a card for an audience with the Holy Father.[45] After Mass, the setting out with Jeanne B— for the Vatican, the arrival in the Court of St. Damasus, and our entry into the hall of the Consistory. We waited an hour sitting in the second row, opposite the papal chair, in the midst of the somber and thoughtful people. Greeted with acclamation, the Pope appeared, in a chair borne by men clothed in striking red velvet; he mounted the steps of the throne, seated himself, and I was able to contemplate at length that thin transparent face, fine with intelligence and goodness, with unusual eyes full of life, suggesting a world of thought and a strong will. His entire soul lived within those eyes.

He spoke to us for a few moments, telling us how much he loved France, and that this great nation ought not to lose the traditions that had made its strength and beauty, and he ended by giving the apostolic benediction to us and to our families.

Greatly touched, I bowed down before this old man, this father, the trustee of the Eternal Word, and in my thoughts I presented all whom I love for his benediction, the living and the dead, and also the new life opening before me. Then we filed in front of him and I kissed that large white hand that is lifted only

[45] Pope Leo XIII (1810-1903).

to bless. After a last farewell the Holy Father mounted his chair, with more acclamations, and disappeared. Just as the chair turned he leaned toward us, with much feeling, and with an affectionate gesture of his hand.

I looked for the last time on his incomparable face and said "*Adieu*" from the bottom of my heart, knowing well I should not see him again. I was not wrong, for last Monday, July 20, after long agony, Leo XIII died, and that great light went out, or rather went to shine above our shades, in the One Eternal Light.

The second ineffaceable memory is my morning at St. Peter's, the following Wednesday, April 22. I set out alone for St. Peter's, and after going to Confession to a French-speaking priest, I went to Communion in the chapel of the Blessed Sacrament. Those moments were completely and supernaturally happy.

I felt in myself the living presence of the blessed Christ, of God Himself, bringing me an ineffable love; this incomparable Soul spoke to mine, and all the infinite tenderness of the Savior passed for an instant into me. Never will this divine trace be effaced. The triumphant Christ, the eternal Word, He who as man has suffered and loved, the one living God, took possession of my soul for all eternity in that unforgettable moment. I felt myself renewed to my very depths by Him, ready for a new life, for duty, for the work intended by His Providence. I gave myself without reserve, and I gave Him the future.

I then heard Mass in another chapel, in profound joy and peace. I prayed again, and then I knelt close to the Confession,[46] in a last intimate and solemn consecration.

On my return I found myself in an atmosphere of irony, criticism, and indifference. But nothing mattered; the flame of Christ was still burning within me.

---

[46] *Confession* here refers to a place in St. Peter's where the relics of the saint were venerated.

30

How many memories of that journey crowd themselves upon me! The visit to the church of St. Paul of the Three Fountains on the day of our arrival, the calm and poetry of that spot where I wished to stay and pray at length.

The next day, Palm Sunday, the first visit to St. Peter's, during High Mass, and one moment of joyful recollectedness alone; the loveliness of the palms, yellow and green.

All Holy Week; Friday, the end of the day in St. Peter's; Easter Sunday at St. John Lateran and St. Peter's in the morning; afterward, a Mass held at the *Trinità de'Monti.*

Then the visit to the catacombs and churches and all Christian Rome; and to the ancient Rome that is also so interesting, but in another way.

And then the departure, with loving memories of this city unique among cities, where each inch of territory recalls something, where the stones have a soul; this city that is truly royal first by force and then by love, and which, victorious, was vanquished by that strange Conqueror who said "Love ye one another."[47] A Conqueror so powerful that for twenty centuries He has been adored and will be still when numberless centuries have passed over humanity.

Since our return, many trials for me, as if God would accomplish my purification through suffering: Maurice's illness, terrible anxiety for Juliette's[48] health and that of some others, physical fatigue and suffering; and then the feeling, sharper and more painful than ever, of the great spiritual separation between myself and Felix and many of those around me. How unhappy it is to see all that one loves and lives by misunderstood or attacked by prejudice and hatred, or even to feel others'

---

[47] John 13:34.

[48] Her second sister, already attacked by the malady that was to cause her death less than two years later in April 1905.

complete indifference toward the greatest things of life and
the soul!

Through this trial God imposes on me perpetual efforts
and the deepest suffering, all the better for being known alone
to Him, and a sort of withdrawal into myself, to the depths of
my soul, where He lives. If only these dear ones about me, especially my best beloved, knew the depth of my tenderness for
them, and what joy it would be for me to open wide my soul
to them!

For the moment it may not be. O Lord, once more I implore
Thee to come to him, to come to them, and let them live, let
them live the interior life deeply, and also an outer life renewed
by Christianity. The harvest is plentiful; my God, let them be
blessed laborers in it; let their life and mine be a work of beauty
and love, and let us labor together for the coming of Thy Kingdom in the world and in souls.

⚓

August 11, 1903

A good, long conversation with the Abbé V—. He has a
warm, keen heart, such as I would like to see in every priest, in
every Christian. He understands what is imperishable and profound in Catholicism and that wonderful domain of souls that so
few know how to explore. Without suspecting it, he has renewed
my fervor and made me resolve to work more than ever for the
material and moral welfare of everyone, and above all for those
dear people who are so mistaken and yet so interesting. To know
how to understand them will be one part of the task, to love them
deeply will be another, but to love them for themselves alone and
for God, without counting on a single recompense or sweetness,
simply because they are souls and because Christ, the adored
Master, in looking upon them one day uttered this tender

remark: "I will have pity upon the multitude."[49] Let us also know how to have pity.

⌘

August 24, 1903

Thanks to God, progress in my mastery of self, in spite of my wretched state of health; many preoccupations through Mother and Juliette, and much deep sadness poured out before God alone. To acquire more and more of the complete serenity that one must beg from God, and to know how to sacrifice all I had desired, and to endure the privation of all human support and strong Christian sympathy. Father H—'s absence deprives me of rare but precious conversations, and lacking any strong human voice to console me, I turn to the great heart of Christ, who is the best Friend and who knows how to comfort and strengthen. With His aid I will be able to come to the help of so many souls about me, for whose sake I must only forget my weakness, my suffering, and my longing for deep sympathy.

⌘

November 3, 1903

More than two painful months in the dejection of almost continual physical suffering, and with terrible anxiety on Juliette's account; the miserable belief that my illness will last as long as I do, always impeding my life. Complete resignation, but without joy or any inner consolation. The resolve to use my misfortunes for the good of souls. To fill my life with prayer, work, and charity. To maintain serenity through everything. To love more than ever those who are the dear companions of my life.

A great trial in being unable to occupy myself actively now in the works that I am interested in.

---

[49] Mark 8:2.

⚛

December 3, 1903

To prepare myself for Christmas by prayer and work and by furthering my interior life.

To call upon Christ from the bottom of my heart to make me live fully my spiritual life and to work in me so complete an interior renewal that others shall feel its influence.

To act above all through this divine influence that lives in me, and to ask the blessed Master to enlighten other souls through me.

Christmas: feast of humility and sweetness and love, feast of the little ones and of the poor. One of the three great stages in the Redemption.

⚛

December 9, 1903

Through the uncertainty of the future of those I love, and in spite of suffering and the absence of a life such as I dream of, to anchor myself firmly in God.

The more I meditate on the Gospel, the more I understand all its beauty. I want my soul and my life to be so filled with it that both will be a living preaching of it.

⚛

January 20, 1904

A new year begins, which I entrust to God.

A fuller life, a deep constant feeling of the presence of God in me. Regrets only for all the pressing duties and difficulties that impede my activities and prevent me from occupying myself more completely with the religious and social work that interests me so much. To offer God this sacrifice and await the time when I can do more.

This morning at Charonne I made the acquaintance of the little girls who were making their first Communion. In those souls I will sow the seed, and leave to the Savior the care of the harvest.

❧

March 9, 1904

Great suffering, on Juliette's account and through my usual trials; a scattered life, often occupied more fully than I would wish. But intense prayer, and an inner life full of God, in spite of weaknesses and faults.

To try as much as possible not to sacrifice my daily meditation, in spite of active occupations and duties. In that meditation and close contact with God my soul finds greater strength to perform the wearisome, monotonous tasks of every day, to act. Those things are better carried out that have first been prepared in deliberation with the Master and the Friend, and the soul remains at peace in the midst of every agitation and grief.

To go more and more to souls, approaching them with respect and delicacy, touching them with love. To try always to understand everything and everyone. Not to argue; to work instead through contact and example; to dissipate prejudice, to reveal God and make Him felt without speaking of Him; to strengthen one's intelligence, to enlarge one's soul more and more; to love without tiring, in spite of disappointment and indifference. Above all, to draw to oneself the humble and the little ones so as to lead them to Him who loves them so much.

Deep, unalterable respect for souls; never to do them violence, however gentle one tries to be, but to open wide one's soul to show the light in it and the truth that lives there, and to let that creative truth enlighten and transform, without any merit of our own but simply by the fact of its presence in us.

Nothing singular, mean, or equivocal in one's attitude. Straightforwardness, simplicity, and, when necessary, the quiet statement of one's convictions. But never any ostentation in that statement. No extremes or partisanship. Never to show the wounds that are caused by certain hostilities, declarations, or misunderstandings; to offer them for those who cause this suffering.

To exercise one's will; to work with hands and brain; to acquire knowledge. To fortify one's thoughts, one's will, and even one's feelings and yet preserve all their gentleness and depth. To Jesus my Savior and Master I offer all these resolutions, having been to Confession and preparing to receive Him this week. May He help me to follow in my soul and in my life the ways of the ideal Christian, to be completely Catholic, and to work for the coming of His Kingdom.

⚜

April 7, 1904

My Easter week was good indeed. Communion on Wednesday with great joy, and again on Easter. After this year, which seems to me (after having received so many graces) to have been a year of preparation — by suffering and activity — for my new life, another spiritual year begins for me, which with God's help will bring me more grace and strength and during which I will try to do the most good possible and to fulfill my task courageously.

⚜

May 3, 1904

Has my life known any unhappier time than this? My happiness last spring was indeed what Mme. Swetchine[50] has called

---

[50] Madame Swetchine, born Anne Sophie Soymanov (1782-1857), Russian-French author, convert to Catholicism, organizer of a famous Parisian salon. Her works are notable for their mysticism.

the "Viaticum of Sorrow."[51] The cruel, lacerating, and ongoing trial of Juliette's illness and the fear of the future, the painful knowledge of our poor mother's grief, my usual afflictions, a bad state of health, and a painful oppression of mind and body — all this now makes of my life a sacrifice that I offer to God in silence for Juliette, for those I love, and for all souls.

It is a great and double affliction that I offer: my life and the great solitude of my soul, so different from what I would have wished. To be always with dear ones or friends to whom one can never open one's heart even for an instant, to whom one can never reveal anything of one's inmost being, is an intense grief. Jesus Christ must have known it, He who had so much to give of Himself and who endured painful rebuffs and reverses beside which the ones I sometimes suffer are nothing.

And yet through all these trials and in spite of the lack of interior joy, there is in my soul some central place, which all these waves of sorrow cannot reach. In this place is hidden all my inner life; there I can feel how completely united I am to God, and I regain strength and serenity in the Heart of Christ. My God, give health and happiness to those I love, and give us all true light and charity.

Public events also would be saddening if I had not firm confidence in the future of Christ's Church and a great hope for the future of our country. How heartrending to see the poor ignorant masses deceived and driven to evil and hate! My God, give us "sons of light";[52] let there arise apostles with burning hearts to go to the little ones wholeheartedly and bring them truth and love. Thou alone canst save and transform. Give to me, weak

---

[51] *Le viatique de la douleur.* The term *Viaticum* refers to the Holy Communion that is given to those in danger of immediate death, to strengthen them with grace for their journey into eternity.

[52] Cf. John 12:36; 1 Thess. 5:5.

and little as I am, some of Thy divine strength, and come to me so that I may do much good to souls.

I am going to try again to act with renewed strength; at any rate, I know, thanks to the wonderful Communion of Saints, that I can certainly act through my present suffering, and God will do with it what work He wills.

⁂

May 25, 1904

No relief, no glimmer of joy on the horizon.

I must defend myself forcefully against outside excitement and dispersion. Have too much neglected my morning meditation.

To put away the obsession with the future, and to try more than in the past to be calm and smiling to all, more constantly to practice a charity that is lively and forgetful of one's unhappy self.

To live each day fully and to look to the future only in order to prepare the soul so as to make it fruitful.

⁂

July 4, 1904

Painful time of illness. Always the same uncertain future. Yesterday, a spell of weakness and tears, which I regret. Today the resolution, with God's help, to be cowardly no more; to become joyful again; to subdue the body through the soul, which belongs more than ever to God, in suffering more than in joy.

My God, give health and happiness to those I love; give them faith and love, the life of the soul, and I ask for nothing more.

A day of great joy: a present of a lovely little bureau from Felix, accompanied by words that moved me to the very bottom of my heart. His affection is the greatest happiness of my life.

To hold firmly each day to my resolutions: daily meditation, regular and thorough work, and quiet action. Not to give way to the indolence of mind and body that come inevitably with a poorer state of health; to keep up my energy and to force myself to be neither sad nor discouraged.

In eight days, departure for Jougne. Sadness to leave Mother and Juliette. Joy to have Felix near me and to occupy myself with the children. I give these months into the hands of God, and also the winter that I see coming.

⚘

August 31, 1904

We returned last night from Jougne; after a rough start because of the illnesses of Juliette and my mother-in-law, we had three good weeks in which I fully appreciated that lovely country and the full, sweet life that can be led there.

To have the children near me, to occupy myself with them, to try to raise them in the noblest sense of that term and to impress on those little souls things that will never be effaced; to interest myself a bit in everyone and to make our home into a living center, to give it a soul — all this has filled my days, and I will always keep the happy memory of this time. Our departure and return were sad, aggravated by physical fatigue.

With all my soul I thank God for the graces He granted to us during these six weeks, and I ask from Him pardon for my weaknesses and faults.

I have made several resolutions, which I place in the Heart of Jesus. To begin a work that will make Him better known and loved. To give myself regularly and wholeheartedly to the two tasks in which I am engaged. To make our home more Christian. To fill my days and my life with prayer, meditation, and work, and a stronger and more lively charity.

❧

September 13, 1904

I am going to take advantage of a rare day of calm in my increasingly troubled and scattered life to make a serious examination of conscience and meditation. And first I want to write a little in this journal; it will do me good, for I feel a great solitude in my soul, humanly speaking, and a word of faith or of charity, falling from human lips, would bring warmth to my heart.

It is God's will that, until my most intense wish is granted, I should walk alone in the path of suffering that He has shown us, and that He has made quite rough for me lately. And yet He is more than ever close to me and supporting me.

From the human point of view, no light is visible. Sadness in the present, anxiety for the future, frequent impediments in everything through my illness, the privation of all that could have transformed my life: good and fruitful work, reading — and this because of more immediate and humble duties. Absence of the consolation that contact with people of intelligence, faith, and truly Christian love always brings; physical discomfort — all these at present make a dull, sad atmosphere in my soul.

Today in recollection and humble prayer I will implore the divine aid I need so much, and plan out my life for this winter, such as it presents itself to me. First, I must firmly renounce the concrete visible good I would so much have liked to do; my duty to my dear invalids comes before all, and since I believe in the Communion of Saints, I will ask God to apply to those I love and to souls the sacrifice of this inaction. I must learn to use stray moments to write and work. I must not neglect to meditate daily, for that is so necessary to me, and I will do it when and how I can.

To return to greater serenity, inner and outer; to struggle against absorption in beloved ones' suffering; to avoid speaking of my miseries, which is harmful to inner concentration. To be severe with myself and to try to acquire more indulgence for others.

Not to dwell upon the little wounds that my feelings and convictions perpetually suffer, but to offer them "manfully" to God. Not to give way to discouragement and a type of moral lassitude as a result of emotional sadness and bodily trials, but to keep alive in myself supernatural joy and the will to act, without any care to know the result of my action and efforts.

⚭

October 18, 1904

My birthday the day before yesterday. How many useless or evil years! In the future, at least, to make of these, and of however many more God will give me, a work of holiness. To be truly Christian, another Christ, as is demanded of every child of the Church. To be an apostle — what a word! And what a task, impossible to perform alone!

Resolution to be always amiable, without trying too obviously. If I wish to avoid all useless controversy and fruitless expense of energy, I must nevertheless know how to make myself all things to all men and interest myself in things that sometimes seem childish, and sadden me by their contrast with my own state of mind. Often people are like great children, but Jesus has said that what is done for children is done for Him.[53]

So let us show indulgence to childishness and to the incredible light-mindedness of so many about us, and insofar as it is useful, let us learn how to become little with all types of "little ones,"[54] even the little of soul. Let us try to speak the language they can understand, and with them stammer eternal truths. Has

[53] Cf. Matt. 25:40.
[54] Cf. Matt. 10:42.

not God done the same with us, and has He not placed in our souls only as much light as we can bear?

⅋

October 24, 1904

One of those blessed days of which the memory is never effaced. Alone — it would have been happier if there had been two of us, and one day I shall have that joy — I went from Moulins to Paray-le-Monial,[55] and there, after a few purchases intended as souvenirs of this visit, I went and prayed in the church for a moment. It is a twelfth-century church with a beautiful exterior — finer, I think, than the interior. Then I went to the little chapel of the Visitation, where so many prayers have been placed that it is, as it were, impregnated with them. I stayed there a long time, and I left in the Heart of Christ the petition that was the chief motive of my visit: Juliette's recovery. I confided to Him many other wishes, and I prayed for our dear country and for the Church.

I brought away with me some of the blessed peace that is to be found only before the tabernacle, because there lives, ready to answer us, the most holy Soul that earth has possessed, who alone can understand us because He has known all human distress and yet possesses, by the eternal Word, all divine knowledge.

The day was supernaturally complete because a great grief awaited my return — suffering all the more keen because it

---

[55] Her husband had gone to Moulins for a few days for a lawsuit, and, as they were never separated, she had gone with him. One day when Felix was detained at the lawcourts in Moulins, she made this rapid afternoon excursion. (The Visitation convent at Paray-le-Monial is the place where St. Margaret Mary Alacoque (1647-1690) received her revelations regarding devotion to the Sacred Heart of Christ.)

struck him whom I love above all. I offered it to God for him, for Juliette, for all I love, and I felt peace again.

❧

November 21, 1904

The tremendous longing to be an apostle, renewed love of souls — all this through the divine grace I have lately been conscious of. But how much there is in that thought: to be a Christian, to be an apostle, and how little worthy I am of these two titles!

God has not done so much for me without expecting something from my free and humble cooperation. With all my soul I give myself to Him; from today I consecrate my life to Christ and to souls. Lord, Thy Kingdom come in the world, in souls, and in me to whom Thou hast given so much, and who would wish to be less unworthy of the Master and Savior Jesus Christ.

❧

December 3, 1904

The moments spent with Juliette are among the best of my life. The dear little woman moves and edifies me more than I can say. I love her soul, and I think she understands mine. This is a great sweetness, because of those who surround me, apart from Mother, my sisters, and my dear Felix, no one knows my inner self. And the whole of my Christian life will be understood by my beloved one only later, when God will have chased the shadows from him and made the light shine.

On Wednesday I had a striking example of what divine grace can do, and I saw how abundantly it is given to us in the sacraments. I had spent the morning in a state of extreme prostration and sadness; during the day I went to Confession, and I was at peace again; I seemed to be — and indeed I was — renewed by a strength other than my own. The feeling of forgiveness and spiritual renewal in the sacrament of Penance is a wonderful thing.

And yesterday morning I went to Communion in the same peace and the same abandonment to God. I felt Christ Jesus truly living in me, and now I want to become different, to be wholly Christian, with all that that word means of forgetfulness of self, strength, serenity, and love.

That others may see in me Thy apostle, may Thou alone, my God, know my faults and weaknesses, as Thou alone canst pardon them.

*

January 11, 1905

The new year begun in the sadness of Juliette's illness, the uncertainty of the future, but in the renewed giving of my soul and my life to God.

Dear feast of Christmas, in which I can offer to God only my trials and my good will.

May God grant Juliette's recovery, and my life will be more than ever consecrated to Him.

*

February 11, 1905

A succession of emotions, the same heartrending trouble, a grievous blow from someone whom I do not think I ever deliberately harmed — that is the balance sheet of the new year. Not enough deep recollectedness, partly through circumstances, partly through defective will. Today there is exterior calm; I enter in upon myself, I feel myself nearer to God. Next week I will receive Communion again and draw a little divine grace from that contact with our Savior.

I will destroy egotism in myself, all "touchiness" and pride, and I will try to be gentle and humble even toward those who cause me pain and affliction. Besides, I, too, have done wrong by them; I have not been sufficiently good and openhearted toward them. If they misunderstand me, so much the better — I shall have less pride, and it will be for God alone and through supernatural charity that I will try to work good among them.

Not to give way, in moments of fatigue or sadness, to the temptation to slacken my efforts; to remain valiant at whatever sacrifice, and in times such as this to invoke more than ever the strength that is not of this world, but which is given to us.

To apply myself soon to hard intellectual work, so useful to me, and to maintain equilibrium in my mind and in my life, which is haunted by too many cares at present.

To be unswervingly faithful to the daily task, in big and little things, in work, in painful inaction, in illness and suffering as much as in joy and health. May those who draw near to my soul sense that it is rooted firmly in God, and is peaceful and lively because of it.

The restless waves that sometimes beat against my soul are human things that come to it from outside; may others see in me only what is permanent and true; never may any soul hold back discouraged from mine because agitations and worldly complications have hidden the way of approach; may my soul be as smiling as my lips toward all, and may Thy Word, O my God, inspire my humble word and make it fruitful.

❦

February 18, 1905

My Confession on Wednesday did me good and the sacrament of Penance brought me consolation and peace.

Yesterday I went to Communion with joy and renewed the offering of my life to Jesus my Savior. May He give me grace to be His apostle and to make known to souls, by my example and my deeds, the strength and life He gives to a soul and how He can transform a human being even as weak as I. The divine Spirit, who out of ignorant fishermen made Apostles of burning zeal, can make use of me to do a little good, and I fervently ask for this from Him.

⚙

March 20, 1905

Lord, I cry to Thee from depths of anguish and sadness such as I have not known before. Thou alone canst save her whom we love and keep our hearts from breaking — hearts that entrust themselves to Thy love. Thou art the All-Powerful and the All-Loving; O my God, do that which it is in Thy power to do, and give us joy again in giving life and healing to my beloved sister. She is to me a child, a friend, and a sister, the person whom, with Felix and Mother, I love above all.

⚙

May the twenty-fifth of May,[56] which draws near, be a holy and blessed day and find us all reunited and happy.

My God and my Savior, I consecrate to Thee my future, my words, my actions, and all the good works I can ever do, begging that I may be used in Thy service to make Thee known and loved.

⚙

March 25, 1905

A sweet and peaceful Communion today, in thanksgiving for this blessed anniversary and to obtain Juliette's recovery. My God, grant us this grace, and then make of me an apostle all my life.

I must strive, with divine grace, to make myself a new soul for a new life.

---

[56] This was the day on which her niece Marie was to make her first Holy Communion.

46

❧
April 4, 1905

I suffer, I adore, and I pray.

O Jesus, in that garden where Thou didst see the last night of Thy life descend upon men, and a still darker night upon Thine own soul, Thou didst suffer alone. Even those who loved Thee failed in that critical hour to understand Thee and Thy torture.

O my Savior, all humanity experiences that agony in the Garden of Olives, all Christian souls go through the ineffable crisis of suffering and desolation. And, like Thee, the Christian soul is always alone in the garden of Gethsemane, in spite of tenderness and pity sleeping close at hand. No heart can penetrate deeply enough another's pain, to pour soothing balm over it, and those who touch it sometimes only hurt the more.

Remember, then, adored Master, what that hour was to Thee; have pity on our weakness, and do Thou, who art the only Consoler, the only Heart that can share and understand, come and appease and strengthen us, and help us to make our grief a work of salvation and of love, a living preaching of the Gospel.

O Lord, she whom I love is ill.
Thou alone canst save her.
May that be Thy will!

Have pity on us!

❧
April 13, 1905[57]

---

[57] The death of her sister Juliette.

⚭

July 4, 1905

It is three months exactly since I wrote these last lines and uttered the cry of anguish that Thou hast heard, O my God. Thou hast not granted the supreme prayer that went out from my tortured heart, or rather, Thou hast granted it differently and better. All that I desired for my beloved (with what ardor Thou knowest!), all that I hoped for her of human joys and health and sweetness, all the life that I begged Thee to allow her, and the final happiness, all these Thou hast given to her in taking her, in drawing her, to Thyself.

Oh, I cannot believe that my constant ardent prayers, and those of others for her, and all the sacrifices offered and the tears shed, and so much suffering accepted, could all be useless. I do not believe that all her trials, her life of privation and grief ended by a sweet and holy death could be without fruit.

If earthly happiness was denied to her, if she knew bitter and sad separations, and if in the end she was taken from us, it is that a better life awaited her than on this earth, it is that joy out of all comparison with her cruel suffering was prepared for her by the God of love, and that God wished her to know all beauty and all good and to give her His light, and that her dear soul was purified and holy enough to enter into the domain of sanctity.

My God, Thou hast wished, no doubt, to purify us also, to lay a heavy cross upon our shoulders, and to transform us through suffering. I can only say to Thee with all my soul, which is Thine, the words I wrote on April 4: "My God, I suffer, I adore, and I pray."

I adore because I believe, because I have seen and felt what lies at the bottom of suffering, because my soul is forever rooted in Thee, my God, unless Thy grace abandons me. I adore because Thou art Goodness, Beauty, Light, and Life; because Thou

art the Father full of love and pity; because Thou art the
Friend and only Consoler, O Jesus Christ!

But I suffer because she whom Thou hast taken was the
friend of my heart and the gentle confidant of my faith and
thoughts, because I have passed with her some of the best hours
of my life, because I loved her like a sister and like a dear child
at the same time, because we prayed, suffered, and loved together,
and because her affection was a part of my life, of my happiness,
of my heart.

And now, humanly speaking, my life is broken; part of my
heart has gone with my dear sister to live in Thee. Already my
earthly happiness was only the happiness of those I love, for little by little all my human hopes had become, as I wrote to our
sister, supernatural and Christian ones.

My share in human happiness has been Felix's love and my
dear ones' affection, a share so great that I give thanks for it
and accept the moral and physical trials that my life has known.
Those trials seem little now beside the grief that has struck us,
which nothing can console. May we one day, at any rate, be all
reunited where there is no weeping, grief, or separation.

Later on, with God's help, I hope I shall write of the last days
and the peaceful end of our Juliette;[58] she had every holy consolation and grace up until the last minute; she went to God on
Thursday, April 13, six weeks before that first Communion she
had so looked forward to, and which she witnessed from eternity,
more united to us than she would have been here below lying on
her dear bed of pain. The week of the retreat and the first Communion was one of peace and recollectedness. Marie was charming and full of feeling, and I shall never forget that Communion

[58] She did so, and published the book anonymously for her
mother, her family, and her friends, under the title of A Soul:
Memories Recalled by a Sister. The book was never offered for
sale.

when we all prayed and adored together. I gave myself to God for a new life, and upheld more than ever by our angel's prayers, I want to become an apostle and to transform myself.

How can I say what Felix was to me and to all of us during April, and also at the time of the first Communion? My beloved, since I have no better way of showing my affection, let me write here, in my name and in the name of her to whom you did so much good, a solemn benediction. May it bring you divine grace, and may you become a Christian and a saint. Juliette loved you greatly; she offered for you a part of her sufferings; may my sweet beloved one obtain true happiness and life for him who has my greatest affection on earth.

And may she obtain for our poor afflicted mother, whom I love more than I can ever say, the supernatural peace and consolation that come from God alone. May she be the dear protectress of those children she cherished and wished to be Christians, and may she protect me who am so feeble, to whom her tender words and example did so much good.

With Louis Veuillot I say, "Let God give me strength and leave me my grief."[59] May I not slacken at my task, and may my sufferings be transformed into charity and supernatural love for those who belong to me, for little ones, for the poor, and for all who do not know God.

My dear one, my Juliette, may your soul still be the friend of my soul. Pray for me and remember that you said to me one day, with such a tender look and tone, that you could "no longer do without me." I do not ask to shorten by one hour the time that I must spend on earth. "All is brief that has an ending," whether it be days or years. I know with perfect faith what awaits us at

---

[59] Louis Veuillot (1813-1883), French writer, the author of novels, poems, and polemical essays, and editor of the periodical *L'Univers Religieux*.

the end. But I ask you to support me and to accompany me in my pilgrimage, to pray that I be faithful and strong, and to welcome me when the hour appointed by God shall come.

My beloved, I believe the joy of reunion will surpass the pain of separation and waiting, and that then we shall live. You who can see and know, obtain for us a feeble ray of this eternal light to guide and illuminate us.

⁂

October 2, 1905

After a stay at Jougne, in great restfulness of body and soul, the return here was full of pain. To resume ordinary existence without the dear being who filled it seemed a task almost beyond my power. But did I not count on my own strength instead of relying on the fatherly Providence that has never failed me? Once again that Providence has aided me, for in the midst of all my grief and frequent bodily misery I was still able to remain closely united to the divine Will.

As Juliette used to say, I want to "reform my life." That is, without any great external change or singular behavior, to establish firmly in my soul more serenity, true humility, and charity. I want to be more and more true, and it is sometimes more difficult than it seems. Even if my grief is inconsolable and has totally changed my life, I must not give way to depressing and sinful sorrow. Since I cannot altogether live the life I would wish for, I must make my actual life better and more fruitful for God and for the souls who have been entrusted to me.

After all, the workman does not choose his task; the child submits to the tender will of the father. The only important thing is to perform my task; the circumstances and the means offered to me matter little. It is true that I shall have less human joy and comfort than if I lived in the midst of Christian friends and hearts; but I know by experience how God supplies all that is lacking and with what generosity He gives us what outward circumstances deny us. With Him and by Him I must become more tender, strong, and peaceful, to live more in the soul and yet give myself more to those I love and to all whom Providence has put or will put in my way.

To speak little of my bodily suffering and yet give myself necessary and reasonable care. To expect nothing from those whom I will try to benefit, except, of course, those whom I know thoroughly; to accept in silence the disappointments, the misunderstandings, and even the scorn that always come to those in whose depths others discern — and think they can attack — God. To live in memories, in prayer and action, and in hope and expectation. To be Christian — fully, reasonably, supernaturally Christian. To pray, to act, to work, to love.

⚬

October 7, 1905

Firmer resolution to have deep inner stability, and to accept as a trial that does not touch the depths this assault of troubles, agitations, and confusions that, to be sure, have their cause in my health, and also the painful disappointments caused by certain persons. To love those who have betrayed my confidence and made me suffer, or at least to pardon them fully. Not to assign to others my own faults, but to accept the humiliation of having given my confidence too quickly and of having committed these faults. For the future, without discouragement or bitterness, to practice great prudence in regard to work and new connections, and in all things to observe the greatest moderation. To give myself to everyone in charity, but not to let everyone enter into my heart, which I must not open too lightly. To welcome an affection only when I have solidly proved its value, and yet to have kindness for all. Never to compromise with ideas and principles, and yet to be full of indulgence for those who differ most widely from me in their point of view. To maintain, by prayer and daily effort, integrity of will and moral energy in spite of the oppression and failure caused by ill-health. It was, I think, Bichat who said, "The soul makes its body."[60] And when God dwells in the soul, how shall it not be stronger than the very evil that acts upon its body and sometimes overwhelms it?

⚭

October 17, 1905

Thirty-nine years old yesterday! And even if I live a long time, the greater part of my life behind me!

It will be three years in April since I solemnly offered my being and my life to God, before the tomb of His Apostle after an unforgettable Communion. How often I have thought of those blessed hours, which were for me the Viaticum of Sorrow![61] How plainly visible is Providence in the history of my soul and of my life! It must be the same for all, if one knows how to discern its beneficent action; when I look back, in spite of misfortunes and tears, I can only bless and adore. I begin this new period of life — long or short, calm or sorrowful, according to God's will — with these words from the depths of my soul: I believe, I adore, I hope.

I want to be Christian, Christian to the marrow, and transformed by grace. This year I will accept and offer to God for beloved souls and for the Church the trial of external distraction and agitation, which aggravates pain. I certainly will defend my home and myself from all who are unworthy, for that is a duty. But in spite of my natural aversion, increased by inconsolable grief, I must not give way to my immense longing for repose and withdrawal. To live a life of work and activity, in an atmosphere

---

[60] Probably Marie François Xavier Bichat (1771-1802), French pioneer in scientific histology and pathological anatomy.

[61] See May 3, 1904.

of faith, with Felix, in the midst of dear affections and friendships — that is my dream. But if that dream came true, it would
be a bit of Heaven already — and this earth is not Heaven. And
yet I must say in all humility what trouble I have in making the
necessary effort and how I suffer through my existence, which is
too varied for my liking and in which there comes from outside
no glimmer of faith or consolation. Perhaps that is why God has
made Himself everything to me, why He has supplied every one
of my needs and accomplished everything in me.

But I would be ungrateful if I did not say what a great happiness my dear mother's affection is. To talk to her is for me both
a great good and a sweet renewal of departed hours. May she be
blessed for what she is and does for me. May God keep her in
peace and sanctity!

May God help me to accomplish my resolutions and give me
His grace! May He do a little good through me!

❧

All Saints, November 1, 1905
After a painful period of exhaustion during which I had
to struggle against myself and against moral lassitude, God has
blessed my feeble efforts, and I have just made one of those
blessed Communions of incomparable joy in which one is truly
conscious of the divine presence. I renewed my offering for God
and souls; I gave thanks for all, even for suffering, and I again
asked pardon. Then I prayed for my beloved ones, especially
those who have left us, for my dear sister.

This is a sweet feast, the feast of those who already live in
God, those whom we have loved and who have attained to
happiness and light; it is the feast of eternity. And what a fine
idea to make the feast of the dead follow so soon! During these
two days a vast stream of prayer and love flows through the three
worlds: between the Church in Heaven, the Church on earth,

and the Church in which souls wait and expiate. The Communion of Saints seems doubly close and doubly fruitful. We feel that all souls and all those we love are close to us in God; and this living dogma by divine grace gives life to many souls on earth and in Purgatory. Not one of our tears, not one of our prayers is lost, and they have a power that many people never suspect.

I want to pass this month in prayer, memories, the thought of Heaven, and also in charity and peaceful and valiant activity.

⁂

November 13, 1905

Seven months today since our beloved one left us! And I suffer as on the first day, or even more, because around me indifferent people have forgotten that I could suffer still and because my external life allows me less quiet and recollection. I have let my calm be troubled by outside influences, and by anxiety for Mother's health, and for the future; but my deeper calm is untouched, because more than ever I feel abandoned to God and anxious to sacrifice all for Him and for the good of those I love most of all.

But too many things still agitate this exterior part of my soul and make it suffer. Worries, sad memories, an atmosphere of unbelief, indifference, or scorn, and the painful awareness of never being able to make either one's God or one's soul known to others — all this has beaten me and cast me on the ground, bruised like the gentle Savior. But all this ends in a humble act of faith, love, and acceptance, and in a new resolution to be more brave, to establish myself in peace, and to submit to these offenses without revealing the suffering they cause me.

With Felix I should be more even-tempered, more truly strong; with Mother more tender and attentive; with everyone kind and forgetful of myself. My weakness is great. I have had new experience of it, but I must say with St. Paul, "I can do all things in Him who strengthens me."[62]

My beloved Felix has cares, Mother has a great grief; their dear souls have need of mine, or rather — since the soul needs only God — by my sufferings and sacrifices I can obtain for them transformation of life. Is not this a task to make me sacrifice "hateful self" and offer up all that attacks this self and wounds it? My God, assist her who in spite of her faults desires above everything to make Thee known and loved.

⁂

January 3, 1906

This sad year is over! I ended it on my knees in my little oratory, offering myself to God with all my soul, confiding to Him those I love and the Church.

May this be a good year for souls and for me; may at least one heart know and love Jesus Christ through me. For that it would be well worthwhile to live and suffer and wait.

I went to Communion on Christmas Eve and on Christmas Day, and drew strength and peace from that blessed contact with the Savior.

Yet now I suffer from great physical exhaustion; and longing for the things I lack — candor, recollectedness, and Christian action — is causing me pain. In spite of my resolves I have allowed my peace to be troubled a little by certain offenses and excitements.

My God, I thirst;[63] grant me Thy peace and this infinite joy that Thou sometimes dost grant me, this beautiful light that enlightens and transforms all. To possess even a glimmer of it is already a small portion of Heaven, and it is for this reason, no

---

[62] Phil. 4:13.
[63] Cf. John 19:28.

doubt, that Thou dost give it all the more infrequently as the soul loves Thee more deeply and progresses further in Thy way.

Through suffering and in silence I want to pray, love, and act. It is best for God alone to dispose of what we offer Him; if we knew the result of our efforts, if the mysterious influence worked by our sacrifice and prayer were revealed to us, pride, always near, would have its way.

In eternity we shall have these consoling revelations. I shall know all that Juliette has been to me, and all that she has obtained for me, and perhaps I shall have the joy of seeing that one of my sacrifices offered for her obtained for her in the supreme hour a little peace and divine grace.

O my beloved one, for whom I have prayed and who, I hope, knows my spirit now — pray for me, and ask for me only the grace to love God more and more and to be a most humble apostle of Jesus Christ.

⚬

January 31, 1906

I interrupt my meditation to write down an idea that it just suggested to me.

For some time I have gradually been giving out too much of my being and of my interior life. It used not to be thus; the work of my soul was done in solitude in the sight of God and known only to my spiritual father — as much as those things can ever be revealed.

But under the influence of grief and the tenderness and sympathy that then enveloped me, I gave way to this sort of appeal from without and came to speak too easily of myself, my sorrow, and my illnesses, and even of my soul and of the graces I have received. I have even spoken too much of Thee, my God, for it is true that in this world that does not know Thee, one should weigh well one's words concerning Thee.

Some reflections made regarding this, and the attitude of some who are dear to me, have already given me a useful lesson in humility and reminded me of the duty of silence.

And this is the resolve of this meditation: silence in regard to my trials, silence about my interior life and what God has done unceasingly for me, silence about my soul and all supernatural things, about my hopes and my faith. I believe it is my duty in awaiting the divine hour to preach Jesus Christ only through my prayers, my sufferings, and my example.

The adored Guest of my soul must be guessed at rather than plainly seen; every part of me must speak of Him without my saying His name; I must be an influence, without ever being a profession of faith.

Anything that even in the most subtle or indirect way gives rise to pride and egotism must be banished without pity from my heart and conversation; is there not a little self-absorption even in the slightest display of oneself?

I do not want to be a spiritual chatterer, and except when charity makes it a duty, I want to keep this great silence of the soul, this encounter of myself alone with God alone, which guards one's strength and interior fortitude. Nothing must be dispersed, not even one's soul; one must direct it entirely to God, so that it may shine all the farther.

⁂

February 21, 1906

I have kept my resolve of silence fairly well, but I have let myself be too much dominated by an exhausting combination of irritation and dejection resulting from bad health.

But what a great thing the soul is, and how distinct from and independent of the body! In depression and physical pain, when our poor mental faculties share the lassitude of the body, the soul is still free and continues to live its own life, and upheld by a force that it knows to come from above, it dominates the body and keeps it in its place. But how we need God! And how quickly we should be conquered without His grace!

New resolution of silence, work, and quiet action. Resolution to do what God wills, not desiring the task that does not belong to me.

To pray and to offer my trials more than ever to obtain for him and for those I love the grace that has been given to me, which is the incessant desire of my soul and the goal of my life.

❦

February 27, 1906

Tomorrow Lent begins. I have just made a short meditation and made my resolves for this time of grace. I want to practice recollectedness, penance, and charity.

Recollectedness of soul, which can exist in the midst of exterior occupations and duties from which, less than any other woman, I can excuse myself. The soul can be a cell as white and empty of worldly influence as the cell of a monk. The crucifix and some books — that is to say, God and work: this is what fills the solitude of nuns and monks; this is what can make a solitary of the woman who is completely beset by external noise and activity.

Secondly, penance. Apart from penances prescribed by the Church, I must perform my own, unlike other people's. I will accept and offer to God those visits and receptions, the contact with indifferent people, those material occupations that are more painful to me than ever during this month when I would have liked to live with my dear memories. I will do it so that God only, I hope, will know what it costs me. And in the trials of my life or the misery of ill-health I shall have plenty of opportunities to mortify myself.

Lastly, charity. More and more to make myself all things to all men, to forget myself for others, to be always indulgent and affable, to show more tenderness to those about me, to go more to little ones and to the humble. Even in times of debility and physical exhaustion, I must not be as slack as I have been recently. I must take up my work again with prudence, but with more ardor and perseverance.

And then silence always, unless there is good to be done by speech. Not to speak of myself. To be more "amiable" than I have been for some time. To smile and share in the joys and pleasures of others when the body is overcome with fatigue is better than to give oneself in good health, for the effort is greater. May others see in me only that which can bring them comfort or do them some good, and may Thou alone, my God, know the silent battles in my will and my heart. May Lent be for me a time of preparation and sanctification, in order that I may perhaps become, O my God, Thine instrument and Thine apostle with those I love and with the souls Thou lovest.

⁂

April 4, 1906

I will go to Communion tomorrow; and during this week, until my Communion on Holy Thursday, I want to make my spiritual retreat.

I do not know if I shall be able to hear many sermons, but I have made these resolutions: to make a good daily meditation on what should be my apostolate; to practice penance and charity without being noticed; to finish my retreat with my Holy Week and Easter Communions.

It will be a wholly interior retreat, for my second resolution is that no one shall know what I am doing or suffer for my spiritual gain. I must, on the contrary, try to be more cheerful and serenely gentle, so that if anyone should by chance guess that God has been this way, such a discovery would not dishonor Him. It is a year since I wrote for the last time in this journal, before April 13. "*Fiat* for us, *alleluia* for her." O my God, give her happiness, and leave us our suffering and our memories, and let us all love one another one day close to Thee.

⸿

August 11, 1906

Before God, I close this journal in which for seven years I have noted the stages of my life and my soul. That outpouring was good for me while Providence was performing "in me, without me," a work that I understood only later. Now that I have come to maturity of age, when the day of the divine harvest dawns, a day prepared for in struggle and in pain, casting my eyes over the past and looking toward the future with serenity, this future that can no longer bring any true sorrow, because God is my horizon everywhere, I make an act of great faith, supernatural hope, adoration, and of gratitude, too, for all the tremendous graces that have been granted to me. Thy gift, my God, has been entirely free, and Thou hast made me a "privileged child."

On the threshold of my new life, I offer Thee, in humble but loving oblation, all my past existence — my childhood and youth; these fourteen years with their joys, sufferings, and faults; the trials Thou knowest of, which have made my life somewhat exceptional, but less exceptional than Thy graces, O my God. I offer also these two past years, sorrowful and yet transformed after unforgettable hours, all this time of purification and suffering, ending with the greatest trial of my life; these last months in which Thou hast worked upon and refined my soul, perfecting the instrument, as has been said to me, to use it in Thine own way for the good of souls and of those who are dear to me. As our Juliette has said, "I love Thee and abandon myself to Thee."

And now I offer Thee the new existence that has opened before me. Sustained by Thy grace I want to become another woman, a Christian, an apostle; and I take these resolutions in order to attain this goal, and to fulfill the mission that I see clearly to be mine.

First, *silence:* never to speak of my soul, my interior life, or of my trials except for some charitable necessity. To cover with the same reserve any manifestations of my piety; to let my Communions, prayers, and meditations be known as little as possible, that I may remain humble, and so that I may not provoke the spirit of obstinacy and ignorance with which I am surrounded.

Then, *work.* Material work and spiritual duties. Study, the cultivation of my mind. Intellectual apostolate, too, which God seems to will for me and for which He has prepared me. To complete one work and pass on to another. Never to remain idle or leave this land uncultivated.

Charity. To go from the near duty to the far one. To set priorities for my action: duties to my husband first, then all who belong to us, our friends, and those who depend on me. Charitable or social work, after the duties of my state; to be sure to continue with these, and in the presence of others to maintain the silence about them about which I have spoken. To keep humble and yet act distinctly and firmly.

Resolutions in regard to myself and others:

For myself. To be very severe. To maintain energetically as the basis of my whole exterior life the practices of my spiritual life: daily prayers, meditation, Communion as frequently as possible. These things are such a great sweetness and source of life to the soul. To accept troubles, sadness, suffering, and to practice voluntary mortification, all in the spirit of penance and reparation, and for souls.

For others. Not to speak of myself and my spiritual life, to keep silence about my good deeds. To be simple, true, always humble. To maintain calm always and never to betray physical suffering, anguish, or sadness. To be friendly and full of sympathy for men and ideas, to try to enter into and understand them. To be kind, with that true kindness that comes not from the lips but from the heart. To devote myself, to pour myself out, all without excitement or useless dispersion.

And in view of a greater good and for a higher purpose, even to watch over my bearing and my dress; to make myself attractive for our good God's sake. To make my home pleasant, that it may be a center of good and salutary influence; to let diverse spirits and hearts congregate there and to make every effort to raise and enlighten them.

To sum up: To *reserve* for God alone the depths of my soul and my interior life as a Christian. To *give* to others serenity, charm, kindness, useful words and deeds. To make Christian truth loved through me, but to speak of it only at an explicit demand or at a need so clear as to seem truly providential. To preach by prayer, sacrifice, and example. To be *austere* to myself, and as *attractive* as possible to others.

Those are my resolves, my God. I place them in the dear protection of my blessed sisters, of those I love who live in Thee. I confide them to my guardian angel, to the holy souls in whom I have special confidence — my sweet patron, St. Teresa, St. Catherine of Siena, and others as well. I confide them above all to thee, Mary, Mother and blessed protectress. Through thee I offer them to God, and I wish in the future to live only for my dear affections, for souls, in the peaceful expectation of eternity, when we shall at last have happiness and where, loving us, Thou shalt be adored forever, O Jesus Christ, my Savior and my God!

✂

Book of Resolutions
1906-1912

To re-establish all things in Christ.

Ephesians 1:10

(October-November 1906)[64]

This rule, which I now write down so that I can better examine my soul before God, should not be too rigidly interpreted by me.

The milieu in which I live, certain people's hostility, the variety and sometimes the complication of my duties, the influence I can have on the hearts who love my own heart and on the spirits who come to me with confidence: all demand great circumspection from me. If I must be so exact as not to neglect the smallest detail of my rule when I alone am concerned, it would not do to act in the same way when a neighbor is in question. My resolutions should therefore be adaptable to circumstances. The precept of charity should come before any measure intended to ensure the solidity and intensity of my spiritual life.

I place this project and these resolutions under the protection of Mary, my beloved Mother, and of my guardian angel, of my holy patron and the saints I especially honor, and also of the beloved souls whom God has taken to Himself and will give back to me in eternity.

In an act of faith and love, after giving thanks for all that God has done for me, I offer and consecrate myself to Him, asking for

---

[64] Dates given by the author in her manuscript are printed without parentheses at the head of each entry. Dates added by others have been placed in parentheses.

myself only one grace: to love Him more and more and to be His apostle to those I love and to souls.

RULE OF LIFE
Each day:

Morning and evening prayer.

Meditation. Meditation is necessary to my soul; it is daily food, without which my spiritual life would weaken. Meditation prepares the daily toil; to be alone with God helps us later in the midst of people, and enables us to distribute among them some of our morning provision.

To be present sometimes at the Holy Sacrifice of the Mass, especially on Fridays.

To go to Confession and Communion every two weeks if possible. To receive Communion more frequently whenever it can be done without troubling or displeasing anyone.

Holy Communion is a happiness that I would give myself more often if it were not my duty to deprive myself of it sometimes, in order to avoid offending prejudice. The strength God brings to the soul, the sweetness of His presence, the vitality communicated by that blessed contact with Him can neither be described nor explained. To those who marvel at this miracle of divine love one can only say "Taste and see."[65]

Blessed art thou, O my God, for those hours I have known in which my weary heart has lain against Thy Heart, and drawn from it peace, charity, the knowledge of things divine, and through the latter the knowledge of poor humanity, weakness, and the manifold forms of suffering. Through Thy pity, Thy power of consolation, and Thy tenderness Thou hast taught me, my adored Savior, how to sympathize, pacify, and love. How could I not love souls, especially those that are most weak and guilty — I

---

[65] Ps. 33:9 (RSV = Ps. 34:8).

who, weak and guilty too, have known the depth of Thy love and the fullness of Thy pardon?

Each month:

Give one day to a little spiritual retreat; go to Mass and if possible to Communion.

On this day, to abstain as far as possible from going out and from worldly contacts. More complete meditation. Examine my conscience and my life. Make on this day my preparation for death.

Each year:

Make a few days' spiritual retreat — as complete as possible, at least in a state of great interior recollectedness.

A retreat is to the whole of life what meditation is to each day. The soul gathers new strength and, transformed and sanctified, returns to the tasks and duties that fill up our lives. Giving oneself is easier when the soul has renewed its interior provision.

I do not include here all those precepts that each of us should observe unless especially dispensed from doing so. These resolutions have in view only the evangelical counsels. They have for their goal Christian perfection and seek that which will help me to draw closer to this ideal, which is still so distant.

After these resolutions concerning piety, I come to the resolutions that concern my exterior life and my relations with my neighbor.

First my duty to my dear husband: tenderness that has not even the merit of duty, constant care to be useful and gracious to him. Above all, to be extremely reserved concerning matters of faith, which are still veiled to him. If a quiet statement should sometimes be necessary, or if I can fruitfully show him a little of what is in my heart, that must at least be a rare event, done after careful thought, performed in all gentleness and serenity.

Let him see the fruit but not the sap, my life but not the faith that transforms it, the light that is in me but not a word of Him who brings it to my soul; let him see God without hearing His name. Only on those lines, I think, must I hope for the conversion and sanctity of the dear companion of my life, my beloved Felix.

Duty to my two families, especially to the young, to whom I will open wide my mind and my home. Duty to set an example, to pray, to exercise an influence. Duty to those whom Providence has put in my path and seems intentionally to have confided to my care. Never to anticipate a new task or duty, but as soon as one presents itself with a clearly providential character, to welcome it and never forsake it.

Duty of consolation and tenderness to my dear mother.

Duty in work. To undertake only a little and only what I can really accomplish. To speak of it little or not at all. To be occupied with it only during those days and hours when it will inconvenience no one around me and not interfere with the duties of my state. To bring to it all humility and charity, as well as a clear mind and an understanding of spiritual and social needs. In dealing with the poor, to avoid familiarity or haughtiness, or excess of any kind.

⚭

Three General Resolutions

Silence. To avoid speaking of myself, my troubles, my illnesses, and especially of my soul and the graces I have received from God. The abuse of confidences and indiscreet conversation easily lead to pride or to an egotistical absorption in oneself — an absorption, moreover, that does not help but, rather, hinders true recollectedness. To abandon this reserve only in those rare cases when the good of a soul seems truly to demand it or when some compelling opportunity for edification or counsel presents itself to me. Even then to speak of myself and my soul only with perfect truth and simplicity, without affectation or secret seeking after praise, wishing to glorify what is divine by belittling myself, or, rather, by letting myself be seen with all my weaknesses and faults.

Giving myself. Not only in doing my duty to all, not only in charitable works, not only in prayer, but in my whole attitude and way of life. Great and holy ideas and profound convictions often reach souls only through the personal charm and attraction of those who present them. "By their fruits you shall know them,"[66] our Savior has said — by the fruits of devotion, charity, and radiant faith, and also by those flowers that first strike the eye and precede the fruit; those flowers are called sweetness, charm, nobility and exterior distinction of manners and ways, serenity, equanimity, friendliness, smiles, and simplicity.

A deep and sanctified soul — perfect mistress, by divine grace, of the body and its obstacles — such a soul, without ever pouring itself out, shines forth and sheds upon everything the delicate perfume of these flowers of which I speak. Such a one attracts hearts and by its gentle influence prepares them for the coming of the Master, which she obtains for them eventually by her prayers.

Personal austerity. By austerity I do not mean, of course, anything harmful to the body or to health. I must, on the contrary, watch out for and try to improve my health, since it may be an instrument in the service of God and of souls. But in this illness that I am afflicted with, the precautions I am obliged to take,

[66] Matt. 7:16.

71

the discomforts it brings, and the privations it sometimes imposes on me (or at least may in future impose on me), there is
a plentiful source of mortification. Apart from that there are
numerous opportunities for self-sacrifice, without anyone knowing of it or suffering because of it; on the contrary, our personal
immolation will often be of actual benefit to others. To perform
these mortifications and sacrifices in a spirit of penance, of reparation to God and to the Heart of Jesus, and to obtain the salvation of sinners.

⚘

Intellectual apostolate

This is perhaps what God especially intends for me. He has
treated me like a "privileged child"; the word has been spoken
to me and I know its profound truth; He has arranged everything
in me and about me to prepare me for this form of apostolate.
In making known to me His intimate and personal action in the
depths of the human soul, in obliging me to live in the midst of
total negation and indifference and that impenetrable ignorance
of divine things that oppresses so many unfortunate people, He
has doubtless intended that I should understand the most widely
differing states of mind, that I should have compassion for, share
myself with, and turn toward those who blaspheme and doubt
with more pity and love.

To be the good Samaritan to so many discontented hearts,
uneasy minds, and troubled consciences; to have delicate respect
for souls and knowledge of them; to try to approach them gently;
to pour upon them healing oil or strengthening wine according
to their weakness or the gravity of their wound; to show God to
them only by letting Him shine forth from our soul where He
lives; to be all things to all men and thus conquer hearts for
Jesus Christ: this is the apostle's task, which I accept from
Thee, O my God, in spite of my unworthiness.

But I know well what this word *apostle* means and all the obligations it creates. First, the necessity of an interior life that becomes stronger all the time, of drawing more than ever charity and humble serenity from the Eucharist and from prayer, as well as of giving a wholly spiritual end to my intentions.

Then, to cultivate my mind, methodically to increase my knowledge of all those subjects that my mind is ready to seize upon and study; to do nothing in a hurry or superficially; to acquire, as much as is possible for me, competence in the subjects I take up. To transform and sanctify this intellectual industry by giving it a spiritual motive, performing it humbly without any thought for myself, but exclusively for the benefit of souls.

To bring to all conversation and discussion a tranquil sweetness, a firmness, and a friendliness that will banish bitterness or irritation from the opponent's mind; never to capitulate where principles are concerned, but to have extreme leniency and indulgence for people. Above all, to try, after discovering the vulnerable spot, to present the divine, unchanging Truth to each one in such a way as to make it understood and loved by him.

To bring great liberty of mind and clarity of judgment to any purely intellectual matter. Each time the conversation leads me to speak of faith, I will do so simply, but in a direct and firm way that will leave no doubt as to my convictions. Cleverness is nothing in such things; I am struck with the fact that unbelievers have more sympathy with people of deep faith than with those of variable and utilitarian views. These dear unbelievers attend more to those who are "intransigent" regarding the Faith than to those who by subtlety and compromise hope to bring them to accept the Faith. And yet the bold statement must be made with the most intelligent sympathy and the liveliest and most delicate charity.

To beg God to give me more and more knowledge of souls. To go to them through intelligence, through the heart; to strengthen my mind and rekindle my heart for that end. To work and act with serenity.

Every morning to offer to God, as I already do, all the indulgences I can gain during the day for the souls that are in Purgatory, especially those who are dear to me; to offer my active day and my *suffering* day for various intentions: for those I love, for souls, for the Church.

More frequent Communion, since circumstances allow of this — and as much as they will allow of it.

The Holy Eucharist is indeed food for the soul; to say so is a commonplace, but how true! Apart from the conscious joy it sometimes brings, even lacking that joy, the soul is left stronger and more alive; the Eucharist transforms it, although the soul may not be aware of this mysterious operation at the time.

This incorporation into us of the divine substance, this assimilation of the Being *par excellence* with our being, this eternal Life penetrating our lives, this close contact with the most holy and tender Soul of all, with this spiritualized humanity, as St. Paul says,[67] works within us and, if our will belongs to God, deeply renews us.

Anyone who has received Communion for many months or years without being changed inwardly and outwardly has assuredly not brought to the Holy Table the humility and childlike simplicity that is blessed by our Savior. This renewal is independent of all conscious sweetness and exterior joy; the sweet feeling of Jesus Christ's real presence is a grace sometimes bestowed by Him upon our soul, but it does not necessarily contribute to our

[67] Cf. 1 Cor. 2:15.

spiritual progress. It is one thing to love God, and another thing actually to feel the happiness of His presence.

To put a veil between my suffering and the outside world. Illness, sadness, the absence of a Christian atmosphere, which my heart and mind feels so much; the sorrow that, although it has lost its first intense bitterness, is still and will always be the great grief of my heart — the loss of that dear presence and that affection that have been my joy: in the future all these things must be a hidden treasure, concealed from indifferent glances. Excepting those whose rare affection makes them see through appearances, no one must know of my suffering, nor of the sacrifice I make in concealing it.

I must be all things to all men, occupied only with others' griefs, not saddening or troubling anyone around me with mine. To let my faith be seen only in the works inspired by it, and my sorrow only in the sanctification of my soul. To know how to smile, sympathize, share; but to keep the weight of my burden from all but God. Not to be ungrateful, to rejoice simply, with gratitude, in the great affections and delights that Providence has accorded me.

To ask God to draw on the interior reserve of suffering that I bear within the depths of my soul, in favor of souls and of those I love. Always to welcome trials, little or big, to accept them and offer them. Then, to keep silence and continue to act in all gentleness and serenity.

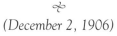

(December 2, 1906)
Resolutions for this time of Advent:
Prayer. More intimate, more profound. Frequent Holy Communion. Meditation.

Penance. In a spirit of reparation. Mortifications sought out and offered up. All hidden, done for God alone.

Charity. More lively, more forgetful of self, more supernatural. May the exterior be more attractive, more gentle toward all, in proportion as there is more interior detachment.

(End of December 1906)

Renewal of the foregoing resolutions now when a new year is about to begin. To implore divine grace and, sustained by it, to work during this year for my interior perfection. To ask God to grow in my soul and to transform it, while I myself, on the contrary, diminish through humility, penance, and silence. To make myself all things to all men without a single hope of human recompense; to work for the good of souls with Jesus and for Him.

Let inner austerity have a veil of smiles and gracious words. Let unfailing indulgence toward men excuse in me the unflinching fidelity to doctrine, the strict application to my life of the principles that inspire my soul.

To neglect not even the smallest duty.

Communion at least weekly. To keep up my daily meditation. Frequent visits to the Blessed Sacrament. Mortifications. A spirit of reparation.

Greater efforts than ever to efface from my heart and hide from the outside the hurt caused by many people's hostility, ignorance, and disdain of my faith. To offer up these frequent and painful stings, which sometimes strike to the quick, for the benefit of those who inflict them, for my dear souls, and also in a spirit of reparation.

Never to betray the confidence that another heart has entrusted to us. For the intimate outpourings, the confidences of the soul, the giving of oneself, there should be secrecy as of the confessional.

In work for souls, to guard carefully against all pride and egotism. Not to forget that we are the humble intermediary between God and souls, the dull instrument Providence makes use of, and that all our duty consists in perfecting this instrument, for which we still need grace.

✧

(February 13, 1907)

Resolution to sanctify myself during this Lent, and to work for the sanctification of souls and those I love, through penance.

Penance, humble, hidden, authentic; austere penance, without ever harming my health or drawing other people's attention.

To abstain from my pride, egotism, laziness. To practice mortification. To offer my sufferings in a spirit of expiation and reparation.

To try to make my charity more intense, more sweet; to ask God to augment the supernatural life in me.

In awaiting the divine hour for my beloved ones, to look to the Heart of Jesus alone for sympathy, comfort, and peace.

To give myself to others generously, with joy, without seeking or expecting anything in return, not even a clear-sighted look into my own soul. God sees me, I am His privileged child; may He make me His apostle, and that is enough for me.

✧

(June 1907)

During the month of the Sacred Heart, to meditate every day on the beauty, love, and holiness of the Heart of Jesus. To offer

Him in a spirit of reparation a part of the suffering and privation I now endure, consecrating the rest of my privations and activity to other intentions: the conversion and sanctification of those who are dear to me, the salvation of souls, the good of the Church. In the absence of all conscious joy, to establish myself more strongly than ever, by divine grace, in perfect serenity. Never to show by irritation or, what is more likely with me, by outward exhaustion, the moral and physical fatigue caused by certain difficulties and by long illness. To do everything to guard and improve my health, and to make of this care, which is often disagreeable, even morally, the best of mortifications.

To learn from the Heart of Jesus the secret of love for souls and deep knowledge of them: how to touch their hurts without making them smart and to dress their wounds without reopening them; to give oneself to them and yet reserve oneself; to disclose Truth in its entirety and yet to make it known according to the degree of light that each soul can bear. The knowledge required for the apostolate can be had only from Jesus Christ, by encountering Him in the Eucharist and in prayer.

(July-August 1907)

Resolution during this vacation: to persevere steadily with my daily prayers and meditations, my Communions at least weekly, to increase and strengthen, by divine grace, my spiritual life.

To be all things to all men, and in all circumstances to remain gentle, serene, full of sympathy for those around me. By example, by my words and acts to try to make Jesus Christ known and loved; through Him (or rather to beg that He do through me) to do good to those souls for whom I can be the instrument of Providence. Each day to work first for God and then for my neighbor. To pray, to act. To speak to each one the language he can understand. To be in the depths of my soul and to proclaim myself before all, yet in all simplicity, a child of Christ and of His Church, and to make my outer life harmonize with this high claim.

To maintain always exterior calm and evenness of temper.

Not to hope too ardently for the realization of my wishes, even those that are wholly spiritual; to consider that God is the master of His own action; to await the hour willed by Him for the souls I love; to hasten Him not by action that is perhaps indiscreet, but by prayer, by the gift of my suffering, and by a charity that does not calculate results and is free of all pride and egotism.

To put into all my words, acts, and gestures even, a modera-tion, a peaceful gentleness, which will be a constant sign of my interior serenity. In this way to show God always working in me to calm me, to soothe me, and to give me every strength.

Renewed resolve, after failure, of silence about myself, my soul, my sufferings, and the graces I have received, and of great reserve with those souls not yet decisively touched by grace. It is a mistake to suppose that our efforts will take effect before God's chosen time. Let us speak only insofar as it seems provi-dentially intended, when our words will be an answer to the call of a soul.

⚶

August 23, 1907
After a meditation on the
Gospel account of the Transfiguration:

Consecration, absolute gift of myself to Jesus Christ. He took me with Him, led me apart, and that is where I wish to stay — *apart from evil* forever; *apart from the world and human things* insofar as the duties of charity and of my state do not oblige me to lend my outward self. Never again to give them my soul.

Renewed consecration of my life to Jesus Christ.

To live in the future for Him alone; to preserve in Him my affections and friendships, more sanctified each day.

To love souls with a more lively and devoted love; to practice the threefold apostolate of prayer, of atoning penance, and of action through good works, words, writing, and example.

⚶

I take as a motto for my whole life those words recalled by the Holy Father: *Instaurare omnia in Christo* (to re-establish all things in Christ).[68]

First, to re-establish my soul in Christ, by prayer, Communion, and meditation; then, my whole life, by penance, charity, and the exercise of humility.

To re-establish in people's minds the idea of duty and of family; to prepare their souls for the return of faith and for supernatural life; to solicit the divine summons by my fervent prayers, my sacrifices, and my trials.

To make Jesus Christ loved and His Church known; to pour out untiringly, without looking for any result of my efforts, all that has been given to me; to make of all my actions, words, and affections so many different forms of apostolate.

[68] Eph. 1:10.

(October 1907)

A new life is imposed on me by the divine Will — a sedentary life, which resembles a sort of spiritual retreat offered to my soul by Providence at a time when my years enter into maturity.

Here are my resolutions for this period of my life:

First, *deeper recollectedness* — more authentic, imbued with prayer, meditation, and the constant thought of God; abiding recollectedness from which my soul shall draw its strength.

To be an *apostle by prayer*, that high and fruitful form of action, the only activity allowed me, the more secure because it is unknown and works with God for souls.

To *make amends* by suffering, sacrifice, and the mortifications that will arise daily or that I can take on voluntarily.

As exterior activity is forbidden me, to try to act by words and example upon those who come to me.

To keep my soul always open to those souls who wish to confide in me, but not to open it completely; always to keep the greatest intimacy in reserve for God alone.

To welcome my daily visitors with serenity, trying to be all things to all men, in the manner and to the degree fitting to each one.

To be pleasant, but with all discretion and simplicity.

To work and read seriously that I may improve and elevate my mind.

In spiritual things: to go to Communion every Sunday, as that will be the only day I can go; to go to Confession whenever I can.

To offer for my usual intentions and for souls this privation of Communion, of the spiritual consolations that have been so sweet and good for me, especially during this last year.

To be severe with myself, still more than in the past; on the outside, to make myself attractive so as to draw other hearts to the Master of whose goodness so many unfortunate people are ignorant.

The love of souls for and through Jesus Christ, without a single personal motive and without anything that could feed pride or egotism.

To give myself generously, and not to expect or calculate on the least return for this gift or the faintest satisfaction; not to desire affection, esteem, or sympathy or, still less, praise.

To practice my humble apostolate for God alone, in an unbounded charity that is mortified, lively, disinterested.

The two foundations of all Christian life:
Penance and humility.
The formula of all Christian life:
Contemplation, then action, in sacrifice.

Prayer is the higher form of activity; through it we act directly upon God, while the outward act is directed solely to our fellow human beings. We are sure of the result of our prayer; we can doubt that of our actions — unless their supernatural intention makes them another form of prayer. To pray, therefore, without ever tiring.

To love for those who hate, to suffer for those who rejoice, to give oneself for those who hold back.

More than ever, to practice Christian austerity: in my acts, in my food, and in the fulfillment of the duties of my state. To do it without injuring my health, reasonably at the same time as supernaturally. And to cover my sacrifices and freely chosen mortifications with a veil of smiles and cheerfulness that will keep them unknown. In my home, my dress, my manners, my welcome, to have nothing but grace and sweetness.

God has deprived me of all the aids of religion; for nearly three weeks my health has allowed me to go neither to Mass nor to Communion. That is the great, the only true privation, the oblation I can offer in a spirit of penance and reparation, the prayer that will obtain from our Savior, I hope, the graces so desired for others.

To be silent and to live in interior recollectedness. To pray and to practice mortification, for that is all God seems to want of me now. To ask nothing from outside in the way of human or spiritual consolation; to look to Jesus alone for everything.

On the outside, to give to those who come to me a gentle welcome, serenity, the word that is fitting for each. But much reserve. To do without haste the daily task, and to avoid the subtle forms of pride: love of our good deeds, of the influence we exercise, of inspiring others with our attractiveness. To hunt down "self" to its last perfidious hiding place.

Complete union with God; abandonment and full consent to His will in present illness and inactivity. To pray and to suffer, since activity is forbidden me; to give to my sufferings and prayers a supernatural intention; may they become, in silence and humility, a better form of activity, that thus, by divine grace, I may work unceasingly for the good of souls, performing also a work of reparation to God.

To speak as little as possible of myself, and yet without affection. Always to take part in others' joy and sadness. Not to allow this prostration, this slackness, which continuous illness and a confined existence make only too easy. To renew myself, therefore, each day by prayer, meditation, and voluntary mortification, which will help me to endure the mortifications sent by God.

To offer to God as the greatest and purest sacrifice the privation of outside spiritual help that I must endure, especially the most unhappy of all privations that could beset me, that of the Eucharist. O Lord, that is indeed abstinence, the severest penance, and the most painful trial of all. And it is suffering that many often do not know or understand.

Purify and transform me by this trial! Perfect Thy humble instrument! Give me the only grace I desire: to be Thine apostle with those who are dear to me, with the souls that Thou hast placed in my path, and other souls, too, distant and unknown, for whom my prayers and suffering will obtain from Thee salvation.

During days of illness and physical exhaustion, one must do everything with even greater calm and purpose, and guard oneself from exterior agitation by an even greater recollectedness.

Not to allow myself the slightest movement of impatience, and to fight unceasingly against every inner temptation to irritability. To punish and humble myself for it afterward.

To ask Jesus to put in me and allow to shine from me a little of the sweetness and gentleness of His Heart. To make myself all things to all men and to forget myself for all. To renew every day from our Savior my too-soon-exhausted store of tranquil affection, strength, and serenity.

To increase in gentleness; and to make myself more welcoming to all when, as now, I long ardently for solitude, silence, and rest. Nevertheless to arrange to have as much time for recollection as possible, so that my soul may have the nourishment of which it has so great a need, and which makes it stronger, more peaceful, and more filled with spiritual life.

✂

(April and May 1908)

A long time of illness, during which I could only live united by the deepest intimacy of my soul with God, forcing myself to accept and offer Him my sufferings. May He let them serve in expiation of my faults and accept all my intentions for them.

Most painful privation of many spiritual helps. And yet great joy, for the Savior comes each week to visit me and brings me, with the sweetness of His presence, a strength I could never have alone.

There are so many painful things in the empty monotony and distraction of those times when we are ill. God alone can make of this emptiness, of these little sacrifices and successive privations, a work of redemption for me and for others. Is there no sweetness in being on our Savior's Cross and, so close to Him, obtaining the grace of salvation or conversion for others, for souls that are greatly loved?

❧

(April and May 1908)

The two months just passed have been fruitful for my soul, I can now see. The apparent inertia, the inner destitution, the humiliating prostration of body and mind were all covering and hiding a mysterious work of grace that was taking place in the depths of my soul. And now I state with joy that God has made me take a great step forward in the way of renunciation and self-denial, teaching me even to do without His sweet consolations.

I want to love Thee and Thee alone, O my Savior — not the great joys Thy child sometimes receives from Thee. Help me to detach myself more and more from passing things and to attach myself to Thee. Give me the grace of being — by prayer at least, and by suffering —Thine instrument with souls, those who are dear to me, and those whom I do not know but who need my humble intercession with Thee.

And then, O Lord, give me the grace I long for, and make Thyself known to and loved by him whom I love best here below. Give all Thy light and Thy peace to my mother, and sanctify those I love, especially those children whom I beg Thee to make into apostles with valiant souls. I give myself to Thee and renew at Thy feet the resolutions of these last months and of all my illness.

❧

October 2, 1908

Renewed offering of myself and consecration of my life to God.[69] Renewal of baptismal vows. Consecration to the Blessed Virgin. Resolution to practice, with divine grace, evangelical perfection according to the duties of my state, to lead an apostolic

[69] In the church at Jougne.

life of prayer, penance, and charity. To make reparation for myself and for all.

A holy day, which completes that innermost consecration begun at the tomb of the Apostles, starting a new era in my spiritual life, and binding me irrevocably to the way of the evangelical counsels, the only one in which my soul can breathe now.

(November 1908)
Resolutions for this winter:

Mass and Holy Communion three times a week.

Confession every two or three weeks
according to circumstance.

Daily meditation.

Morning offering of my day, active and suffering,
for special intentions, for souls, for the Church.

Offering of the day's indulgences
for the souls in Purgatory.

At least a decade of the Rosary each day.

Intellectual work.

Correspondence and charitable works.

Practice of mortification and acceptance of suffering.

To have nothing but sweetness, amiability, and serenity for all, however I really feel, whether I am suffering or physically exhausted. To be joyful with the deep and radiant joy drawn from God in the Eucharist. To love with more intense affection the dear ones around me who cherish me.

Not to speak of myself, to interest myself in everyone. To give myself to others, keeping my best for God.

To count more on prayer than on action, on God more than on myself, on the tremendous power of suffering more than on human energy or personal effort.

Prayer is an all-powerful force that, coming through the Heart of Jesus right into the very bosom of God, seizes, attracts, and in some way plunges grace into souls. Suffering and the practice of charity are other and equally powerful forms of our prayer.

It is quite clear to me that the divine Will does not intend me for action. Until a new command is given to me, I should confine myself almost exclusively to prayer and strive to have more of the spirit of sacrifice. Perhaps God deprives me of outward activity in order to subdue in me all inclination to pride, even the subtle pride of doing good. In prayer we do not see the result of our efforts, however certain they may be; we are truly instruments in the hands of the divine Artist. We can remain humble even while knowing the great joy of working for God's glory and the good of souls. Let that, O Lord, be my portion and my task, and in silence let me do Thy will alone.

(January 1909)
The word of command from our Savior to my soul for this year:
Prayer and penance.

I want to give myself the great joy of sometimes choosing a soul, apart from the dear souls entrusted to me, for whom I pray incessantly — some guilty or hostile soul, preferably — and of adopting it spiritually. In a special way, with pious persistence, I will often offer for that soul part of the day's activities or sufferings and will pray and practice mortifications for it. It would be a very humble, hidden apostolate, which divine grace could make most fruitful. Does it not fit in exactly with my vocation, which seems above all contemplative and inclined to prayer and sacrifice?

I have just chosen such a soul for adoption and will never abandon it before God, while not neglecting the sweet burden of souls — those of all our brothers and of those who do not believe — I already carry to Him in prayer.

Contrition of heart, mortification of the body, the two elements of penance, which must not be separated as long as the soul is not separated from the body. Living charity as a foundation.

(February 24, 1909)
During this Lent:
Prayer — that is, my precious Communions, Holy Mass, visits to the Blessed Sacrament, meditation, liturgical prayers.

Fasting — that is, the abstinence prescribed for me, mortifications accepted or voluntary, sufferings sent by God, sacrifices. Abstinence above all from pride, egotism, and sensuality.

Alms — of money, but still more of time, trouble, my personal satisfaction (given for the benefit of others), my intelligence, my heart, and my home. Almsgiving of words, smiles, cheerfulness, and sweetness.

Great calm and reserve; silence always about myself and my concerns. A spirit of reparation.

Humble and complete renunciation of all honor, joy, and success, even in spiritual things and in my work for souls. To give my time, my trouble, my words, and my work; to open my heart to all who come to me; then if I seem to fail in my poor apostolate, if disappointments and griefs multiply, to redouble my prayers and penances and, entering once again into that habitual silence that I wish to practice more than ever, to confide to God the souls I love and am concerned about, remembering that I am an instrument that Providence may sometimes wish to use, but could easily dispense with, to achieve its ends.

To be humble, mortified, even in the zeal to hide mortifications and acts of humility.

(July-August 1909)
Resolutions for this vacation:
Humility, charity to all, silence. Less dwelling on myself, to make myself less the "center," not to speak of myself.

Within, close union with Jesus Christ: Communion three times a week, meditation, prayer. Great interior recollectedness. A little more austerity to make up for the unavoidable outside diversions. But nothing obvious: good spirits and smiles covering efforts and sacrifices.

To confide my vacation, those I love, and myself to the Heart of Jesus, which is more and more for me the Heart of the Friend and the beloved Master.

(January 1910)
The word of command for this year:
To try to give our Lord Jesus Christ to souls by the most humble and courageous practice of charity, by suffering and mortification, above all by prayer. That is in a special way my "vocation."

To combat pride in myself by the exercise of humility, egotism by forgetting myself within and offering myself without, and sensuality by silence in what concerns me, by mortification, and by the renunciation even of spiritual joys.

To hold in check my longing, which is sometimes so strong, for a life that is different from my own, for calm and recollection and silence. To keep within wise limits my growing dislike of the world, of external excitement.

To accept the suffering caused so often by hostility, indifference, or incomprehension of religious things. To wish strongly, humbly, and solely for God's will and to live through Him and for Him in the world that I would like to flee from for the solitude that I cannot have.

Not to neglect the duties of my state, all the while maintaining as the basis of my life and my days the religious exercises my soul has so much need of, which are its strength and its joy. To be gentle and smiling outside, keeping for God alone the inner life, the life that is "hidden" in His heart.

&cx;

In what concerns God: To suffer and to offer.
In what concerns others: To give myself, to pour myself out.
In what concerns me: To be silent and to forget myself.

&cx;

(February 8, 1910)
This Lent I renew the resolutions of last year. To practice the same privations in regard to food; they do good for the body, all the while being beneficial for the soul. Austerity for myself, great and loving charity for all.

Prayer — Penance — Charity.

O my God, Thou dost not refuse me suffering. For some time Thou hast accustomed me to love Thee in the privation of all sensible joys, in a suffering heart and, often enough, in an exhausted body. I accept all from Thy hand and unite myself to Thy will. Is it not just that having received all from Thee I should give Thee something in my turn, and that I should offer Thee the trials, prayers, sacrifices, and humble activity that is Thy daily design for me? Through all I want to try, by divine grace, to maintain joy of the spirit.

O Lord, for some time Thou hast allowed me the grace of suffering: mental trials, the renunciation of my desires and tastes, deeply felt solitude of soul, and now the illness of my dear sister.[70] How well Thou knowest how to choose for us the most salutary suffering, the one that crucifies us and allows the least possibility of egotism and pride. In my illness there were still subtle temptations for me, and satisfactions that were legitimate and yet too much of this world. In leaving me this physical misery, with the inconveniences and humiliations it brings, Thou hast again hidden this from the eyes of others, and hast sent me other trials, which are also very painful, but truly known only to Thee.

From the bottom of my soul I say to Thee "Thank you." Blessed art Thou, O Lord, for all this pain, through which Thou hast allowed me to expiate my faults, draw near to Thy Heart,

---

[70] The serious illness of her younger sister Amélie beginning in May 1910. The cure of this sister was one of the three objects of her pilgrimage to Lourdes. See *In Memoriam*.

and also to obtain, I hope, many spiritual graces for souls and for those I love.

My God, help me to carry the cross Thou hast offered me, and let none of this precious grace of suffering be lost to me or to the souls Thou lovest.

(July-August 1910)
Resolutions for this vacation:
Confession every two weeks.
Communion three times a week.
Each day:
Morning and evening prayer.
Meditation.
Offering of my day and of daily indulgences.
A decade of the Rosary.
Without:
Forgetfulness of self, giving of myself to others, apostolate.
Within:
Recollectedness, interior union with God.

Always to speak calmly, and to put gentleness in my gestures.

(October 1910)
Resolution, word of command for this winter: *A spirit of prayer and charity.* Interior union with God, daily prayers, meditation, my Confessions, and my usual precious Communions, the wholly supernatural intention given to my daily trials and my actions — that is what will sustain the spirit of prayer in my soul and make it shine in my life. Friendliness, gentleness, the constant effort to understand the most diverse minds and to give

them the truest sympathy, forgetfulness of self concealed by smiles, the giving of my heart and understanding in the service of souls, indulgence of others acting as a cloak for my severity to myself — this is what it will be for me to practice charity.

To ask God to give me a soul great enough to love Him ardently, to serve Him with joy, and to shine forth with His light.

To avoid carefully all discussion on religious subjects. Prayer, example, words, and deeds filled with charity and intelligence — these are the elements of fruitful controversy. The combat of intellects will never open the way to God, but a ray of charity sometimes illumines the path from which some poor distressed heart is wandering and leads it to its destination.

Renewal of my consecration to Jesus Christ, act of complete abandonment to His will, offering of myself for special intentions.

After our sweet return to the Faith and the inexpressible joy of union with God, after He has given us everything, the time comes for us to give Him something in our turn. There comes a second period, more grave, more austere: the period of loss and interior deprivation, of dryness even and sometimes real distress. We can then show our Savior the depth of our love; we expiate past faults and offer the purest reparation to Him whom we have offended; we can also offer reparation for others, make our interior trials serve other souls, and acquire more inner strength. From a spiritual perspective, we attain to manhood, and, as St. Francis de Sales says so well, God weans us from the milk of infants to give us the wine of the strong. Through all suffering and darkness of the spirit one feels a great sweetness to be doing something at last for God, showing Him that one loves Him truly — Him, and not His consolations, of which He was so prodigal not so long ago. The unachieved *Alleluia* ends in a *Fiat* that, in spite of all, is still joyful.

My God, I belong, and wish always to belong, to Thee, in suffering or in pain, in spiritual aridity or in joy, in illness or in health, in life or in death. I want one thing only: that Thy Will may be done in me and by me. More and more, I seek, and desire to seek, only one end: to promote Thy greater glory by the realization of Thy designs for me.

I offer myself to Thee in wholehearted interior immolation and implore Thee to dispose of me as of the commonest, most useless instrument, in favor of the souls Thou lovest, for Thy service. Make of me a being either passive or active, practicing in turn and as the hour requires the contemplation I love best and other good works according to Thy Will.

Let me be always austere with myself, more and more gentle, sweet, and helpful to others, to make Thee loved through me, always hiding my efforts, prayers, and mortifications. Make me very humble, and draw my heart to Thine, my beloved Savior and God.

Catholic Liturgy has a great charm for me; I love to live, in the course of the year, the great collective life of the Church, uniting myself with its joys and sorrows, joining my feeble prayers with its prayers, my weak voice with its powerful voice. It is sweet to me to go through the liturgical cycle, reliving our Savior's life, from His Incarnation to His death and Ascension; through the mouths of the prophets, fathers, and saints of all ages to tell Him my faith and my love; to adore Him in company with those who have adored Him through the centuries; to offer myself to Him with shepherds, disciples, and martyrs, with souls of all times; to feel myself a living cell in the great Catholic union; and to come, after so many others, and before so many who will follow me, with my homage to the Infant God, the suffering Christ, the risen Lord.

How I pity with all my devoted sympathy those who are ig-norant of all these traditions and of our Christian joys, who have rejected them with contempt or even with hate, because they have not sufficiently understood or experienced them in the past! How I regret that I cannot draw these souls to Jesus, and how fervently I resolve to pray, suffer, and act with more ardor and humility than ever for these poor misguided hearts!

When we feel impotent against hostility and indifference, when it is impossible to speak of God or the spiritual life, when many hearts brush against ours without penetrating it, then we must enter peacefully into ourselves in the sweet company that our souls never lack; and to others we must give only prayers and the quiet example of our lives and the secret immolation that makes the most fruitful apostolate. All our explanations, words, and efforts are not worth the feeblest ray of the Holy Spirit in en-lightening a soul, but they may obtain all His light for this soul.

There are moments in life when we must look neither ahead nor behind nor to the side, but contemplate only the cross God of-fers us, from which will flow great graces for ourselves and others.

To practice sacrifice in love. Resolution made after Confession today, and suggested by these words of the priest. More humility, sweetness, and serenity than I have practiced lately; more generosity. To love Christ who loved me *even unto sacrifice, the crown of thorns, and death*. To love souls for Him and in Him, and to sacrifice myself for them humbly and joyfully, in secret, by prayer, suffering, and action.

Much sadness and disappointment and those intimate sufferings that escape the eyes of others and are all the more salutary for it. O Lord, I offer Thee all; make of my trials a work of expiation, reparation, and prayer; help me to practice complete renunciation and to preserve peace of heart; make me know how to be all things to all men without looking for any human return for my devotion or efforts; teach me that prayer, all-powerful with Thy Heart, which is made of faith, humility, and confident surrender; teach me the silent and constant practice of mortification; give me the spirit of sacrifice, and renew my soul deeply so as to make of it the living victim in which Thou wilt be always present and which Thou wilt offer unceasingly to the greater glory of Thy Father. I place this prayer, and myself too, under the special protection of the Blessed Virgin Mary, my beloved Mother, whom I wish to love and confide in more.

⚘

(November 1910)

Change of abode,[71] a new life, which must be directed to a greater degree toward God.

To recollect myself more; yet to be all things to all men in devoting myself, in giving myself generously to those around me, to little ones, to the poor and afflicted, above all to souls.

---

[71] At the end of October 1910, she and her husband left the apartment they had inhabited for twelve years, in which the evolution and sanctification of her soul had taken place, for a new home from which, three and a half years later, God was to take her to Himself.

And to maintain more than ever silence about my spiritual life, my pain, my health. Silence is the safe guardian of humility. Never to be silent, on the other hand, when it is a question of others' pain, or generous praise of one's neighbor, or of doing good.

It is marvelous how well God knows how to try a soul — how, after captivating it by the sweetness and blessed charm of His consolations, He despoils it, imposes upon it one renunciation after another, takes away from it sensible joy, and leads it little by little to the true love of Himself, the love that no longer reckons joy or pain, good or ill health, death or life, and which does not even seek any longer the conscious sweetness that was its light in the beginning of its conversion.

Bitter suffering of an evening spent in hearing my faith and spiritual things mocked at, attacked, and criticized. God helped me to maintain interior charity and exterior calm; to deny or betray nothing, and yet not to irritate by too rigid assertions. But how much effort and inner distress this involves, and how necessary is divine grace to assist my weakness!

My God, wilt Thou give me one day . . . soon . . . the immense joy of full spiritual communion with my dear husband, of the same faith, and, for him as for me, of a life turned toward Thee?

I will redouble my prayers for this intention; more than ever will I supplicate, suffer, and offer to God Communions and sacrifices to obtain this greatly desired grace.

A ray of light in the midst of the bitterness caused by these conversations with my friends: a young Jewish woman, a convert, is entering the Carmelite convent to make reparation in the name of her brothers and of all of us who are sinners, and to offer to God an oblation of love and supplication.

Lord, Thy Kingdom come, in the world, in souls, in all the souls Thou hast entrusted to me or that are dear to me, in the soul that is the dearest of all to me. And may Thy Kingdom be completely, deeply, and exclusively established within my soul, which renews its whole consecration to Thee. Make me Thine instrument, and use me for the good of all persons and for Thy glory, adored Master, my Savior and my God!

⚜

(December 1910)

Lord, I offer Thee my spiritual aridity and privations. I offer Thee the interior sadness, the injuries, the disappointments of my heart, so many anxieties for dear souls and for the health of those precious to me, and all the many sufferings of life.

I offer Thee darkness of mind, faintness of will, inner vexations and griefs.

I offer Thee the physical misery, this unhappy infirmity with which Thou hast impeded my exterior life, the discomforts and weariness, too, that my illnesses bring upon me sometimes, at this very moment even.

I bind these things into a sheaf, Lord, and come humbly behind the shepherds to lay it in the manger. Little Child, all love, all purity, all sweetness, give me purity of heart, sweetness, and charity. Accept my burden of afflictions and use them for the good of souls and for Thy glory.

May Thy blessed hands help me to carry it, and may Thy love and the close union of Thy Heart with mine sweeten this unhappy solitude of mine. Let this solitude come to an end one day when, by Thy grace, Thou shalt convert and sanctify those near and dear persons whom I implore Thee to make Christians and apostles, O Jesus Christ, my Lord and my God!

December 31, 1910

The last day of a year of which the chief characteristic for
me has been privation.

God willed it to be full enough of suffering, renunciation,
sadness of every kind, and in a spiritual way arid, with the destitution of the manger, without the sweet joys that make the hour
of the divine dawning in our souls so radiant. But the Blessed
Master taught me stronger, deeper love, stripped of conscious
happiness; and it is from the bottom of my heart that I offer
Him the year that is gone and the one that is to come.

I consecrate myself to Him and accept beforehand all that
He wants of me, through me, or for me: joy or sorrow, health or
illness, poverty or riches, and also life or death, according to
what He shall judge to be for the greatest good of souls and in
His interest and for His glory.

O Lord, I abandon myself to Thee and wish to love Thee still
more. Give health and holiness to those I love, salvation and all
Thy graces to souls, and peace and expansion to Thy Church.

For myself I ask one thing: let me love Thee, without joy or
comfort if need be, and use me for the spreading of Thy spiritual
Kingdom in souls, Jesus my Savior.

It is a source of pain and difficult sacrifice to have to divide
one's life so much, and always to give to each one less than he
expects. This sometimes leads to a feeling in others that not
enough is being done for them, and they perhaps show some
sadness or regret, which becomes a bitter trial to her who is
the involuntary cause of it.

And then one's self-love does not like a state of things that
makes one less esteemed and appreciated and apparently unequal to one's task. That perhaps is the true, hidden fruit of this

trial: a little useful humiliation, less dangerous sympathy and admiration, very deep pain that does not elicit any praise.

To make myself do my duty amply, to give generously to each one my efforts, time, affection, a warm and equable welcome, even at the price of sacrifice and renunciation.

To offer God my incapacity and joyfully to endure being a little misunderstood, or, rather, to endure being truly understood with my weaknesses, my laziness, my numberless imperfections. Without this drop of bitterness, the sweetness of the affection surrounding me might make me slide into laxity and self-satisfaction.

My God, I accept my dispersed life, so often contrary to my wishes — this sometimes fatiguing variety of occupations, acquaintances that do not attract me, cares. Help me to perform all the duties of my state and yet to safeguard my spiritual life. Let the warmth of my welcome, the serenity of my bearing, the friendliness of my words always hide from everyone the miseries of my poor body, and the efforts and sacrifices of my soul. Teach me to be all things to all men, and to be more austere within, to myself alone. To practice greater mortification, especially in a spirit of reparation.

Meditated on the miracle of the multiplication of the loaves. Jesus Christ takes this lifeless thing, this tiny, coarse object, this bread, and by His blessing, it becomes food and life for the entire crowd.

Why should I not be, in these same divine hands, the poor instrument for another such work? Why should I not be given by God to souls to uphold and revive them? I am only feebleness, but strength will come from Him alone who uses me; I will let myself be distributed by Him to souls, and will serve them only in the measure that He wills. Sweet divine benediction, descend upon me! Multiply my prayers, sacrifices, and acts of charity! Let these fragments of Thy love in me become warmth and comfort for the spiritually starved, until the blessed time when Thou, the one living Bread, shalt come Thyself to revive and save them.

People in the world do not realize that one can be very detached from all human things and live a keen spiritual life, and yet find sweetness in the interests, occupations, and joys of life. However, it is only when one has rooted oneself in eternity that one can let one's humble little barque float upon the surface of the waves and rejoice fully in the view from earthly rivers. Storms no longer frighten one; the clear sky makes one more bold. The sun is always shining behind the clouds; the light, for all its beauty, does not conceal the eternal and splendid light that guides us to port and waits for us there.

Joys of life — affection, the beauty of nature, and the splendors of art: as much as or more than anyone I rejoice in you, for you are a reflection of the Beauty and Love that have taken possession of my heart. Sorrows of life — trials, illness, and painful infirmities: dear companions who have been so faithful to me, I do not reject you; I love you, because you are other aspects of the one true Love; because, united to the holy Cross, you become good workers for the salvation and conversion of souls and for my own expiation; because, thanks to you, I can sometimes show my tender gratitude to Him who has done so much, who has done *everything* for me.

May God be praised for all: joys and griefs. May He help me, by the spiritual joy that exists even in the midst of interior gloom, to praise and glorify Him until I breathe no more, until I enter eternity.

To preserve, by prayer and constant efforts, unalterable exterior serenity and continual gentleness. To keep calm on the outside when inwardly one is painfully assailed and shaken, and to maintain always the equilibrium of these two duties, these two needs of my being: interior recollectedness and the giving of myself to others. Before all, prayer and meditation; then activity.

Resolution to make each of my days a resumé of my whole life by putting in each one first of all prayer — prayer of the heart, entirely mental and interior — meditation, habitual devotions, Communion three times a week.

Next, penance by the acceptance of daily suffering and voluntary mortification — not neglecting mortification in the matter of food.

Finally, by the humble and constant exercise of *charity*: to be kind, gentle, to speak to each person the language of his soul.

I want to try to work among the poor once more, as far as my health and the duties of my state will allow. In any case, to go always first to the humble and afflicted, and to accept peacefully the inability to do *all* I want to do for my neighbor and for souls. To offer for them my powerlessness, my prayers, my sacrifices, and to impress on myself the thought that prayer is more powerful than action.

To have more and more, by the grace implored from God, a spirit of reparation.

Not to forget that by His choice graces, by exceptional trials, and by the wonderful strength of His love, God has called me to a vocation of usefulness to Him for souls. All the miseries of my life are nothing beside this grace of which I was and am so entirely unworthy.

O Lord, teach me to make reparation and to use Thy poor instrument in Thy service for Thy glory.

☙

My present trial[72] seems to me a somewhat painful one, and I have the humiliation of knowing how badly I bore it at first. I now want to accept and to carry this little cross joyfully, to carry it silently, with a smile in my heart and on my lips, in union with the Cross of Christ. This involuntary "hair shirt" will replace that which I would never be allowed to wear, and I will thus discipline my pride, egotism, and laxity. My God, blessed be Thou; accept from me each day the embarrassment, inconvenience, and pain this misery causes me. May it become a prayer and an act of reparation.

☙

(March 1, 1911)

Beginning of Lent: time of recollectedness and penance. To withdraw into solitude, not outward but inward. To seek for true sanctification, and at the end of this period, a more complete consecration to God.

To *fast*, spiritually, by more constant efforts with myself, by sacrifices and suffering; physically by self-denial in food, by privations and all my bodily misery.

To *pray*, by Confession, more fervent and recollected Communions, meditation on the Passion, visits to the Blessed Sacrament, the Rosary, the penitential Psalms, the Way of the Cross; by more constant and peaceful union of my soul with God; and to attend, when I can, sermons and other pious devotions.

Almsgiving, of a little money, but also of my time, my heart, my prayers, and my suffering. To place in my heart or, rather, with the help of divine grace, to cause to descend into it by

[72] Either in late 1910 or early 1911, Elisabeth noticed a small tumor on her chest. Her doctors required her to wear a painfully tight apparatus about her chest, hoping thereby to eliminate the need for surgery.

prayer and the sacraments, a boundless charity, a charity that is sweet, tender, strong, always active and directed toward everyone, more perhaps toward those who do not humanly attract me.

To become humbler, more silent about myself, my trials, and my spiritual life; to practice greater bodily mortification, as I resolved before God. And to follow strictly the counsel of the Master: to conceal greater austerity beneath a more smiling, cheerful, and gracious appearance. "Not to look dejected,"[73] not to bear the heart's fasting from human satisfactions as if it were a heavy burden; but to let my interior joy shine forth on all, the fruit of renunciation and penance.

⤸

Means of sanctification in Lent:

Fasting — to the extent that is possible for me, by the suppression of whatever is not necessary to my health in food or other material things; by bodily and spiritual mortifications.

Prayer — by the Eucharist: Communion, attendance at the Holy Sacrifice of the Mass, visits to the Blessed Sacrament, meditation on the Passion, union with Jesus Christ suffering and crucified, by my usual pious devotions carried out with greater fervor, recollectedness, and calm.

Charity — by giving myself to everyone, by material and spiritual almsgiving. Great humility, silence, and gentleness.

Intellectual work, or the modest duties of my state, transformed and sanctified by the supernatural intention.

⤸

March 17, 1911
Special prayer.

[73] Cf. Matt. 6:16.

An intimate compact between my soul and God, my heart and the heart of Jesus,[74] through the intercession of the Blessed Virgin and under the protection of St. Joseph and St. Teresa. Confidence this time of being heard again. Now, O Lord, I await the fulfillment of Thy blessed promises, and I wish to receive faithfully what they bring me in Thy name.

May God be blessed!

❧

April 9, 1911[75]

May God's will be done.

Be Thou blessed for everything, O Lord;

and give me Thy pardon and Thy grace.

Bless my beloved ones, all of them;

grant to their souls conversion and holiness.

May my dear nephews and my niece

be Christians and apostles.

Give Thy grace to the souls I love,

light and supernatural life to every soul.

Bless and guide Thy Church

and sanctify Her priests,

my spiritual father among them.

And take me altogether to Thyself,

in life, in death, and for eternity.

Amen.

[74] A pact by which she offered to God the sacrifice of her life, as she writes below in the entry of April 9, to obtain from God certain supernatural intentions that were particularly dear to her, chiefly the conversion of her husband. See *In Memoriam* and the second part of the *Journal* (October 19, November 5, 1911; March 6, 1912; and June 14, 1913, especially).

[75] Palm Sunday, the day of Elisabeth's entry into the nursing home where the next day she was operated on for the tumor mentioned above.

O Lord, I offer Thee this trial for the intentions Thou knowest. Let it bear fruit a hundredfold, and let me lay in Thy Heart my sufferings, desires, and prayers, to be disposed of as I have asked of Thee.

O Mary, pray for me, for us, now and at the hour of our death. Amen.

June 8, 1911

Thanksgiving to God for the success of this operation, for so many graces received, for the sweetness of such dear tenderness and such precious affection.

Resolution to employ my life — what Providence leaves me of it yet — in the service of our Lord; to put His interests and the good of souls before everything; to live a more recollected and stronger spiritual life; to be more all things to all men and to fill my existence and my days with prayer, suffering, and charity; to practice humility and silence and to accept with a joyful heart this new physical "ugliness" — out of which God will make beauty and supernatural light for the souls that are so dear to me.

Thought and resolution suggested by our Lord
during my visit to the Blessed Sacrament:
To expiate for others and for myself.
To merit for others and for myself.
To obtain for others and for myself.

O Lord, Thou hast laid Thy Cross on my soul, on my heart, on my body. Of all sufferings, Thou givest me that which pierces my heart the most. Help me to carry this cross without bitterness, without falling, without egotistical thoughts of self. In spite of failings and humiliating weaknesses, I seem to be advancing little by little in the way of renunciation and entire abandonment.

My God, let me renew my prayer to Thee: that for those I love there may be neither sin nor suffering, that Thy light may shine on them, that their souls may be sanctified by Thee. To Thy care I confide them, and to Thee I abandon myself, placing my burden in your Heart and surrendering all to it — sufferings, desires, prayers. For Thee I will keep the tears of my heart, giving to others only the smiles in my eyes; it is with Thee alone that I want to carry the Cross, letting nothing be seen of my interior misery but the light of Tabor,[76] the light that once rekindled me and that has now been extinguished to give place to the shadows of the Cross. On Calvary Jesus carried out His work of redemption; it is in suffering that souls chosen by Him can likewise do their work, in desolation and humiliation.

⚬

(November 1911)

Resolution for this year, in the beginning of this winter:

To be *joyful* and to *practice spiritual poverty.* Joyful in spite of, or even because of, this prostration, discomfort, and lassitude into which my physical miseries sometimes plunge me. Serenity within, and always gentleness and smiles without, amiable when I feel bad-tempered, welcoming when I long for solitude, patient and cheerful when I feel weary and tense.

To be spiritually poor, detached from all that is purely human, and to the extent possible with the duties of my state, to practice a little [physical] poverty in what concerns me alone. Poverty of spiritual joys, of the heart, of life's satisfactions, deprivation, abandonment.

[76] Mark 9:1-8.

At the same time, more tenderness of heart, more warm and supernatural affections, more sympathy for all, more compassion for those who suffer, more kindness and delicate attentiveness to my dear people. Not to repulse, scorn, or neglect anyone. Not to allow the slightest sign of bitterness or irritation.

To suffer seems to be my true vocation and the interior call of God in my soul. Suffering enables me to do the work of reparation; to obtain, I hope, the great graces I desire so much for my dear souls, for all souls. Suffering is the reply to my abandonment of myself to the divine Master for my dear ones, for souls, and for the Church. If I am heard, no grief will seem to me to have been too great, and I will sing a joyous canticle of thanks here below and for all eternity.

My adored Savior, I give myself to Thee, and renew my intentions, my prayers, my complete consecration.

(Christmas 1911)

At the approach of this sweet feast of Christmas I ask the dear Child Jesus for His most far-reaching blessings upon everyone.

To put more supernatural spirit, more of the spirit of prayer, into my life; and through penance of the heart and of action to attain the interior joy that is its fruit.

(February 21, 1912)
Resolutions for this Lent:

Fasting — (as much as I can): by the prescribed abstinences; my chosen mortifications in the matter of food, such as cannot harm my health; other spiritual and bodily mortifications, accepted or voluntary.

Prayer — by my precious Communions, the sacrament of Penance, attendance at Mass, visits to the Blessed Sacrament, the Way of the Cross, daily meditation — especially on the Passion; by prayer both silent and spoken, the constant union of my soul with Jesus Christ, and interior recollectedness.

Almsgiving — by the gift of my money, my time, my heart, first for those closest to me, then for the neighbor who is further away — especially for the poor, the humble, the suffering, for souls.

Greater austerity for myself; on the outside, more abandonment, sweetness, friendliness, gaiety, remembering that our Savior wants a cheerful countenance and a radiant joy in times of fasting and mortification.

To hide from everyone my interior recollectedness, my prayers, my poor penances, my small attempts at charity.

Union with Jesus Christ, which we shall realize in Heaven in joy and vision, is already possible for us on earth in suffering. That is why all souls in love with Jesus, those souls that have heard the mysterious and irresistible call of Christ, love suffering and, far from rejecting it with an entirely human horror, ask for it, desire it as the sweet forerunner of the Master, as that which ushers us into His presence. It is suffering that reveals the Cross to us, that opens the divine Heart to us, that enables us to enter into this supernatural world that no human thing can reach, which we will know only in eternity, but from which a glimmer shines over us through the grace of suffering and the radiance of the Cross.

Thou lovest me, O my God, for I have from Thee two unmistakable proofs of Thy love: exceptional graces and extraordinary trials. Be Thou blessed for this precious double gift. Help me to make it bear a hundredfold for the souls that are dear to me, for all Thou lovest.

St. Joseph: life hidden in God, close to the Heart of Jesus, beneath the gentle gaze of Mary, in silent contemplation and humble activity, doing the daily duty with good heart, doing it joyfully, and with a completely supernatural intention.

May 18, 1912
O my God, through the precious Blood of Jesus
and His five blessed Wounds,
grant me today five graces:
the conversion of a sinner;
the conversion of a heretic, infidel, or Jew;
the salvation of someone dying in peril of everlasting death;
a vocation to the priesthood or to religious life;
and, for some new soul,
the grace of entering into
and savoring the mystery of the Eucharist.
(The prayer that our Lord suggested to me after Communion
this morning, which I will try to say each day.)

To offer the morning with its prayers, thoughts, words, actions, pains, sufferings, and privations for those who are to die that day.

To offer the afternoon in the same way for the Church and for souls.

To offer the evening and night for all souls dear to me, for the spiritual and temporal interests of those I love.

☙

July 18, 1912

My God, I lay at Thy feet my burden of suffering, sadness, and renunciation; I offer all through the heart of Jesus; and I ask Thy Love to transform these trials into joy and holiness for those I love, grace for souls, and precious gifts for Thy Church. Into this abyss of physical prostration, discomfort, and moral weariness, into these shadows into which Thou hast plunged me, let a glimmer of Thy triumphant brightness shine. Or rather, since the shadows of Gethsemane and Calvary are fruitful, use all this ill for the good of everyone. Help me to hide my inner desolation and spiritual poverty beneath the riches of smiles and the splendors of charity. When the Cross grows heavier, put Thy gentle hand under the burden Thou hast laid on my soul and on my aching body.

O Lord, I adore Thee, and I am still, and always, in Thy debt, for against my sufferings Thou hast put the Holy Eucharist and Heaven.

Alleluia!

⚭

The Journal, Part 2
1911-1914

And I live, now not I; but Christ liveth
in me. And that I live now in the flesh:
I live in the faith of the Son of God,
who loved me, and delivered Himself for me.

Galatians 2:20

October 19, 1911

Three days ago, on my birthday, a new year began for me and I feel the need of making an act of adoration and thanksgiving, of confessing my faith and in a certain way of confessing myself, by declaring both what God has been to me and what I have failed to do in His service, first through my ignorance, then through my tremendous weakness.

When I look at the past, I see all my childhood and youth, even the beginnings of maturity, passed in ignorance of and estrangement from God. I see the first graces received while I was still young, although they did not sink in deeply; flashes from on high streaking a path of indifference and superficiality; this call, a fugitive light glimpsed in the years of youth and swiftly extinguished, perhaps by a mysterious divine Will; the breaking of every link, even the external ones, with God and the total forgetfulness of Him in my heart; then the slow, silent action of Providence in me and for me; the wonderful work of inner conversion, begun, guided, completed by God alone, outside all human influence or contact, sometimes by the very means that should have caused me to lose all of my religious faith,[77] an action whose intelligent and loving beauty one could discern only when it was completed.

[77] See the history of this crisis in *In Memoriam*.

Then, when that divine task was done, the friend and guide of my soul[78] was put in my way by circumstances that were truly but gently providential.

Then my reconciliation with God, the journey to Rome, and, at the tomb of St. Peter, my consecration to Jesus Christ, whom I carried in my heart by Communion; then years of trial, and the greatest grief of my life up to this time,[79] and my ill-health; and the decisive consecration of myself on October 2, 1908, in the dear church at Jougne, where I left so many prayers.

Finally, this last year full of suffering: spiritual sufferings and deprivations, blows that went straight to my heart, trials with my health, progress sometimes slow and feeble through the cruel paths of renunciation; then renewed peace, the feeling of having progressed in God's service in spite of all my struggles and weaknesses; my entire abandonment to Jesus Christ in confidence and love, offering myself in the future for "all that He might want of me," asking of Him in return the graces that I desire deeply and whose complete accomplishment I hope for from Him, for the souls dear to me, for all souls, and for the Church.

That is a swift review of my life. But what I cannot say, my God, what will be known only in eternity, is the greatness of Thy love, the wonderful graces Thou hast favored me with, which I never did anything to deserve. Neither can I tell the extent of my misery and weakness, which is known to Thy heart alone.

Be Thou blessed for all — even for my faults, since they have served to humble and transform me — for Thy gifts and Thy unspeakable mercy. Be Thou blessed for the affection Thou hast

[78] Father R. P. Hébert, O.P., who instructed the young man (a colleague of Felix Leseur) at whose baptism Elisabeth served as godmother on March 25, 1903.

[79] The death of her sister Juliette in 1905.

put in my way; for the trials that were perhaps an even greater grace from Thee.

Receive the renewed gift I offer Thee of myself, my soul, my life, wishing to love and serve Thee alone, joyfully, everywhere, always, with all my being, wishing to do nothing but Thy Will "in health or illness, poverty or riches, happiness or suffering, life or death," and asking Thee only to use me as the most humble instrument for the good of souls and for Thy glory.

May my grief and supernatural joy, my whole life and even my death proclaim the greatness of divine love, the holiness of the Church, the tenderness and sweetness of the Heart of Jesus, the existence and the beauty of the supernatural life, the reality of our Christian hopes.

I believe, I adore, I put myself under the special protection of the Blessed Virgin, and I have the sweet confidence that, offered by her, my humble oblation, with divine grace, will serve the Church, souls, and those who are so entirely dear to me on earth.

❧

October 21, 1911

What will this winter bring to me: sickness or health, joy or suffering? I do not know; but I know that I shall welcome all, because all will come from God for my good and the good of those souls for whom I have surrendered myself into the hands of the adored Master.

In my weakness and weariness, by divine grace, I want to be always joyful, to have smiles for all, and to hide my pain as much as possible; to forget myself, to give myself, and to try to be charming — that the honor of this good grace may fall wholly upon our good God.

I occupy myself with clothes and furs . . . and talk about them, so as to give no hint of austerities. How afraid the world is of suffering and penance, and how carefully I must hide both of these, as much as possible, from the eyes of my neighbor! My friendliness and charity will with God's help draw hearts to Him who is so good; my sufferings will accomplish His conquest of them; my prayers will give them to Him. Or rather, it is He who will do this blessed work of conversion and sanctification through my prayers, my trials, and my humble efforts at charity.

My Savior, I am all alone, as Thou knowest, in spiritual things; Thou knowest, too, what I suffer from the hostility or indifference of certain persons. I think that is why Thou hast done so much for me and given me so much in Thy goodness. And now with Thy gentle gaze Thou art dispersing the clouds that in these last months have often darkened my soul; Thou art kindling it again after leaving it in painful aridity; Thou art chasing away the shadows and the confusion. I give Thee thanks, my beloved Savior, my God! I know that grief will return, for effort and struggle are Thy will for the souls Thy love hast conquered; but I know that Thou wilt not abandon me and that deep peace will remain with me. To love amidst the storm is very sweet, and my love emerges stronger from each sorrow, each setback. Complete abandonment of myself to Thy Will, offering of my heart and my life in Thy service and for souls.

✂

November 5, 1911

I try to keep my resolution of outward "worldliness." When my soul longs for recollectedness and prayer, when I want to act, but act by deeds, for God and my neighbor, when I hope for a life totally detached from the world, made up of contemplation and fruitful activity, devoted to my dear ones, to the poor, and to souls, in order to fulfill the divine Will and do my real duty, I must give myself to people, occupations, and even pleasures that are entirely superficial.

What a mortification in my secret heart — with God for its only witness and confidant! He wants me to have joy and comfort only from Him. Perhaps He will wait until He has taken me to Heaven and pressed me against His Heart before giving faith to those I love; and perhaps He will then grant me the unspeakable joy of seeing in His light what my sufferings, privations, and spiritual isolation will have obtained for these dear souls. This morning, coming from church after Communion, and thinking of Felix and my great longing for his conversion, I said more explicitly to our Lord what I let Him see unceasingly in the silent depths of my soul — I offered myself to Him entirely, for this soul, dear above all others.

November 14, 1911

I renew my resolution of silence, seeing more clearly than ever the necessity of reserve with everyone, especially concerning God. I must hide from everyone my soul, my spiritual life and the graces I have received, and speak as little as possible of my trials and bad health. The edification of another person, which (apart from less pure motives) sometimes tempts me to expand, should be only a result and not an end in itself, as Father Faber says so well.[80] The only end I want to have in view is the will of God, and my surrender should be complete, humble, and full of love.

Other people's absolute incomprehension or ignorance of much that concerns the supernatural life is a good reason for practicing the silence that is recommended so much by the

---

[80] Frederick William Faber (1814-1863), English Oratorian and hymn writer, who converted to Catholicism under the influence of John Henry Cardinal Newman. He was the author of many widely read devotional books, including *All for Jesus* (1853) and *Growth in Holiness* (1854).

ascetic writers. Interiorly, then, I want to practice more complete recollectedness and to be in closer union with our Lord. Exteriorly, I want to devote myself more, "squander" myself, become more cheerful and smiling. And when my task of humble charity and daily effort is done, God will know how to dispose of it for souls and for His glory. For me, the labor, unknown to others; for Him, the realization of the good I long for, of the spiritual work that all my poor efforts have in view. The workman brings his work; the master disposes of it in his own way. Let it suffice for me to know that this work is never unfruitful.

To work, then — and joyfully. And if I must still suffer because of my faith, because of the isolation of my soul, I will offer these trials with serenity for my usual intentions and in a spirit of reparation.

⳨

January 3, 1912

A change of year, which will be, by divine grace, the beginning of a real change in my soul and in my life.

For this year I ask of God, of the divine Child, the grace of an inner life that is stronger and entirely supernatural and an outer life entirely devoted to my beloved neighbor. May the serenity of my heart be strengthened and shine upon all; and while being more austere within, may I become more welcoming to each one, and gentle toward life, other persons, and trials. Use me, O my adored Master, according to Thy will, for souls, and for Thy glory.

To be silent, to hide myself. To be quiet about divine grace, and to hide my spiritual life. For others, to give words and actions, to be amiable, even at the price of great effort.

With God's help and by the gift of myself, I have been seemingly worldly and outwardly gay; I have renounced much for some time and especially during these last days. And while I talk and smile and force myself to be gracious, in the depths of my soul there is an unspeakable longing for solitude and recollectedness, and I cry from within to the kind Master, "Thou seest how I thirst for prayer and calm, and how ardently I desire to live only for Thee and for a few persons who are dear to me. Thou knowest how heavily the world weighs upon me, how I hold the spirit of it in horror; but since it is Thy Will that I should live not for the world but in the world, since the duties of my state and my ardent desire for the apostolate keep me there in spite of all my longing to be free, then permit these many sacrifices, these constant efforts, these renunciations, and these profound sufferings to accomplish Thy work with souls and to obtain grace for them. It is for this that I offer Thee so much conversation without interest, so many activities devoid of consolation for me, so much costly amiability. Accept it all, take it all, use it all for souls and for those I love."

Then at the first opportunity I retire quickly into my inner "cell," and there I pray and adore and lie at the feet of my Savior. My three Communions each week and the few minutes of meditation each morning prepare me for my daily activity; and every day when I offer Him in advance all the activity and suffering that makes up my days, everything that later happens is gathered up by our good God, and nothing is lost; no, nothing, not even this great boredom with worldly occupations hidden beneath the veil of charity.

Tender confidence in Mary; abandonment of myself to God; prayer, mortification, charity.

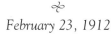

February 23, 1912

I have noted down in my little book[81] my Lenten resolutions, but I want to confirm them here. I must truly renew my life, and

---

[81] See the *Book of Resolutions*, February 21, 1912.

it is the adored Master whom I humbly ask to transform my soul; I want to live interiorly more supernaturally, exteriorly more gently and charitably, so as to make better loved He who is the beginning and end of my spiritual life. More than ever I want to hide in the Heart of Jesus my good works, my prayers, my mortifications, to preach only by example, to speak not at all of myself and little of God, since in this unhappy world one only gives scandal or annoys others by showing one's love for Him.

But whenever a soul approaches me, or whenever, too, it seems God's will that I should approach a soul, I will work very humbly, very discreetly, effacing myself and disappearing as soon as the task is done, mixing no thought of self with the action performed for God alone. And should I be misunderstood, criticized, and judged unfavorably, I will try to rejoice in remembering our divine Exemplar, and I will make myself as nothing in the eyes of others, I who am in fact so poor and little in the eyes of God.

⌘

March 6, 1912

A short conversation with my dear Felix a little while ago deeply stirred the hopes and desires of my soul concerning that dear soul. Oh yes, my God, I must have it, Thou must have it, this straight, true soul; he must know Thee and love Thee, become the humble instrument of Thy glory, and do the work of an apostle. Take him entirely to Thyself. Make of my trials, my sufferings, and my renunciations the road by which Thou shalt come to this dear heart. Is there anything that belongs to me alone that I would not be ready to offer Thee to obtain this conversion, this grace so longed for? My sweet Savior, between Thy Heart and mine there must be this compact of love, which will give Thee a soul and will give me for eternity him whom I cherish, whom I want to be with me in Thy Heaven.

⁕

March 27, 1912

"While the angels fulfill at our sides their function of tender watchfulness, they never cease to contemplate God." This thought of Father Faber struck me during my meditation and made me take a new resolve: to imitate, in my little earthly domain, our dear friends the angels. Before all activities, even during all activities, to keep united to God, to dwell in His presence and to offer Him everything: words, charitable deeds, work.

⁕

April 20, 1912

Lord, permit that after my spiritual death and entombment with Thee, I may rise again to a new and completely supernatural life.

I want — and this is my humble resolution this Eastertime — to become both more "interior" and more "exterior," however paradoxical that may seem. My soul should live in a more complete, intimate union with God; prayer should be the foundation of my spiritual life, my surest means of apostolate, my best form of charity; my suffering, with my habitual or voluntary mortifications, will also be the means I will take for doing good to souls and drawing near to the heart of God.

But exteriorly I will make myself, through divine grace, more gentle, more loving, occupied always and exclusively for others, their pleasure, their good, and above all, their souls. This in all humility, effacing myself, and making of my entire spiritual life a life hidden in Jesus Christ.

And then I want more and more through prayer and my humble effort to establish in myself and shed forth upon others the joy, the holy, sweet, unspeakable joy of Jesus. My immense weakness allows me to approach Him only with great effort. The blessed Master makes me walk often in the shadows, on a dry path where the flowers of joy can scarcely grow. Yet my will to be His is stronger than ever, and He will deign to accept, as a sacrifice of love, the gift of these struggles, these multiple sufferings that He sends me.

The isolation of my soul, the constant and painful injuries caused by those who are hostile or indifferent, especially when they are near and dear to me, the sadness of feeling unequal to the great task to be accomplished, the sufferings of my heart, the difficulties of my life, the misery of physical weakness — this is the rugged soil, my God, in which Thou wilt cause joy to grow. And out of all of this Thou wilt make for souls, salvation and graces of every kind; for me, expiation and holiness; for Thyself, glory.

All my work of reparation will be accomplished, too, according to my vocation, between my soul and Thy Heart, by these sufferings, by prayer, and by whatever humble living charity Thou wilt put into my heart and enable me to pour forth for others.

⸎

May 18, 1912

Unhappy days of Maurice's illness.[82] Renewal of my offering. This morning, Communion, with all the conscious sweetness that the divine Presence has rarely allowed me for many months.

⸎

September 25, 1912

Return to Paris, where much sadness awaited me. Sweet and fervent Communion this morning. I asked Jesus for the virtues

---

[82] Her younger sister Amélie's son, Maurice Duron. In playing with a toy gun, which he charged with caps, he badly injured his right hand, and complications were feared that would have led to the amputation of his arm. Ultimately, he was cured, and Elisabeth went with her sister and nephew to thank the Blessed Virgin at Lourdes in June 1912.

dear to His Heart, His own virtues, without which there is
no true spiritual life:

Purity of heart, renewed often in the sacrament of Penance, and each day by contrition and a spirit of repentance;

Gentleness, unalterable, strong, and peaceful, in spite of
all exterior and interior agitations;

Patience, in spite of all, toward all, toward myself, very
sweetly;

Obedience to God, to my spiritual superiors, and to my temporal superiors in all but matters of conscience, with regard to
the divine Will revealed in all the events of life;

Humility, the foundation of all interior life, the virtue dear
to the Heart of Jesus; humility of soul; outward humility, too;

Mortification, through daily circumstances, through ill-health,
through others, through penances carefully chosen and silently
performed;

Spiritual poverty, by inner privation, and, as far as is consistent
with the duties of my state, renunciation that shall be made
effective by carefully concealed personal poverty and detachment. To sacrifice none of my duties; on the contrary, to be more
vigilant about externals — clothes, care of the house, food, even
elegance — to make myself more attractive, the better to hide
my personal austerities.

Renewal of my offering, complete and without reserve.

I want to dedicate this year to the conquest for God of the
souls I love, by prayer and by suffering especially: my husband,
my mother, my dear nephews and niece, my sister, all the dear
relations I wish to give to Jesus, *at the cost of all;* that is the object
of my life, and along with these beloved souls, I wish to give
others, by the same means, to our Lord.

I will, therefore, redouble my prayers and sacrifices, and will
begin truly to practice penance for sinners, for the dying (for
whom I feel a special tenderness), for the souls of unbelievers,

and also for the souls in Purgatory, all of whom I especially
love.

⚶

October 7, 1912

To love, to practice humility. To efface and simplify myself,
to go joyfully to God, seeking nothing for myself, with complete
abandonment.

Never to lose sight for a moment of the intentions for which
the beloved Master wishes me to pray, to suffer, and to act. In
the midst of exterior occupations and the faithfully performed
duties of my state, to keep my inner attention fixed on God, to
offer everything for the souls that belong to me, the souls that
Jesus wants, the Church.

To be always ready to obey the inner call of this gentle Jesus
to action or to suffering, or to eternity, too, when He wills, and to
reply always with joy and generosity, "Here I am, Lord, ready to
do Thy will."

The day will come, will it not, O Lord, when it will be Thy
Will that I go to Thee, when the shadows, the sorrows, shall
vanish, and the burden of the body will no longer weigh upon
the soul, which will fly at last, free and pure, to Thy Beauty, to
plunge itself into Thy Holiness, to drink in Thy Love; when this
soul, now delivered, will love inexpressibly in Thee all those it
will have rejoined, and those it will have left here below; when
the true life will finally begin, to last forever.

Blessed dawn of eternity, I greet you, not knowing whether
from near or far! I must not hope for you, because my only wish
is to do the divine Will "in life or in death." I know that one
must first climb up to Calvary and hang upon the Cross before
knowing the sweetness of union with the divine; I know that I
possess, and hope to possess still more here below, this union by
the grace of God, in a great spirit of abandonment.

I wait and, like the workman who does not know when he will receive his supreme reward, I want in the meantime to perform my task radiantly and peacefully for the love alone of Him who has given everything and done everything for me.

October 17, 1912

My birthday yesterday: behind me, a great stretch of time almost bare of merit or good works, filled only with an abundance of divine grace. O Lord, may the future, short or long, with Thy help be rich in effort, sacrifice, and prayer. I ask Thee nothing for myself, no, not even spiritual joys. I ask of Thee with all abandonment only the fulfillment of our secret compact, the realization of all that I hope for from Thee, and all that I will then owe to Thee.

And now, beloved Master, take first Thy payment, if that is Thy Will, and leave the fulfillment of Thy blessed promises until afterward. Should it only be from Heaven or from an abyss of suffering that I behold the realization of my wishes, be Thou praised in advance for having heard me. I renew all, offer all, ask all. For these intentions, for souls, and for the Church, I give myself to Thee, my Savior and my God.

In what relates to God: Recollectedness and prayer.
In what relates to my neighbor: Charity and loving devotion.
In what relates to myself: Penance and austerity.

A spirit of reparation.
Reparation by prayer,
suffering, mortification,
and by good works.

�֍

October 20, 1912

Spoke too much of myself; too much self-absorption, in which I caused others to share. Renewed resolution of silence, mortification, spiritual and, to the extent possible, even actual poverty.

Complete abandonment and offering of myself to God. More amiability and friendliness with my neighbor. Nothing hard or austere with others. Greater severity and austerity with myself alone.

✶

November 16, 1912

To try this year to increase in myself the supernatural spirit by prayer and mortification.

✶

January 15, 1913

A new year has begun, which seems as if it must bring the fulfillment of the compact between my soul and God, or at any rate my part of it. Let all Thy Will for me be done, O Lord, if Thou, too, wilt fulfill Thy blessed promises for the dear objects of my offering, for souls, and the Church. I abandon myself to Thee and desire that Thy Will may be done: suffering, poverty, illness, life or death as Thou wilt, action or fruitful inactivity, and all surrendered to Thy good pleasure. Is not this inactivity the image, the reflection of Thy blessed Passion, more powerful with Thee than all our good works?

Thou knowest the three graces that I beg of Thy Heart this year for the souls of my husband and my mother, and for the happiness of my dear little Marie.[83] If Thou givest me these Thou

---

[83] Her niece had met the young man she later married (the marriage took place during the war, in August 1915, during a

canst indeed ask much from me; and I prepare myself to give Thee *all*.

Give me also many souls, or rather take them Thyself, the souls everywhere that I love with Thee and for Thee. Grant many graces to Thy beloved Church, and pour out unto Her sanctity and life. Recollectedness, prayer, union of my soul with God and with the Heart of Jesus; confidence in and filial love for Mary, my Mother; to root my soul deep in Heaven, to make it live in the Eucharist, to let it be gently inclined toward my neighbor and toward the souls on whom may fall its overflow of light and love that the gentle Savior has placed in it.

⚜

January 29, 1913

Suffering and renunciation through the burdensomeness, discomforts, and exhaustion of the body, through the darkness or at least the dimness of the mind, and through the interior suffering of spiritual solitude and aridity. Pure and solid faith. To ask, as I have been told, the grace of "simplicity in suffering."

Material occupations, sometimes too heavy for my already burdened body, time frittered away, relations that have no charm for me with people who have nothing to give me from the moral point of view, the effort to be amiable and smiling when all my inner being longs for recollectedness and for only deep affections — all this constitutes my hidden cross, the best cross, which does not attract sympathy or admiration as illness or misfortune does.

Well, I will carry it "joyfully," until the day when God will change the form of the duties of my state. Yes, joyfully in spite

leave, when he was a lieutenant in the artillery at the front); but as he was then still a student at the École Polytechnique, the engagement was announced only some months later. This was the writer's last great joy.

of aridity, weariness, at the cost of all efforts, gently united to the Heart of Jesus, aided by Mary, my Mother, firmly adhering to my habitual rule of pious devotions, meditation, etc., always severe with myself alone, making myself more friendly to all, careful to keep my soul open with trust and abandonment, without narrowness, egotism, or subtlety.

To accept as a trial the impossibility of a life that is active through good deeds, relationships, and regular work as well as the impossibility of a wholly contemplative life, which the duties of my state, the tastes of those about me, and circumstances prohibit. To do all I can for others and for the good of souls, to take refuge often in my "inner cell" to pray, to adore, and to unite myself to the beloved Master. To make of all — prayer, suffering, mortification, and action — an interior offering to God for souls and for His glory, and also for those who are dear to me.

O my God, "give me an adoring soul, an atoning soul, the soul of an apostle," and dispose of me according to Thy Will and according to my compact with Thee.

⁂

February 6, 1913

In my meditation I saw clearly what remains of worldliness in me. In asking God, this Lent, for a spirit of withdrawal, I resolved to pray, suffer, and act in union with the divine Will, for the glory of God alone. May His Will be done *in me,* in my soul; *for me,* in my whole life; *by me,* in regard to my neighbor and souls.

To live spiritually hidden; to fast as much as possible, to abstain faithfully, to seek mortification and endure it silently; to speak no more of my suffering, my pain, myself, and to accept the real humiliation of looking so well when I am overcome with fatigue. To be gracious, completely serene, and to practice the forms of charity and almsgiving that are most difficult for me — of which contact with the world will be one.

Lord, Thou hast tried me lately by inner deprivation, suffering, and painful hardships. I think that Thou art preparing me for an end known only to Thee; whatever it may be I accept it from Thy Heart and wish that all Thy Will may be done; sanctify me if Thy blessed design is to give Thy Heaven to me; sanctify me if Thy Will is to leave me here to labor and bear the Cross. Use me for Thy glory: that is all I ask; and let me love Thee more and more, uniting myself to Thee completely and forever.

❧

February 17, 1913

The Cross lies heavily upon my body and my soul. May all be as God wills, provided that I am heard. To love, suffer, and pray, always with the joy that comes from Jesus.

Fiat!

Deo gratias!

I want to be a eucharistic soul, a hidden apostle of the divine Heart. To practice complete, confident, and loving abandonment. To go to God by means of the Cross, through the Heart of Jesus, under the sweet maternal protection of Mary. Whatever it may be, let the future be welcome, since it comes from the heavenly Father and the one Friend. As the future becomes the present, it will bring me its own necessary graces. Until then and even afterward I must remember that "sufficient unto the day is the evil thereof"[84] and that the present day is the one during which I can work and suffer for souls, for the glory of God.

❧

February 19, 1913

This morning, after Communion, in a passing vision I thought of the three tabernacles that Jesus deigns to inhabit.

---

[84] Matt. 6:34.

First, *the depths of Heaven,* the bosom of the inaccessible Trinity, in the ineffable union of His humanity and divinity; this is the tabernacle of His glory, where we can contemplate Him only after having shed our mortal clothing.

Then *the Host,* in which He veils Himself in order to come to us and live in our midst, always ready to welcome us and hear us; this is the tabernacle of His love.

Lastly, *our soul,* where He comes in Communion, wonderfully uniting Himself to it, making Himself its guest, its friend, its spiritual food, living on in it spiritually after the actual presence has ceased; this is the tabernacle of His Heart, the place of His delights, His repose, and His joy.

Oh, how I long for my soul to be for Him at once a Heaven, a tabernacle, and that holy appearance under which He comes to me! From beneath this veil where my Savior will hide, I will let Him shine forth, drawing souls to Him, the dear souls He wants to save.

⚬

February 20, 1913

More and more I see that God does not want me to be active, unless a new state of affairs should arise. What He seems to expect from me is an apostolate of prayer and suffering. What a blessed vocation, and how much I will try to respond better to it than in the past, loving the Cross of Jesus, "carrying it daily,"[85] always placing in the divine Heart my burden of pains, privations, and weaknesses!

Austere to myself, I want to have nothing but sweetness and tenderness for my neighbor. To live in interior spiritual union with our Lord, and to make of all the monotony, triviality, and humble duties of my life so many prayers for souls. To have a

---

[85] Cf. Luke 9:23.

eucharistic soul, never to lose sight of my vocation of prayer, suffering, and reparation.

Holy Thursday, March 20, 1913

How well Thou knowest, O Lord, how to try souls, and what a tool for purification in Thy hands is suffering! Perhaps Thou hast deigned to accept my interior offering. In spite of inexpressible vexations, trials, and privations of soul and body, I can say a joyful *fiat,* if by so many crucifying pains I obtain from Thee the fulfillment of my desires and all the graces I have hoped for, and if my sufferings serve souls. I offer all to Thee, beloved Master: dryness, deprivation, solitude of soul, my present lack of religious help, overwhelming bodily miseries.

To others I must speak of only a part of these trials; the best will be for Thee, and Thou alone wilt know what certain efforts cost me, how certain weaknesses humiliate me. Even to these I must give a good welcome, and I must be cheerful and smiling with my neighbor, toward suffering, for everything and for everyone.

During these four painful weeks,[86] a visit from our Lord illuminated my life and my heart. I am at present an exile from the tabernacle, and I hunger for Jesus in the Eucharist. Will I be able to go to Him on Sunday to tell Him my joy in the Resurrection and renew for Him the offering of my trials? I shall spend these holy days in spiritual isolation, in privations, in destitution. . . .

Yes, but my beloved Savior is close to my heart, my soul is united to the Cross, and I wish only for the fulfillment in me, for me, through me, of the divine Will.

---

[86] First attack of the generalized cancer that was to reappear in July and prove fatal after ten months of suffering.

Is it not a great honor to be chosen by our Lord to suffer, on the blessed anniversary of His Passion and death on the Cross?

Yes, through all the blows, pains, and sacrifices of life, of soul and body, I want to give God from the deepest recesses of my being complete and joyous assent to His holy and ever beloved Will.

⚛

March 25, 1913

Today is the tenth anniversary of the blessed day when I began my new life. I thank Thee, my God, from the bottom of my heart, for so many graces. What charity and sacrifice could pay my debt of gratitude? The Heart of Jesus alone can accomplish this task; it is to it that I confide my sweet burden of thanksgiving.

Yesterday I was able to go to Mass for the lovely, great feast of Easter; my fatigue and physical weakness deprived me of any conscious joy in Communion, but the action in me of the beloved Master will only have been the greater, as I can feel today. And that is enough. What does even spiritual joy matter to one who feels alive?

In my meditation, I made the following resolutions for this joyful Eastertime; may God help me to fulfill them, despite the great fatigue and discomfort of my aching body.

Toward God: More tender and confident love.

In myself: Greater inner peace and joy, in spite of all.

Toward my neighbor: More amiability than in these last weeks, a friendlier and more smiling exterior; to forget myself more so that I may think of others; to think and speak of myself as little as possible, and yet to take care not to attract attention by an air of exaggerated silence or indifference to my own sufferings.

Lord, help my weakness!

❧

April 22, 1913

Ten years ago today, I experienced some of the sweetest and, to be sure, most solemn moments of my life. That morning at St. Peter's in Rome, my Communion in profound closeness to Jesus, the decisive consecration of my soul and my life to God, all the joy, all the love, and all the sweetness of that hour when I knelt at the tomb of the Apostle: how can I thank Thee for all of this, O Lord? How can I express to Thee my gratitude?

I tried to say something of it this morning in Communion; but it is by my love, my deeds, and my sacrifices that I will try to discharge my immense debt. It is only through the Heart of Jesus that I will be able to pay all of it, by the gift of His tenderness and holiness. To work, then, to act and suffer, according to the divine Will!

❧

Ascension Day, May 1, 1913

Sharp, intense pain, going straight to the core of my heart, is what I have had to offer to Jesus glorified, together with the struggle against myself and outside agitations. During this month devoted to Mary, which is also devoted to Jesus in the Blessed Sacrament, to the Sacred Heart, and to the Holy Spirit, I want to make a courageous effort toward holiness. To be silent, to forget myself; to think of others and devote myself to them; to care for and accomplish nothing but the divine Will; to be the apostle of the Sacred Heart, an adoring and atoning soul; my eyes and my heart fixed on the tabernacle and on Heaven, to seek there only Jesus and to lead to Him all of the souls He will place in my path.

Above all, an apostolate of prayer and suffering. Humble, discreet action; unalterable gentleness, friendliness, and kindness.

⚜

June 14, 1913

My God, be Thou blessed for all the graces Thou hast lately granted me: temporal graces through the happiness of my dear niece[87] and sweet family joys; spiritual graces through much consolation, supernatural joy, and inward illumination, and the compassionate kindness to me Thou hast inspired in my spiritual father, which has done so much good to my soul. What a debt of gratitude I owe to Thee, my God!

Grant the fulfillment of the three spiritual graces and the temporal grace I have asked of Thee for this year; grant health and real sanctification to those I love; save and convert many souls, especially those Thou hast confided to me; pour out Thy greatest blessings on Thy beloved Church. Then, Lord, accept my offering, keep all of our compact, do with me as Thou wilt. I ask only Thy love and grace, with the deep and lasting peace necessary for the flourishing of my soul. Even as it has been said to me, I want to abandon myself to Thee with confidence, to bring Thee an ample soul, always peaceful, and to think less of my faults than of Thy love. Thou art my Father, my Friend; be Thou also, O Jesus, the "Companion of my solitude." Thou knowest how spiritual isolation weighs upon me; with Thee I shall never again feel alone. If I am not on earth to see my beloved ones united to me in my inner life, may I from Heaven unite myself with their dear souls, which shall then be conquered and sanctified by Thee.

⚜

June 26, 1913

I have lately been able to live a more active life and keep some of the resolutions I made regarding this.

---

[87] The official announcement of the engagement of her niece, Marie Duron, was made May 14, 1913.

In the future I want to be amiable to everyone; to show more interest in the exterior things and trivialities of life that occupy so many people; to look after my home, my clothes; to leave no duty of my state undone. No one must suspect the trouble and sacrifices that this charitable effort means for me.

And deep in my heart I will keep that full, sweet union with God, which is my life. Be Thou, Lord, the dear Companion of my inner solitude, the divine Guest of my soul; live in my soul, and in Communion and prayer give it Thy most interior graces. Make me the apostle of Thy Heart by prayer, suffering, and action.

⤝

July 16, 1913

Lord, be Thou blessed for my present suffering, because I dare to hope that it is the gentle answer of Thy Heart.[88] I offer it all to Thee, all of it: sufferings of body, heart, and soul, all my privations, my interior desolation, my great spiritual solitude. Use these humble offerings for the intentions and substitutions Thou knowest, for souls, and for the Church. Accept a tithe of it in expiation of my sins and for the work of reparation that Thou dost entrust to souls that are dearest to Thee.

It is not pride, is it, Lord, thus to call myself Thy friend, the one Thou hast called, Thy chosen friend? Because everywhere in my life I see the traces of Thy love, everywhere the divine call, everywhere the supernatural vocation. Thou hast made use of

---

[88] She had taken to her bed on July 6, 1913, struck down by her fatal cancer. When she wrote these lines in bed, in pencil, she had already passed through crises of suffering that were extremely painful. She grew worse, and her state aroused the gravest anxiety at the end of August and at the beginning of September. In October, she was so much better that she was believed to be cured. On November 12, the illness reappeared and sent her back to bed.

trials, suffering, and illness to take me entirely to Thyself and
to sanctify me, first drawing me to Thee solely by Thine action
within me. Thou hast done *all*.

Now complete Thy work; make me holy insofar as Thou wilt;
use me for souls, for my beloved ones, for all Thy interests; use me
for Thy greater glory, and let all be done in silence, in an intimate
heart-to-Heart encounter of my soul alone with Thee alone.

From the depths of my being and my misery I say to Thee,
"Lord, what wilt Thou have me do? Speak, Thy servant listens;
behold the handmaid of the Lord; I come, O Father, ready to do
Thy Will."[89]

Patience, gentleness, humility, silence, amiability. To hide all
that I can of my physical suffering, and all my moral suffering,
my spiritual privations. To cover everything with serenity and
smiles: all my discomforts, sadness, and renunciations. To try to
reconcile the tastes, desires, and needs of each and to count for
nothing myself, not to think of what I myself might wish; to sacrifice even my highest hopes when, misunderstood, they might
irritate or displease another.

I shall have all eternity in which to contemplate Him whom
my soul adores, to unite myself to Him, and to pray. On earth I
must think of my neighbor, of souls; I must sacrifice myself, and
practice contemplation in action. There is matter for plenty of
renunciation and profound and constant mortification in this unending abandonment of all that is the ardent desire, the deepest
longing of my soul.

⚜

January 9, 1914

Six months of suffering: bitter suffering of the body, suffering
of the soul, privations of all sorts, much pain and humiliation.

[89] Cf. Luke 1:35.

Oh, so long as it is the divine response to me —is it not so, Lord? And so long as no least part of my pain is lost! Stronger than my poor action, stronger than my imperfect prayer, may it reach Thy Heart and become the most efficacious form of supplication.

Do not delay; hearken, O my God, to these desires that Thou knowest well. Give great and Christian happiness to these beloved children and sanctify them all. Complete quickly the interior conversion and profound sanctification that I await from Thy grace. Unite with my soul the souls of those I love, the soul I love best of all, and put an end to this grievous solitude of spirit, which weighs on me so much. And then sanctify me, too, by this suffering; bring me close to Thy Heart and teach me to love and serve Thee better. I resolve (imploring divine grace) in the future to give way no more to the lapses I have known in hours of extreme pain, to be always gentle, humble, full of charity.

Help me, dear Savior.[90]

[90] These were the last lines Elisabeth wrote in her journal, during a brief respite. She worsened a few days later, and her suffering lasted four months longer. She died a holy death on Sunday, May 3, 1914, at ten o'clock in the morning, surrounded by her family.

Spiritual Testament

Jesus said to her, "I am the resurrection
and the life; he that believeth in me,
although he be dead, shall live.

And everyone that liveth, and believeth in me,
shall not die forever. Believest thou this?"

She saith to him, "Yea, Lord, I have believed
that Thou art Christ, the Son of the living
God, who art come into this world."

John 11:25-27

✧

For Felix

October 15, 1905

This, my beloved husband, is the testament of my soul.

I wish you to be my chief and dearest heir. Especially to you and to all who love me I leave the task of praying, and having prayers said, for me; and having Holy Mass said for my intention for thirty consecutive days after I am dead, and many times a year as long as you live. May your good works and almsgiving speak to God of her who served Him so imperfectly but who loves Him with all the power of her being and the full affection of her heart.

Try during your life to discharge, as far as a poor human creature can, my immense debt of gratitude to the adored Father, whom you shall know and love through my prayers in Heaven.

When you also shall have become His child, the disciple of Jesus Christ and a living member of His Church, consecrate your existence, transformed by grace, to prayer and the giving of yourself in charity. Be a Christian and an apostle. All that my prayers and trials have asked for our poor brothers here below, try to give them in your turn. Love souls; pray, suffer, and work for them. They deserve all our pains, all our efforts, and all our sacrifices.

I leave to you those whom I love so that you may surround them with your care and affection. Accompany through their lives our nephews and niece, who are also my friends and whom

I love so much. Be their spiritual guide, the friend of their souls, the example of their lives. Help them, morally and materially, at the time of their marriage or vocation. Consider them all as the children of our hearts, and never abandon them. To their parents be always the brother and the loving, devoted friend that you are now, but in a more supernatural way. Even redouble your affection, for I leave you mine to pour out upon them.

If I should die before my mother, I do not need to ask you to care for her; but you will have a great task in regard to her if to your own tenderness you are to add all of mine for my beloved mother.

With your mother, too, who is also so fully mine, I ask you to replace me.

I leave in your hands "Juliette's work," that is, the installation of a chapel in some poor quarter.[91] If the name has not already been used, it should be dedicated to the Holy Spirit, otherwise to St. Teresa or to the Sacred Heart.

I also leave you my various charitable works, and the payment during your life of my regular donations, or others to replace them.

I remind our nephews and niece never to forget, out of what we shall leave them, how much is owed to God and to the poor.

At my burial I want a simple service, without any kind of ostentation, with purely religious music, and no display either at the house or outside the church. I should like the mourners to meet at the church, and that my relatives and friends, instead of sending superfluous flowers, should have Masses said and give some alms for my intention.

---

[91] Elisabeth's sister Juliette had begun to put aside various small sums at her disposal, Christmas and birthday presents, etc., for the purpose of a foundation. Elisabeth continued this work with all possible zeal and devotion.

Spiritual Testament

And now, my beloved Felix, I tell you once more of my great love. And I charge you to tell our relatives and friends how much I loved them all and how much I shall pray for them until the hour of reunion. Close to God, where other dear ones already await us, we shall one day be eternally reunited. I hope for this through my afflictions offered for you and through divine mercy.

Your wife forever,
Elisabeth

✇

Daily Thoughts
1899-1906

Afterward Jesus, knowing that all things were now accomplished, that the Scripture might be fulfilled, said, "I thirst."

John 19:28

And Jesus crying with a loud voice, said, "Father, into Thy hands I commend my spirit."

Luke 23:46

Through the Cross to the Light (Per Crucem ad Lucem)

To pray, to suffer, to act.

The future will be what we make it; let us reflect on this thought so that it may inspire us to act. Above all, let us realize that all collective reform must first be individual reform. Let us apply ourselves to transforming ourselves and our lives. Let us influence those about us, not by vain preaching, but by the irresistible force of upright convictions and the example of our lives.

Let us give ourselves unstintingly and seek to strengthen our faith and enlarge our understanding, sure then that everyone will come to us to be rekindled and to enlighten their hearts and minds.

The world is unable to discern souls; it does not know how to penetrate beyond this covering that shrouds our inmost self. What there is in us of unconquerable strength, purity, and truth is seen in the depths of our conscience only by Him who lives in us and judges us with more justice and love than men. What a reason to be faithful and valiant in daily life! Nothing is overlooked by the eternal Guest, and no less certain is it that our least act has a profound resonance in other souls.

Let us love. Let our souls and our lives be a perpetual song of love for God first of all and for all human beings who suffer, love, and mourn.

Let profound joy live in us. Let us be like the lark, enemy of the night, who always announces the dawn and awakens in each creature the love of light and life. Let us awaken souls.

Why do we wait until tomorrow to do good? Why do we wait to be rich before giving? Is not the gift of ourselves better than money, and is there a day or even an hour in which we could not give a tear or a smile to someone who is suffering? Cannot a word from us strengthen a soul in distress? Cannot an act of pure love coming from the depths of ourselves brighten a sad life?

How many times, O God, have we, forgetful of the divine Word, carelessly neglected one of our brothers and disdained human suffering!

O Light, Beauty, absolute Love, O my God, when will men love Thee, Thee alone, leaving all that draws them away from this pure union with Thee, seeing only one thing: the soul that Thou hast given them and Thee, O my God, who livest in this soul and shouldst be the sole guide and judge of their acts and lives?

Let us try to detach our souls from the vain excitements that so often disturb our lives. May these souls, which are ever more serene and filled with God, be the refuge that is open to every troubled conscience and every weakened will.

Fanaticism fills me with horror, and I cannot understand how it can exist with sincere conviction. Can anyone who loves Christianity passionately and wishes to see it reign in souls think for one moment that he should use any method to achieve this goal other than persuasion? Can one instill conviction through force or deceit? Besides, is there not in the use of such means something completely repugnant to the upright loyal spirit that should mark every sincere Christian? And yet how many little acts of fanaticism we commit unconsciously!

Apart from personal pride, we have the pride of faith, the most perfidious of all. We complacently scorn those of different belief and think ourselves hardly obliged to extend our charity to them. We consider that Jews, Protestants, or atheists are hardly our brothers in the true sense of that word, brothers who are deeply loved, who deserve our self-sacrifice, and upon whom we are obligated to bestow a respectful esteem.

In regard to such as these, we seem to think anything is allowed, even calumny sometimes, and we seem less concerned with convincing them than with offending them. The gentle words of Jesus, and of St. Paul, too, declare that in the future there will be neither Jews nor Gentiles;[92] all that is forgotten. Let those who have engraved upon their hearts the great doctrine of love learn at least to practice it on all their brothers, whoever they may be. Weak and lowly as I am, I will never cease to protest against fanaticism and to proclaim to all Jesus' law of love.

This ardent need for justice, this benevolent flame within us, this deep love for suffering and groaning humanity, all this

[92] Cf. Gal. 3:28.

is and can only be an unconscious turning toward this infinite
Love and infinite Justice, toward this supreme Goodness that
is God.

We must give ourselves; that is, we must bring forth from this
interior sanctuary where we keep the best part of ourselves, some
thoughts, chosen from among the best and most lofty, which,
once they have gone forth from us, will become acts of love and
words of life. We must firmly resolve to try to give our best, to do
all the good we can. The unknown resources of strength, energy,
and nobility lying within our depths must become the property
of our brothers by a valiant effort and a generous surrender of
our inmost personality.

Let us despise nothing: not men, for in the worst of them
there is the divine spark, which can always leap forth; nor ideas,
for in all of them there is a grain of truth, which one must know
how to discover; nor other people's actions, for we often are ignorant of the motive and always of the far-reaching and providential consequences of them.

Sometimes the very desire for action leads to the neglect
of action. Looking for some wonderful opportunity to give
oneself, to devote oneself, one forgets the humble brother
close at hand who is waiting for a word of comfort, a saving
gesture.

Let us not linger in contemplation of the road ahead; let us
follow the narrow path. Let us not look too far or too high, but
right in front of ourselves, right next to ourselves. The good to
be done is perhaps there.

Sincere convictions and the ardent longing that others should share them can coexist with complete respect for every conscience and every conviction.

All that life reveals to us each day, all that we gain by constant, energetic, and persevering work on ourselves, all that constitutes our inner being: all of this should one day be turned into words or actions that reveal our soul. This is truly to give oneself, which is the object of all human life. It is a difficult task, a heroic effort, to bring forth the thought that is in us, but we must do it, breaking our souls as we might break a sacred vase so that others may breathe the divine perfume.

Is it not terrifying to see what the human heart can easily harbor and reveal of fanaticism and hatred? What thoughts and manly resolutions this unhappy state of things should inspire! A sublime task awaits every upright soul imbued with the ideas that Christianity has given to the world: to promote union among men, to sow a little love around one, and to give one's time and trouble and all one's heart to bring to birth the light and life of the spirit.

There is a way of living and thinking that I would call negative, another that I would call active. The first consists in seeing always what is defective in men and institutions, not so much to remedy them as to triumph over them; in always looking behind one, and in seeking by preference whatever separates and disunites. The second consists in looking joyfully at life and its duties; in seeking the good in everyone in order to develop and cultivate it; in never despairing of the future, the fruit of our will; in feeling for human faults and miseries the valiant compassion that leads to action and that no longer allows us to live a useless life.

❧

Whoever seeks the truth will find God.

❧

As we go along, let us cast about us ideas, words, and aspirations, without looking behind us to see who gathers them up. There are so many beggars for ideals!

❧

Our soul is possessed by a desire for truth; we love and search ceaselessly for it, because it is the object of our being. And we will possess it one day, completely. We want to live the life of the soul intensely and deeply, the interior life, the beginning of eternal life, and we wander gropingly over this path of good, which we find most lovely, and upon which we sow our efforts, our struggles, and our desires. A voice calls to us, the all-powerful word of appeal, which lifts us up and transforms us: "I am the Way, the Truth, and the Life."[93] Let us walk in the awareness of this voice. He who can utter such words will never deceive us.

❧

Let us develop in ourselves "divine" sympathy for all men; only thus can it be truly "human."

❧

All that we do to transform and improve our souls serves the divine cause. When our souls become very great, only God can fill them.

[93] John 14:6.

Let us develop our wills to a greater extent; let us try harder to train all the faculties of our being to duty freely accepted and joyfully fulfilled; and let us acquire more gentleness toward souls, more patience and inner serenity.

The disinterested search for beauty, the passionate concern for justice, the love of truth are so many routes that lead to God. Sometimes one makes many detours; one even gets lost a little. And yet one always reaches the goal toward which one marches without knowing it.

There is nothing so great or ideally beautiful as the action of God in the human soul. If we knew how to detect it in ourselves, our lives would be transformed. If we could see it in others we would love still more Him who is always in the midst of us, who works marvels in us, and who effects these spiritual "rejuvenations" of the soul that we shall come to understand only in eternity.

Charity! Saving word, since all light and strength are in it, since it transforms life and the soul, since it means love; and only love will live forever. We must do our task daily, without worrying what God will make of it. For us, work, sacrifice, the offering of ourselves. For God, the immediate or remote effect that the least of our thoughts and actions will have on other souls.

Nothing is lost, and it is this close unity, this solidarity in work and prayer, which makes the wonderful, blessed Communion of Saints.

In spite of sufferings of body and mind, life brings ineffable joys, fleeting glimpses of the supreme joy to come. But these blessed glimpses cannot be life itself; life is effort, firm and persevering action, and duty willed and accomplished, the heroic conquest of the body by the soul, untroubled calm, and the eyes fixed on God. It is charity gradually taking possession of one's being, banishing all else, all that is not love.

Not to accept everything, but to understand everything; not to approve of everything, but to forgive everything; not to adopt everything, but to search for the grain of truth that is contained in everything.

To repulse no idea and no good will, however awkward or feeble.

To love souls as Jesus Christ loved them, unto suffering, unto death.

The first duty now for every soul of good will is perpetual preaching, by word and by example, of the divine law of Charity.

Each Christian should be the voice crying in the desert: "Let us love!" Perhaps some heavenly breeze will carry these words farther than we suspect.

In barren times, when duty seems difficult and the daily task has no charm, when all spiritual consolation is refused us, and the beautiful light that gilds life is veiled, then humble prayer alone can uphold us and give us hour by hour and day by day the will to act "against our will."

To show a part of the good we have done, that others may know who inspires us to all good; and to hide carefully the other part, which shall be for God alone.

Never to speak of one's health, material worries, or moral suffering, for that uses up one's strength to bear them. But always to welcome with kindness the confidences given to us by others and to seek to console their sorrows, thanks to the experience our own sorrows have obtained for us.

How few people know the meaning and value of the word *to live!* To live is to love, to think, to suffer; to give oneself; to make out of everything — joys, desires, affections, and griefs — a kind of sublime poem that will reach the ears of others and perhaps rouse them from sleep, from the moral apathy in which so many unfortunate people live.

A few moments of recollection and meditation each morning in the presence of God transforms and perfumes the whole day, like flowers cast about when night comes, whose fragrance at dawn anoints everything they have touched.

Little duties, little efforts, the better for being seen by no one, except by Him in whose eyes nothing is little.

What unhappiness to be unable to make others understand the beauty of what we love and believe! No one can penetrate the depths of another's soul where love and simple, true ideas are born. He alone who sees and knows can penetrate those depths, He who brings with Him light and life. We have only to make the gesture of appeal and humble supplication: "Come, Lord, to this soul, that it may live."

How can we not try to give when we have received so much? How can we not love when infinite Love has renewed and transformed our life?

The action of God in the soul: something intangible, profound, strong, to be understood fully only when the divine work is finished.

Through all the agitations, all the fatigue, and all the distractions of life, we must try to preserve a certain inner peace, which is not always joy, but which alone gives a noble unity to life and all its courage to the soul, without which in the hour of trouble we would no longer know how to pray or to think or to act.

The farther I go, the more convinced I am of the absolute futility of religious discussions with unbelievers. The intellectual and historical standpoint to which they confine themselves is not sufficient in view of the phenomena of the interior life. All that is profound, subtle, and alive in the human soul is unknown to them — even their own souls are unknown to them. Let us, rather, try to arouse in these poor persons a sense of eternal things; let us search with them for the divine spark; let us open wide for them the path of good, which leads to God, without encumbering them with barriers and obstacles. That will be enough. Then let us ardently pray, and Providence will do the rest.

To give of oneself only what will profit others; to keep the rest jealously hidden in the depths of the soul as the miser guards his treasure, but with the intention of sacrificing it, of giving it up, when the hour comes.

What grief to assuage, misery to relieve, prejudice to destroy, and hate to transform! How many workmen are needed for this work! At least to do all that one can oneself.

Christ, the adored and freely chosen Master of the soul, at the hour of inner renewal and free assent, fashions and transforms our soul in such a way, by a continuous and intangible action, that the saying of St. Paul becomes true and the soul knows its triumphant reality: "And I live, now not I; but Christ liveth in me,"[94] the Christ of inner souls, the Christ of little ones and of the poor, the one and only eternally living Christ, whom one can never forget once one has been in His company and communed with His soul.

The absence of any deep, long, Christian conversation is a great privation. Let us learn to offer it to God, with so many other hidden longings, secret desires, and sad reflections on oneself that each day brings with it.

[94] Gal. 2:20.

The *home* — that marvelous word because of all it expresses of sweetness, affection, intimacy, and charm. I want to make my home a center of light, fine and generous ideas, and deep feeling; to make it loved by Felix and by many young people, upon whom it might exercise an enlivening influence. For that may God make my beloved husband a Christian!

Which of us can pronounce with our whole soul the words of Christ: "I will have pity upon the multitude"?[95] And who, above all, can give life to these words, making them penetrate our being and every one of our actions? Have pity! What meaning in these words!

Never to forget the distinction between the ideas that we have to defend and make others love, and ourselves, who represent them so badly; between the ideas professed by others, and those others themselves, who are our neighbors and who should be loved in spite of all. To treat with deep respect all that belongs to conscience. Never knowingly to wound a sincere conviction. And yet to adhere firmly, without any capitulation, to what we consider truth or duty.

It is a difficult thing to know how to reconcile apparently conflicting duties, to tolerate ignorance and prejudice without, however, seeming to accept them, to discriminate between that which concerns ourselves alone and, as such, should be resolutely sacrificed, and that which is part of absolute truth and

[95] Mark 8:2.

belief and, as such, should be defended through struggle and suffering.

To bring to the organization of one's life a strict method, and to deviate from one's rule, once it is established, only for serious reasons of family or charity. To do as well as possible whatever one is doing, not abandoning it for something else without a real need.

At certain times, when the body and soul are both suffering or the divine Presence seems far off or veiled, we must take refuge in intellectual work or some peaceful action that gradually restores our inner balance.

As far as possible, no one should know of these painful times, nor suffer because of our suffering. We have no right to add to others' burdens. As Christians, we should, on the contrary, seek to lighten these burdens, which will make our own seem less heavy.

To make Christ, always living and present within us, the model of our life and the friend of every hour, the painful hours and the blessed ones as well. To ask Him to make Himself loved by other souls through us, and to be, following a comparison I love, "the rough vessel that contains a brilliant light and through which this light brightens and warms everything around it."

Unalterable calm, true humility, profound charity: the three foundations of all strong and intense interior life.

What a bitter trial is certain people's utter incomprehension of the things of God and the soul! Ignorance, prejudice, and irrational hostility make a heavy weight to lift.

No matter: "The light enlighteneth every man that cometh into this world."[96] Let us strive to dispel the shadows that are in His way.

To take refuge in action in those hours when thought is weary or unhappy, and to lead oneself gently back to interior recollectedness when action becomes too engrossing and threatens to overwhelm our inner life.

Christ must live in us, so that we may give Him to others.

In hours of anguish and suffering, God sometimes grants to the soul — in that place where human torments can no longer strike — movements of joy and an intense awareness of invisible realities, so that one can take up life once again with its struggles and sorrows. The divine illumination has made the road more luminous and enables us to see our destination.

We must know how to discern the important duties contained in the little monotonies of every day, and to transform them by a lively spirit and by love.

[96] John 1:9.

Christ has planted His Cross in humanity, and nothing can uproot it if we do not uproot it ourselves from our hearts. We can attack the outer form of Christianity, impede its exterior manifestations for a time at least, in our efforts to diminish it. But who can attack Christ Himself, living and triumphant within us?

What a wild dream to think one can destroy the Church! It is possible only to those who have not understood the wonderful distinction of her soul and body: the body, which may sometimes appear wounded and weakened but which lives as long as the soul animates it, and the soul, which is immortal.

We should make each day a resumé of our whole life by filling it with prayer, work, and charity.

Let us never expect to see the result of our efforts for souls. It is good not to know it, for if we did know it, pride in doing good, the most subtle pride of all, might follow.

Let us confide to God the disposing of the prayers, sacrifices, and efforts that we offer Him, and with no thought for what we have already done, let us continue to work and to act for our brothers, for souls, and for the coming of God's Kingdom in them.

Not to be understood is a sharp suffering. To know that God understands is a sharper joy than any suffering.

A simple contact can sometimes be the best sermon; a spark can start a great flame.

More and more I understand with what respect one must treat souls and doctrines. In all of these there is a "soul of truth," a spark of life, which must be separated out and revived. That, especially, is gospel work. To perform it, one must be possessed by and imbued with the doctrine of truth and, through knowledge of one's own soul, be able to know and to penetrate other souls.

And then one must love. Charity, always.

"The harvest is great, the laborers are few."[97] The masses are waiting, multitudes of unhappy beings are living in evil and ignorance, and yet we can continue our daily life in indifference.

Oh, the gentle pity of Christ, the tears He shed for the miserable abandoned crowds! Shall we, His disciples, never know how to love with all our soul and act with all our will for those little ones whom Jesus blesses, and whom He wants entirely for Himself?

There is great work to be done. No matter, if each of us does all he can and leaves behind him deeds, words, and prayers that will multiply wondrously until the end of time and do good to distant or unknown souls!

Suffering works mysteriously, first in ourselves by a kind of inner renewal, and also in others, perhaps far away, without our ever knowing here on earth what we are accomplishing by it.

[97] Matt. 9:37; Luke 10:2.

Suffering is an act. Christ on the Cross has perhaps done more for humanity than Christ speaking and acting in Galilee or Jerusalem. Suffering creates life; it transforms all it touches, all it strikes.

"Sufficient unto the day is the evil thereof."[98] We must prepare for "today" in recollectedness and prayer and live it in struggle and suffering.

To shut one's heart to any complaints and regrets that could escape it; to open it wide to all that it can pour forth of human sympathy, strength, and kindness.

Socialism promises to guarantee and transform the future; Christianity transforms the present. Following the expression of Fr. Maumus, it gives humanity its "daily bread," and does so always.

We must never repulse a soul that seeks to approach our own soul; perhaps that soul, consciously or unconsciously, is in quest of the "unknown God"[99] and has sensed in us something that revealed His presence; perhaps it thirsts for truth and feels that we live by this sovereign truth.

The souls that seem to be the most ruined are not always those least accessible to the divine word; when wood is dead it needs only a spark to make a great flame.

[98] Matt. 6:34.
[99] Acts 17:23.

Men live on the surface of their souls, without ever penetrating their profound and sorrowful depths. If we knew how to recollect ourselves, how to look clearly into ourselves, and how to understand the meaning and fruitfulness of suffering, then the slightest gesture, the most imperceptible tremble of the most humble of human beings would reveal to us these abysses of sorrow or tenderness, which remain wide open in a soul until the day when another soul pours light into it and causes life to burst forth from it.

Silence is sometimes an act of energy, and smiling, too.

To defend oneself against the multiplicity of external things and the agitation they bring.

To make firm resolutions and to carry out to the end what was prepared in our meditation.

To look around one for poor proud sufferers in need, to find them and give them the alms of our heart, our time, and our tender respect.

Pride in suffering! To distrust even that.

To let the soul reach full bloom. To repress everything that impoverishes or confines it. No meanness. Life in its fullest and richest expression.

If men tried in all good faith to see their fellows as they really are, and brought a little indulgence into their dealings with them, then hatred and struggles, private or public, would quickly cease. But when we look at others, we are generally short-sighted or far-sighted, and so we either scrutinize their errors at excessively close range, or we exaggerate their faults from afar.

Only charity gives a correct view of men and things.

A thought from without, suggested by some spoken or written word, is received by the intelligence more or less passively. For a long time, that thought remains purely intellectual. Then a day comes when, under the influence of grace, it comes to life, and becomes not only present to the mind but alive for the soul. Does not this explain and justify human intervention in divine work?

Grace alone can bring about a conversion; without it, we can do nothing for a soul. But can we not prepare the materials for grace? Can we not put into people's minds new ideas that, when touched by grace, may one day rise and live? It is a humble work, demanding much patience and tact, and it must be performed without expecting any result but what is willed by God and known only to Him.

To be fruitful, work should be regular and represent real effort and a deep exploration of things. We must guard against the habit of merely skimming things, which is dangerous to the mind and useless.

It seems to me that what is especially lacking to this generation is recollectedness. To meditate presupposes an intellectual strength, a profound insight into spiritual things, of which this generation is, for the most part, incapable. And yet it is only by this means that one can have interior life, of which exterior life is merely an expression; only by this means that action can become fruitful.

What can we give to others when we have gathered nothing for ourselves? Let us first create a reserve of thought, energy, prayer. Our superabundance will flow out to others, and this stream of life will never exhaust itself, because it will have its source in God. Let us each day renew our strength in deep contact with the Eternal. May the Heart of Christ, in a communion that is closer every day with us, tell us some of His divine secrets. May the light of the Spirit guide us. Having God within us, we will surely do the work of God, or rather, He will do it Himself through us and better than we will.

Let us not be dilettantes of divine love, and let us not cultivate even this sort of egotism. We must know how to share with our brothers the gifts that God has given us and to give a tithe of the graces we have received. Perhaps in this effort we will lose a bit of the joys of recollectedness, of interior union with God; it is a sacrifice every Christian must make. That which we give will in this way have only more value. Is this not, to a small extent, what it is "to lose one's soul"[100] for the benefit of another's?

It is comparatively easy not to be absorbed in our own suffering, but the suffering of those we love is apt to become a constant and unhappy obsession, against which we must struggle: first by prayer, confiding those we love to God in complete filial

[100] Cf. Matt. 10:39; Mark 8:35; Luke 9:24.

abandonment, then by work, and also by an occupation chosen outside the center of our thoughts and affections. Finally by doing good to others, we can try to forget a little of our dear ones' burdens, which are a thousand times more painful than the ones we carry alone.

Let us maintain, as much as possible, silence about our sorrows and anguish; and if someone sees that we suffer, may God alone, at least, know the extent and the deepest causes of our suffering.

There are times when we can more fully understand St. Paul's sublime meaning when he tells us to rejoice always.[101] There is a joy that the worst sorrows cannot destroy, a light that shines in the thickest darkness, a strength that upholds all our weakness. Alone, we would fall upon the ground, like Christ carrying His Cross; however, we continue on, or our falls are only passing, and soon we are standing and strong again.

For we "can do all things in Him who strengthens us."[102] Creatures of weakness, we carry infinite Strength within us, and in the depths of our souls shines the Light that is never extinguished. How should we not rejoice, in spite of all, with a supernatural joy, when we have God for life and for eternity?

The influence exercised by a person is something subtle, penetrating; its strength cannot be measured. What powerful preaching there can be in simple contact with a soul! One single

[101] 1 Thess. 5:16.
[102] Phil. 4:13.

soul can change the whole moral atmosphere surrounding it by its solitary light.

Let us not think that by our personal action we can hasten the coming of God's Kingdom in souls. As soon as the divine hour has come, our efforts will be useless, or, rather, they will only be an active prayer, an appeal to Him who transforms and saves.

Nevertheless, let us make this appeal to Him with the humble conviction that He alone will do what must be done and will bring life to the souls for which we act and pray.

What joy suddenly to discover in someone resources that we did not suspect, an instinctive need for the higher life, an unconscious seeking for the unknown God! We must then draw near with respect to give this soul some of our inner treasure, and must offer for it some of our daily suffering and effort.

But with what delicacy must we approach this soul, so as not to impede divine action! A single word that lacks the spirit of the eternal Word might destroy all of this interior working, which God alone brings to completion. We must let Him speak, and we must show by our example and our lives alone the fulfillment of His deep and efficacious action in us.

Never must our wounded sensibilities make us indifferent and hardhearted. The wounds that bleed are still alive; let us rejoice if an unconscious hand by touching our wound proves that the tissues are full of life and will one day have a sweet healing through a continual interior action.

Christ's Church is in need of apostles. But how much is needed before we can earn that name, what subordination of one's sensible being to the strong and sovereign soul, what humble consciousness of failings and faults, what calm intelligence, what burning faith, and, above all, what unalterable and lively charity! We must become "another Christ" among men, bringing like the Divine Model a message of peace, a teaching, and liberty through Truth.

Why search so hard for a heart that understands us and a voice that knows how to speak to us of God and the soul, when the Heart of Christ is open to us and no one in the world knows how to love us and understand us as He does?

Catholic spiritual direction, which is so poorly known or decried, is a wonderful force put at the service of souls; practiced as it should be, it gives to the Christian soul an incomparable fervor and sometimes reveals the soul to itself.

We never speak to God without hearing a response, if the language of our soul is made of humility, suffering, and the longing for good.

Those we encounter along our earthly path cast a distracted look in passing upon the outer wrappings of our being, and go their way, confident of knowing us sufficiently. Let us take care not to act in the same way toward the companions of our life. Even in a brief encounter, we can touch a soul, or, even more, achieve profound insight into that which is hidden beneath appearances: a whole person, a whole life, of which others remain in perpetual ignorance.

❧

I believe in the sovereign action, powerful and constant, of the Holy Spirit in our souls and in the Church.

❧

Practical materialism is as dangerous as philosophical materialism. Every day it makes further inroads among the masses, and without a set agenda, simply through the free play of evil influences, it is now establishing itself in our democracy.

Therefore, in the face of egotism, it is for Christians to proclaim the fundamental notion of sacrifice; in the face of brutal pride — even of the intellectual sort — the idea of humility; in the face of sensuality and indulgence, the law of duty, not made by man but coming from above.

❧

Why should a word, which would at other times remain on the surface of our soul, sometimes sink to a great depth and inflict a cruel wound?

Perhaps in such moments, our soul is already bruised by other sufferings and ready to overflow, and thus finds itself nearer to the exterior, closer to painful blows and brutal incomprehension.

❧

To know how to be silent is often wisdom and an act of virtue.

❧

It is sometimes our duty to disclose more of ourselves than we wish to those who will never completely understand us, and to hide our soul from those to whom we would like to open it wide.

Charity, a supernatural virtue, is rarely considered as such, even by Christians. It is life, love, action; let us guard against practicing it in a manner that is sluggish, passive, lifeless.

To transform one's suffering into joy for others, to cover it with a veil that only allows to show through what could become consolation or affection.

May God alone know that which He alone has willed, and the burden He has given us.

From all quarters, human affairs press upon and engross us, and if our will, sustained by divine grace, does not take serious steps to counteract them, we soon merit the sorrowful reproach our Savior uttered to Peter: "Thou savorest not the things that are of God."[103]

To savor the things that are of God is to have God in our life, to be penetrated through and through with Christianity, to see everything in the light of eternity, which the Holy Spirit never denies us; it is to transform our soul and to establish it in peace and charity; it is to love, along with the works of the human intelligence, the supreme Intelligence from which they spring; it is to try to penetrate below the surface of people, to reach those depths wherein one can gently try to bring them to God; it is, finally, to live, by one's devotion, in sweet, strong

[103] Matt. 16:23; Mark 8:33.

intimacy with Him whom we call our Father, who is the life
of our soul.

There is little suffering that can compare with this: to love,
and to be repaid with hatred or at least hostility; to dream of
doing good for someone, of giving part of oneself, and to find
that this person does not appreciate you, judges you unfairly,
and misunderstands everything about you.

What should one do then? Not be unjust in return; remember that the Master suffered misunderstanding and contempt; and, without reproaches or sorrowful thoughts of self,
continue to speak, act, and love, not to gain the affection
denied us, but in the higher and supernatural thought of
charity.

To think is excellent;
to pray is better;
to love is everything.

We should not scrutinize ourselves too closely while we
are living, but try to live simply, bravely, and joyously beneath
the gaze of God and for Him.

We must always and in spite of everything be indulgent.
In all the wrongs that others do to us, there is always some fault
of our own. May the offense received from our neighbor always
be for us the occasion of a sincere examination of conscience,
and may the wrong of another disappear in what we discover
in ourselves of our own weaknesses and faults.

To know how to forgive is the special mark of the Christian. Forgiveness should not merely be passive; it should be a lively act of love.

Human knowledge becomes finer and more interesting insofar as one imbues it with the light that comes from the Infinite. Second causes, when linked to the first and only Cause, become harmonious. The world, history, are transformed when one realizes the Force that guides them in unknown ways to an end unknown to humanity, but which God knows. Mankind can appear great, to those who know how to discern in it the soul — this soul to whom Infinity lies open, this soul that thinks, loves, and can regard fearlessly everything that happens, sure of its immortality.

The chasm between souls can be filled only by God.

The world approves and countenances nearly everything. To the squandering of time or fortune or one's heart, and even to the most blatant acts of folly and guilt, it closes its eyes or gives its applause. On the other hand, do not think of consecrating any part of yourself or your time or money to the cause of God. Such a thing is not pleasing to this frivolous world, which considers itself to be robbed of all you give to eternal things and to your brothers; and it will not allow such theft. The love of God is the only eccentricity the world does not accept and will never accept.

The intensity of certain sorrows makes them almost sacred and compels them to be hidden from the eyes of men. In the depths of the soul where they take refuge, with God for their sole witness, they can be discovered only by seekers of souls, those who know how to penetrate the living depths of a person and who, as beneficent visitors, leave behind them the alms of religious sympathy. Such well-doers are rare, and "He who seeth in secret"[104] is often enough the only confidant of our interior distress.

The Eucharist truly acts within us to transform us, almost without our knowing it — as bread and wine, human nourishment, strengthens all our body and blood without our being aware of it. By His contact and the grace He leaves in us, Christ gives us moral health and creates for us another soul. It is not in vain that we lean for a moment upon His Heart and confide to Him our burden of suffering, weakness, and anguish.

To refrain from action is sometimes the greatest sacrifice, and the most fruitful of all actions.

God takes upon Himself to do for us, and better than we can, the things we dreamed of doing ourselves. The influence we would like to exert, He uses for the good of souls, while we offer Him only our silence, our weakness, and our apparent sluggishness.

The world does not understand grief; it is ignorant of pity and consolation. How can it discern the infinite in suffering, since there is no infinite in love and joy for it?

[104] Cf. Matt. 6:18.

We must accept in a spirit of humble charity the empty consolations and encouragement that come from the lips only, words that have not sprung from the heart and therefore can never reach our own heart. But we must open our whole souls to the sympathy and words that bring us something of God and speak to us living and eternal words.

April 13, 1905

Per Crucem ad Lucem.[105]

In the final moments of Christ's Passion when, with pierced hands and feet, He poured out all of His precious Blood upon human soil to make it fruitful, lived His last hours, and experienced human suffering to an extent we cannot understand, the Gospel tells us that the earth was covered with darkness. . . .[106]

Lord, in our lives and in our souls, there are also hours completely shrouded in darkness, sorrowful hours in which the veil cast over our hearts hides from us even the sight of those things that could give us comfort, hours in which we suffer in such a way that nothing here on earth could console us.

Happy are those who in such hours and in outer darkness can still at least contemplate Thee, Jesus Christ, the only Life! Happy are those whose weak arms can still clasp the feet upon the Cross, who can lean their weary foreheads against Thy

---

[105] "Through the Cross to the Light." This was the date of the death of Elisabeth's beloved sister Juliette.

[106] Mark 15:33.

pierced hands and their bruised hearts upon the Heart that has suffered so much and that knows how to pity and to love!

⚘

I believe that suffering was accorded by God to man with a great intention of love and mercy.

I believe that Jesus Christ has transformed and sanctified suffering and made it almost divine. I believe that suffering is the great instrument of redemption and sanctification for the soul.

I believe that suffering is fruitful, as much as and sometimes more than our words and deeds, and that the hours of Christ's Passion did more for us and were more powerful with the Father than even His years of preaching and earthly activity.

I believe that there is coursing through souls — those on earth, those in Purgatory, and those who have attained to true life — a great unending stream made up of the sufferings, merits, and love of all these souls, and that our least sorrow, our faintest efforts can by divine action reach certain souls, whether near or far, and bring them light, peace, and holiness.

I believe that in eternity we shall find again the beloved ones who have known and loved the Cross, and that their sufferings and our own will be lost in the infinity of divine Love and the joy of final reunion.

I believe that God is love, and that suffering, in His hand, is the means used by His love to transform and save us.

I believe in the Communion of Saints, the resurrection of the body, and life everlasting.

⚘

Jesus on the Cross said these sublime and sorrowful words: "I thirst."[107] Since then, throughout days and centuries, all of

---

[107] John 19:28.

178

humanity has repeated these words. Lips and souls have cried or murmured it, and every human being in his turn utters it either in despair or faith.

My day has come, O my God! It began to dawn long since, through the sovereign authority of Thy word and the influence of Thy love, and also through the long suffering that Thou hast used for Thy work of renewal.

Misfortune has come, breaking my heart forever, taking from me one of my greatest affections, one that nothing can replace, an affection made of maternity, friendship, and close sisterly feeling.

And now, O Lord, with all my soul I say the sorrowful words: "I thirst."

I thirst for the peace Thou alone canst give, which transforms life; for the stability and living repose that exist only in Thee.

I thirst for light, to know, to see, to possess, as we shall see and possess in eternity.

I thirst for perfect sympathy and the tenderness that can read souls, and for close and strong union in Thee.

My soul thirsts to devote itself, to give itself, to be understood and loved, to understand and partake of everything.

It sighs for that which endures, and it would sometimes shake off the burden of misunderstandings, hostility, and narrowness that weighs upon it and wounds it.

I thirst for immortality, that complete blossoming of the soul that we shall know beyond this transitory world.

I thirst for life, the only Life, full and eternal, with all our affections recovered in the bosom of infinite Love.

O my God, I thirst for Thee!

I utter this cry at this hour; many times again will this cry go out from me, O Jesus, before I come to Thee. I will say it with Thee: "I thirst."

As soon as Thou hadst spoken, Thou hadst done Thy task in this world. Thou hadst prayed, labored, suffered, and "Those whom Thy Father gave Thee hast Thou kept: and none of them is lost."[108] Let it be thus with me, and if in solitude, in those hours when I come to Thee as to a loving friend, I again utter my sorrowful appeal, let me nevertheless, with Thy support, perform my task and be a valiant Christian and apostle. May my secret fervor toward eternal things never make me forget those who suffer on earth. May I always love more and more my human brothers and those who are close to me. Only then will I have the right to say with Thee, "Those whom Thou gavest me have I kept: and none of them is lost."

I have not asked Thee to take me from the world, but to allow me to do Thy will and the work that Thou hast intended for me. Now, having purified me, Thou canst draw me to Thee in Thy light and Thy love, where those I have loved so much already live, and where others will rejoin me one day.

More than ever do I thirst to find them again, my beloved ones; I thirst to live with them, to know, to possess, to love; I thirst for Thee, my God!

Supernatural things have grown so strange to certain people that they imagine that anyone who is called a "mystic" is helpless in practical matters, and their astonishment is great when they see that same mystic capable of bold initiative or persevering will. Ah, poor people! The soul that mounts very high sees earthly things all the more clearly, and as "the soul is mistress of the body it animates," the body obeys its stern commandment.

Continue to trail upon the ground, birds with heavy wings, but let the swift-winged birds fly up into the sky, whence they

[108] Cf. John 17:12.

will return to collect spoils on earth. One can breathe better, on this poor earth, when one has gathered a provision of pure air in the heights.

When prejudice and opposition attack and hurt us, we too easily forget that Jesus Christ suffered even this. He who penetrated everything and could see into all subtleties and nuances of feeling, must greatly have suffered sometimes from the misunderstanding and narrow-mindedness of those whom He yet loved with incomparable tenderness!

And yet we do not know how to endure the least blow, even when those who inflict it are not, as with Jesus Christ, our friends and loved ones.

Let us learn from Him to be sweet and patient always, with men and with ideas.

To give oneself and yet reserve oneself. All Christian duty lies in this.

God, in giving us life, assigns to each one of us a special task to do and a role in the fulfillment of His eternal plan. The important thing, then, above all, is to come to know this particular mission well, to discern the divine Will in our soul and in our life, and then to set ourselves to work, and to make of our entire life and death a means of salvation for ourselves and our brothers.

We are the divine Master's humble workmen, the laborers of the Father, and when the night shall come, we must be able to tell Him with confidence that the harvest is ready and that the living Sun may now cause to grow the seeds that we have sown.

"By their fruits ye shall know them."[109]

God knows our soul in all its depths; He is aware of our least desire, the least impulse of our love, and the least movement of our will. But men see only what we bring forth to the exterior from our inmost being. That is why our acts and words and even our bearing must be the harmonious and truthful expression of our soul. Men will judge this soul, or, what is more important, will judge God on the basis of the fruits He produces in us and the works He inspires in us.

Martha and Mary! The eternal conflict of material life and external existence with the imperishable needs of the soul; the call from without, pressing us to uncover the hidden forces of our soul, to abandon inner recollectedness for the activity that is more pure, more fruitful, or so it seems. But the Master has answered the question and ended the conflict. Mary triumphs; and if our bodies must often be given to the humble tasks of Martha, it is only on condition that our soul, like Mary, devotes itself to the contemplation and adoration of Him who speaks the divine word, and that we know how to listen in silence to that word in the depths of ourselves. The worth of activity lies only in the meditation that has prepared it and in the offering of it to God.

Christianity is based on the idea of sacrifice.

Each Christian in his own time should imitate his Model and should make his sacrifice amid men's silence or indifference, to be joined to that of the Master. He should know Gethsemane

[109] Matt. 7:16, 20.

or Calvary to the small degree that his strength can support. He should offer himself as an oblation for the salvation of all, and stretch out his hands, which are often weary, to the Cross in supplication for all. His lips should proclaim his sublime devotion to the Crucified, and his soul should give what is most pure in itself for sinners and the disinherited.

Souls who have lived for a long time withdrawn into their depths, and who have not been able to pour forth their plenitude, sometimes feel the need to unburden themselves, to give to others a little of their interior treasure. This is the secret of certain writings, and it is perhaps the mysterious reason for this privation of Christian sympathy, which sometimes makes the soul suffer. Exterior deprivations make the interior life more intense and the gift of self richer.

We must give the smallest possible place to "hateful self," avoiding that which only brings us praise and esteem without serving God or our neighbor. And yet we must not neglect the least opportunity for doing good. It is a difficult thing to reconcile these two duties, and yet indispensable, in which the divine light will guide us if we ask for it when it is needed. According to whether the need or duty at hand is one that requires our abnegation or our charity, we must be prepared to sacrifice either our pride or our humility.

When blood no longer flows from an open wound, to the indifferent eye it seems that healing is near. Nothing could be more wrong: the wound that no longer bleeds is one that will never heal.

It is surprising to see the interior progress we make in times
of spiritual privation, when no conscious joy of any kind unites
our souls with God. It is then indeed God Himself that we love,
and not His consolations; and whatever we do then, at the cost
of constant effort and a perpetual appeal to grace, is indeed duty
in all its starkness.

Then, when the dry road is past and the way becomes easier,
we are astonished to see how far we have come; sometimes we
come to a gentle rest, in peace and near the Heart of God.

To be very reserved concerning everything in my interior life.
Whatever I disclose to the outside world, without the absolute
duty of charity, will be of no use to others. We must not rashly
distribute even the small change of our fortune and squander
what the Master has given us.

When physical or mental suffering threatens to reach our
very soul, we must say to it: "Thou shalt go no farther." We must
let the waves from outside beat against our poor soul, without
using too many of its resources to fight them off; on the contrary,
we must avoid any disturbance and fortify our poor assailed soul
against it.

The agitations, bitterness, and all that attacks the soul from
outside or from our sensible being quickly becomes assuaged if
we create in ourselves a little silence and catch our breath in
the presence of God.

If God wills that I should live to be very old, I fully accept
His will, asking only that in the long future years, I may love

Him and work profitably for the coming of His Kingdom in souls and for His Church.

Otherwise, why should one wish the way to be shorter when one knows the end?

I can await the hour appointed for me, for I am confident of finding again, by divine grace, those who have gone before me into eternity.

I know that I cannot now possess complete life, such as we shall know in eternity. My weak soul is bound by a thousand human ties, which do not allow it truly to know, possess, or love. And yet the divine light that illuminates its shadows enables it to wait and hope for everything.

To put more energy into the battle against oneself; not to allow external influences to pass beyond a certain point in the soul, and to fortify this weak soul against the wounds that are endlessly inflicted on it.

One deception alone is praiseworthy: that which allows us to hide the evil done to us, our suffering, and the deep place in the soul that belongs to God alone; the deception that, without hiding what we are, does not reveal us in our entirety, and does not exhaust our reserve of charity, energy, and kindness.

To act while physically exhausted and to suffer without any sensible consolation is perhaps to merit what our prayer would not have been worthy to obtain. Only sacrifice is certain to go straight to the Heart of Jesus.

Silence is a Christian duty.

When it is a question of ourselves, our trials, the graces we have received, we should remain silent, unless charity obliges us to speak. And even when it is a question of divine things, it is well to be very reserved, "to guard these things in our heart,"[110] until the moment when this heart opens itself to someone who is in doubt or unhappiness.

What good is confiding one's pains, miseries, and regrets to those to whom one cannot say at the end, "Pray for me"?

Before acting, to establish oneself in peace; to banish from one's soul by recollectedness all that could trouble or agitate it; to strengthen one's will by prayer and meditation; and then to get to work humbly, manfully, joyfully.

Some laughter is like tears; some tears are like a song of thanksgiving.

Many people know so little of their own souls that it is indeed difficult for them to understand the soul of another.

August 1906

I now cease to write my thoughts here; that evolution is achieved in my soul of which these notes have marked the

[110] Cf. Luke 2:51.

stages. Or at least — for nothing is finished on earth — my soul has entered into this great and divine peace, an unmerited grace for which I must bless Him who has willed and accomplished all.

I believe, I hope, I adore; and it is in a spirit of utmost humility and gratitude that, looking at my life and the benefits I have received, I give to God, I consecrate to Him, my soul and the new life that opens before me.

A Call to the Interior Life

These things I have told you,
that when the hour shall come,
you may remember
that I told you of them.

John 16:4

꧁

At the moment of saying farewell to you, dearest mother, taking with me, thanks to you, a store of physical strength and a heart filled with gratitude for your kindness, I leave you this little book in order that, during our three weeks' separation, it may speak to you of me and, still more, of all that I desire for you.[111]

I need not tell you again that you are one of those whom I love in a special degree and most tenderly; hourly, if not incessantly, some act, prayer, or suffering offered to God on your behalf speaks to Him of your soul, and entrusts Him with your peace of mind. What I cannot do for you, I beg divine grace to accomplish — namely, to transform your pain, calm your mind, and give a supernatural aim to all that is naturally so good in you.

The good that we do, even when it is the outcome of so beautiful a nature as your own, brings no consolation or inner light to our soul unless it is motived by a supernatural intention, and unless our will is united with God's will in accomplishing it. For an action to be completely good, to bear all the fruit possible and to benefit our neighbors, it must be matured and prepared in God's presence. This is effected by means of the recollection that I urge you to practice, being sure that it will be a source of peace to you and in no way hinder your activity.

[111] Elisabeth was on the point of leaving Jougne and returning to Paris, three weeks before her mother and the rest of the family.

I know well enough that your nature shrinks from the thought of contemplation, and that you are alarmed by the very word *meditation*, just as the idea of entering a church would frighten an unbeliever. Nevertheless, you would no doubt tell any unhappy infidel that in the church, where he sees nothing attractive, there is One whom he does not know, and that prayer there is more delightful and fruitful than elsewhere. I can tell you the same thing about meditation; the name repels you, but the thing itself is very beautiful and profound, being the foundation of the Christian life.

But meditation has to be approached, and that requires an effort: in the first place, to set aside each day the time necessary for it, and further, to force oneself to make a meditation regularly, and to persevere when there is no feeling of pleasure and when God withholds all consolation. It behooves us to take the first steps in quest of God, but if we persevere in seeking Him thus, He will someday give us a hundredfold in return, and the reward granted to our labor is very sweet. For many years, St. Teresa awaited God's response to her persevering prayer, which afforded her no consolation, but, when it came, the response was far greater than she could ever have anticipated. We, who are not saints, do not have to wait so long; we receive a great deal in return for a little exertion, and, I can tell you by experience, God is an excellent creditor.

I love you enough, I think, to know you very well, and it seems to me that the two things in which you are deficient are perhaps, from the human point of view, a willingness to discipline yourself and, from the religious point of view, full confidence in God, a spirit of joy and self-abandonment.

Whoever wishes to lead a truly Christian life must first exert his will, and so regulate his existence as to put the most important things foremost. I think that nothing is more important in the use of our days than the time given first of all to God. It may be very short, as a few minutes are enough every morning for us to offer up our thoughts, deeds, and words, and all that wealth of sufferings which becomes daily a source of grace to the souls on whose behalf we offer it. Five minutes spent in this way, and the indulgences of the day devoted to the souls in Purgatory, form a preparation for much good that will be accomplished subsequently unknown to you. Add to this ten minutes or a quarter of an hour devoted to reading and meditating upon some passage, and your morning and night prayers, and all together they do not amount to one hour given to God out of the twenty-four. Is this really too much to ask of so good a Christian as yourself?

I hope that this winter, the nearness of the church will make it easier for you to go to Mass, and will enable you to communicate more often. There, in our Savior's presence, you will find the strength and comfort that all our love is incapable of bestowing on you, so true it is that human nature cannot accomplish this task.

If you, dearest mother, wish to make progress in the Christian life, and at the same time to give me much happiness, force yourself daily to do as I have just said. Do it without any anticipation of finding delight in it, but do it regularly. I would be so glad if the things of the soul and of the inner life became gradually familiar to you, and took complete possession of your good, loving heart, which is restless because God has not yet filled it sufficiently with Himself.

Then all those outward, material things, which often overwhelm you, will resume their proper position, the place of secondary importance, and will no longer be anything but duties quietly performed and reduced to a minimum of what is necessary. The chief place will be assigned to the training of your own soul, to the care of those about you, to good works and prayer. The valiant woman is undoubtedly praised for spinning wool and flax, but still more perhaps because "the heart of her husband trusteth in her."[112]

---

[112] Prov. 31:11.

And then the joy that follows! Yes, it is really joy, an inward happiness proceeding from God Himself, which is increased rather than diminished by trials, for suffering that we accept brings us close to the Eternal, makes us better, and transforms our affections, will, and feelings, without robbing them of the best that they contain from the human point of view. This happiness has nothing to do with the senses; it exists in the midst of moral sufferings, anguish of heart, and bodily weariness; it dwells in our innermost nature and needs for its maintenance the perpetual support of divine grace. Each of our efforts and sorrows adds to it, and nothing can destroy it, because it is based upon faith, hope, and charity.

Cultivate this joy in your heart, beloved mother, and regard as actually sinful everything that might deprive you of your sense of trust in God, and depress you and burden your conscience. Let your soul expand freely, and, in order to advance more quickly along the right way, seek peace as much as the other virtues.

I must stop, for time fails me, and it would take me several hours to tell you all that I have in my mind. What I am anxious to repeat is that we are grateful for all that you have done for us, that our filial love for you is very deep, and that our hearts are united in the precious memory and love of our Juliette, and in the hope of seeing her again. She is waiting for us, and our reunion cannot be far distant, for nothing in life lasts long, and we can calmly await what, by God's help, we are certain someday to possess.

With this beloved name on my lips, I take leave of you, commending the care of your dear soul to your unseen angel guardians, and giving you, darling mother, from Felix and myself a hearty and most affectionate kiss.

Your eldest daughter,
Elisabeth
August 31, 1907

✧

Living the Spiritual Life

As every man hath received grace,
ministering the same one to another,
as good stewards of the
manifold grace of God . . .

1 Peter 4:10

To Madame E— A—,[113]

Every Christian believes that there is a mysterious, supernatural connection between himself and all the other children of the same Father. By virtue of this connection, which we call the Communion of Saints, the efforts, merits, and sufferings of each individual benefit all the rest. A similar law exists in the natural order, and if we reflect a little, we shall be convinced that our words and deeds have a much more profound and far-reaching effect than we are apt to suppose. Hence it is an absolute duty for everyone who understands what *absolute* and *duty* mean to refrain from doing or saying not merely what is bad, but also what is indifferent, since there can be no neutrality in matters of morality.

Moreover, it is also his duty to labor day by day with continuous efforts at his interior perfection, for, whether we wish it or not, the effect that we produce will be the reflection and expression of what we bear within us. Let us lay up for ourselves a store of lofty thoughts, energy, and strong, intense affection, and then we may be sure that sooner or later, perhaps without our being aware of it, the overflow will reach the hearts of others.

I admit that the task is difficult for one who relies only on reason, for reason is itself to some extent an instrument, and many circumstances may falsify it or hinder its action. I have absolute

---

[113] Elisabeth addressed this to a friend who was an unbeliever.

confidence, however, in God's method of dealing with souls, even with those who never mention His name and yet render Him genuine homage by their love of what is good, just, and beautiful. I believe that He prompts and directs all honest reasoning, and everyone who walks in its light. Therefore, setting aside all that belongs to another sphere, I want to limit myself to what is the sphere of all, Christians and unbelievers alike, for a Christian is also a rational "being," and reason carries him just as far as anyone else — to the point of which Pascal said that the last step taken by reason is to recognize the existence of innumerable things beyond its ken.

⚬

Your life must be orderly

Therefore life is for all men a serious matter, and it ought not to be spent recklessly. Whether we regard it as a prelude or outline of the fuller, higher life that we cannot enjoy here below, or whether we look at it by itself as a fruit (a very bitter fruit sometimes) and not as a seed, we arrive at the conclusion that every life involves responsibility, and we are answerable not only for the evil that we do, but also for the good that we fail to do. We become convinced also that the most trifling actions and the most secret sacrifices echo on in time and space, and we continue forever the good or evil that we have once begun.

Consequently, nothing is indifferent in our moral life; the neglect of the smallest duty has results such as we never suspect. This is why we must arrange our life in such a way that no duty, great or small, may be sacrificed, and why we must not allow the aim in view to be lost in the clouds, but set to work at once in order to attain it. The important thing is not so much to succeed at once, but to begin and go on. Therefore, we ought to make each day a sort of summary of life as a whole, and bring into it each of the duties that make up our existence. These are duties toward our family and toward society, and, in your case, I will say moral rather than religious duties.

First of all, we must decide clearly what our real duties are, and here there are two pitfalls to be avoided. We must not be too ready to imagine that certain so-called obligations are really binding upon us, or we shall allow ourselves to be worried and distracted by a multitude of useless trifles; nor, on the other hand, must we neglect what are real duties, from which nothing can dispense us. We should carefully arrange our duties in order, never letting those of lowest rank encroach upon the more important. Highest of all stands moral duty, and, if I give it precedence over the rest, it is because it includes them all, and because the way in which we discharge our other duties will depend upon the way in which we fulfill and understand this one.

Practice meditation and examination of conscience

You must not fancy that the moral life has no need of sustenance; a soul, just as much as a body, can be ill, strong, or anemic. Unless it is to waste away, it must have its daily food, and instead of prayer — that incomparable source of life — two things must be practiced: meditation and examination of conscience. Every soul of any depth recognizes that these things are indispensable, and they were practiced by Marcus Aurelius[114] and Maine de Biran,[115] just as much as by St. Francis de Sales and the lowliest Christian.

Meditation is the withdrawal of oneself into the very depths of one's being, to that point where, as theologians tell us, amid the silence of outward things, we find God; where you will find the source of all good, strength, and beauty (and this is God), where

---

[114] Marcus Aurelius (121-180), Roman emperor.

[115] Maine de Biran (1766-1824), French philosopher.

you will steep yourself in the thought of what is eternal in preparation for the strife of this world; and where you will understand, as your ideal becomes daily more clearly defined, both your own weakness and all that you can do here below in the cause of righteousness. A very definite subject must be taken for meditation, which otherwise is apt to become vague and dreamy, and, in that case, the remedy would be worse than the evil. Meditation should end in a practical resolution that can be applied at once; and it should be made every day, all the more when one is disinclined for it. It is in time of sickness that one most needs a physician.

Examination of conscience is also indispensable every evening; it ought to be sharp and clear, neither vague nor scrupulous. It does not take long to question oneself as to the use of one's time and the discharge of various duties, when these duties are well classified, and a systematic distribution has been made of one's time. This is a fundamental duty tending to restore and strengthen the soul day by day.

Be a light to your children and your neighbors

And next we come to the exterior duties which are, as I have already said, that outward manifestation of our inward condition. You have duties toward your children, and have to look after their mode of life, their work, etc. All this should be done without exaggerating anything, or allowing yourself to be absorbed by one thing at the cost of another, or by one child to the detriment of the rest.

The duty of a mother, who is not dependent upon her own exertions from the material point of view, is to provide for and arrange everything, watching over all, but not claiming the right to do everything herself. These household cares and the organization and arrangement of her home, accounts, etc., do not take up all her thoughts, when things are done regularly day by day, and all is in the right place. What a mother ought to do, and what she alone can do, is to look after her children's moral development, to acquire an insight into their minds, and to awaken in them the highest aspirations. By merely coming into contact with them, she can give them a sense of quiet strength that nothing is able to ruffle, and thus she becomes a second conscience to them. Whoever is happy enough to be able to pass on to her children the results of her own inward experiences is bound to do so.

Toward those whom we call by the pleasant name of neighbors, you, who enjoy a favored existence, have duties and responsibilities. You are responsible because you possess means, intellect, and moral worth. You are an educated woman, whose heart and mind can grasp and sympathize with many things; you enjoy the privilege, in this age of hostility, of hating nothing but hatred, and so you can do much good, if you know where to look. The heart has a power of insight, more or less keen, which enables us to discover needs and sufferings that others would pass unnoticed. My own experience of life has convinced me that never a day goes by without our meeting someone in distress of body or soul, some case of sorrow or poverty, and there must certainly be many such that we overlook. Look around you, my dear friend, and you will soon find out that your good heart does not need spectacles.

Let me give you this little book, written in haste, for in it I have put a scrap of my heart for you. It still contains a reserve of affection, sufferings, and personal experiences, for which it thanks God daily, and which it offers you whenever you like to draw upon it. What proceeds from God must be given back to Him in the form of love for all our fellow travelers on our earthly way; and this is a very pleasant duty in the case of a companion such as yourself.

❧

Litany to Obtain a Conversion

*All expect of Thee that Thou
give them food in season. . . .
When Thou openest Thy hand,
they shall all be filled with good.*

Psalm 103:27-28
(RSV = Psalm 104:27-28)

*The Lord is good to them that hope
in Him, to the soul that seeketh Him.*

Lamentations 3:25

꒦

Litany to Obtain a Conversion

Lord, have mercy upon him.
Christ, have mercy upon him.
Lord, have mercy upon him.

Christ, hear us.
Christ, graciously hear us.

God the Father of Heaven,
have mercy upon him.

God the Son,
Redeemer of the world,
have mercy upon him.

God the Holy Spirit,
have mercy upon him.

Holy Trinity, one God,
have mercy upon him.

Holy Mary,
pray for him.

Holy Mother of God,
pray for him.

Holy Virgin of virgins,
pray for him.

St. Michael,
pray for him.

St. Joseph,
pray for him.

St. Joachim and St. Anne,
pray for him.

St. John the Baptist,
pray for him.

Good thief,
pray for him.

St. Peter,
pray for him.

St. Paul,
pray for him.

St. Stephen,
pray for him.

St. Augustine,
pray for him.

St. Dominic,
pray for him.

St. Francis of Assisi,
pray for him.

St. Ignatius Loyola,
pray for him.

St. Mary Magdalene,
pray for him.

St. Monica,
pray for him.

St. Teresa,
pray for him.

St. Catherine of Siena,
pray for him.

St. Elizabeth,
pray for him.

Holy patron,
pray for him.

Lamb of God, who takest away
the sins of the world,
spare us, O Lord.

Lamb of God, who takest away
the sins of the world,
graciously hear us, O Lord.

Lamb of God, who takest away
the sins of the world,
have mercy upon us.

Christ, hear us.
Christ, graciously hear us.

Grant, we beseech Thee, O Lord, to Thy faithful
people forgiveness of their offenses and true peace,
that, being cleansed from all their sins, they may serve
Thee in peace of mind with holy confidence.
Through our Lord Jesus Christ. Amen.

We witness conversions for which we
cannot account. Grace often works very slowly.
We may trace the successive stages in a soul's progress
toward truth, but there is always a starting point that
we cannot grasp, a sudden movement of grace
before which there is apparently nothing.

Louis Veuillot

✄

Monthly Spiritual Retreat

Seek ye therefore first
the kingdom of God and His justice,
and all these things
shall be added unto you.

Matthew 6:33

❧

I intend each month to make a note of the special resolution which I have formed, and which ought to be the aim of my endeavors.[116] This practice will help me in making my monthly examination of conscience and will show me whether I have made progress or failed continually.

My monthly retreat is never to be neglected, but made in the spirit of faith, charity, and penance.

In the morning:
Whenever I can, I will go to Mass and Holy Communion.
I will communicate at least spiritually when, owing to
illness or circumstances beyond my control,
I am unable to go out.
Meditation on my new resolution.
Preparation for death.
Read a chapter of the *Imitation*.[117]

In the afternoon:
Examination of conscience.
Special resolution.
Read a chapter of the *Imitation*.

[116] This retreat was compiled in late 1909 or early 1910.

[117] *The Imitation of Christ,* a spiritual classic by Thomas à Kempis (c. 1380-1471).

211

In the evening:
Read a chapter of the *Imitation*.
Say the *Miserere*.[118]
Prayer to our Lady.

⁂

First Month: Silence

Silence regarding God, spiritual matters, and my soul, unless speech is necessary to acknowledge my Faith or to do good to the souls of others.

Silence regarding my own soul, the graces that I have received, and my spiritual life, unless charity requires me to break this silence to a very guarded and humble degree.

Silence regarding myself, my trials, privations, and health. I will answer questions truthfully, without affectation, and be silent again.

Silence is good for the soul, essential to recollection, and conducive to humility. Remember our Lord's silence throughout His life and during the hours of His Passion.[119]

When I am in the company of others, for their good, I will talk freely on exalted and serious subjects, the discussion of which cannot fail to enlarge and strengthen both my own soul and theirs.

I will talk about nothing trivial or mean, and no petty grievances. My speech shall be recollected, and my silence living.

⁂

Second Month: Mortification

Penance is obligatory for us all; it is a matter of precept, not of counsel, and our Lord, in the Gospel, lays upon us the duty of doing penance.[120] No Christian can say that this commandment is

---

[118] Ps. 50 (RSV = Ps. 51).
[119] Matt. 26:63; Mark 14:61.
[120] Cf. Matt. 3:2; Mark 1:15.

not binding upon him, nor can he shirk the obligations imposed by the Church: fasting, abstinence and self-sacrifice. Even if some lawful reason renders an individual exempt from the literal fulfillment of these duties, yet the principle remains, and penance is rigorously required.

In the case, however, of those upon whom God lavishes special care and love, whom He has chosen, called, and set apart, counsel becomes precept, and penance ought to be the foundation of their spiritual life.

Lord, I am one of these souls. Thou hast treated me as a favorite child, and hast heaped graces upon me, even when I did not deserve them. In order to overcome me and save me, Thou hast made use of means most carefully chosen and unforeseen.

Therefore Thou desirest something of me, and I am Thy creature, in the fullest sense of the word. Thou art keeping and preparing me to be Thy tool. And first I must discharge the duty laid especially upon those whom Thou hast chosen; I must make reparation — for my own sins and for those of all men, near or distant. By my love and penance, I ought to give consolation to Jesus Christ. Mortification is the manifestation of the spirit of penance.

I must mortify my soul in its pride and selfishness, and struggle against self-love and the subtle assaults of egotism. Means to be employed: humiliations, self-abasement, privations endured or self-imposed. As far as it is possible without attracting attention or failing in my duty to edify others, I will be quick to avail myself of opportunities for remaining in the background, keeping silence or revealing my faults in all that does not affect God's honor. I must aim at making those about me understand that He alone is the author of whatever good there is in me, and that all is bad or weak that proceeds from myself.

I will mortify my body — by enduring the weariness and annoyances of sickness and of daily life; by means of privations, especially by giving up outward gratification and food, insofar as this can be done without injury to my health. Almost every hour of the day supplies some opportunity for mortification.

I will choose by preference mortifications which involve a little humiliation, or which give my soul increased dominion over my body, and accustom my body to submit and to endure ill treatment willingly. I will never speak of these mortifications, but I will offer them up in a spirit of penance and reparation.

In society, I will strive to become more hospitable and accessible, more calm and gentle. I will take an interest in my neighbors and in everything good and beautiful — even in the pleasures of others.

Penance ought to impart additional life to the soul, and, far from making the soul passive, penance should enlarge and strengthen, not restrict and weaken it.

⸙

Third Month: Humility

Humility is the foundation of all solid spiritual life; it and mortification are two pillars supporting the interior temple. No one can think that he has no need to practice it, but it is a duty especially binding upon those who enjoy God's choicest graces. They ought to practice humility in a heroic degree, between their own imperfections and the benefits that they have received.

Our Lord practiced humility; He was humble of heart, humble in all His life, and the innumerable humiliations inflicted upon Him by men were endured with indescribable sweetness and suffered with wonderful courage. He has taught us the way of humble renunciation, being here as everywhere our model, the perfect example that it behooves us to follow from afar.

How can I practice humility? What form should it take?

First and foremost, it should be wholly interior, based on a more and more precise knowledge of myself, my faults and frailties, and my frequent cowardice. All these things are opposed to

God's goodness toward me, and to a clear perception of His love and power, and of all that He has done for me. Examination of conscience and meditation are of assistance in developing humility in our souls. I ought to practice humility discreetly and unostentatiously, by keeping silence regarding my soul and my own affairs, by seeking little humiliations, and by voluntarily remaining in the background when the interests of others do not require me to act otherwise. I ought to display God's way of dealing with me, and lead others to love and admire Him in His work, but I should make myself small in the sight of others and in my own estimation, realizing thus the words of St. John: "He must increase, and I must decrease."[121]

Humility ought to be strong and substantial, one of the best elements of penance, safeguarding prayer and veiling charity.

I shall derive humility from our divine Savior, from His Sacred Heart; from the tabernacle, at Holy Communion; and by prayer. I will ask our Lady to obtain it for me. . . . "The humble shall be exalted."[122] Our Lord said, "Learn of me, for I am meek and humble of heart."[123]

Fourth Month: Renunciation

In the first place, renunciation of evil, always and everywhere, and of all that might, even indirectly, make my soul tend toward evil.

Renunciation of the world, its spirit and works, and of all that belongs solely to this world and will have no place in eternity. I resolve to live for God alone, for souls and for friendships, which become more deep and precious every day in proportion to my

[121] John 3:30.
[122] Matt. 23:12; Luke 14:11.
[123] Matt. 11:30.

rooting them more firmly in God. I must, however, lend myself to the world and to outward things whenever I have to perform any duty imposed by my state in life or by charity.

Renunciation of self is perhaps the most difficult of all. To give up my pride, my egotism, and my self-will, which creeps in everywhere and, under subtle disguises, makes its power felt — a power that is still far too great.

Renunciation of human desires and personal gratification, either for the sake of others or in a spirit of mortification.

Renunciation of spiritual joys and consolation, if such is the will of God; and acceptance, in a spirit of love and penance, of the very real privations involved in recollection, silence, and contemplation, and also of work and action. If God desires nothing more of me, I will at least be in His hands a quiet, unresisting instrument, which He will use for His own glory and the good of souls, availing Himself, as He sees fit, of my prayers, sacrifices, and sufferings.

Renunciation is obtained by prayer, is practiced by means of mortification, and displays itself in charity. It leads us to liberty, the holy liberty of God's children, who are free from all that might impede their progress toward Heaven. It makes us understand and appreciate the eternal truths; it teaches us to love with more genuine and lasting affection those with whom we come in contact, and the souls of our brethren. It makes us adore Jesus Christ and consecrate ourselves irrevocably to Him, our blessed Master and our God.

෴

Fifth Month: Love of souls

I resolve to love souls for the sake of Jesus Christ, because for them, He shed His life-blood, suffered and prayed, and died to give them life.

To know souls. A knowledge of souls, enabling me to do them good and skillfully to probe their wounds, may be acquired by means of a profound knowledge of my own conscience, the habit of meditation, and prayer.

To go out to seek souls. I must begin by welcoming all who come to me, never rebuffing them, but leading them on gently by talking to them in a language that they can understand, although this language must never be false to the eternal truths. In a soul, I ought always to seek the still living point, hidden under the apparent ruin of everything, the faint spark that the Holy Spirit is still able to revive. I must never be weary or discouraged; I must work for souls without trying to ascertain the results of my labor, leaving to God the work of conversion or sanctification, which He alone can accomplish, and looking upon myself as a humble instrument in His hands, an instrument used for purposes of which I myself am ignorant. When it seems to be God's will, I must go in search of souls, and act with all discretion and humility.

To give myself to souls, by means of prayer, suffering, and charity; I must consecrate the best part of my life to this work.

Lord, why didst Thou choose me and treat me with so much love and goodness, when there was nothing in me to justify such treatment? No one can fully know Thy eternal will, but I think, Lord, that while gratifying Thy love and the intense desire Thou feelest for the salvation of even the lowliest of creatures, Thou didst wish to make me Thy instrument. All that is good in me proceeds from Thee; Thou hast done everything in and for me. Continue, therefore, to employ one who before Thy powerful intervention was nothing but evil and weakness. Make me Thy apostle; this is the favor that I crave above all others, and that I implore of Thee, my God.

*Sixth Month: To meditate upon,
love, and serve our crucified Savior*

I will meditate upon Christ crucified, and unite myself with Him in daily meditation, in prayer, and in the contemplation of the sorrowful mysteries. I will steep myself in His Passion, assimilate it in frequent Communion, and gather the fruits of it in the sacraments and by prayer.

I will love Christ crucified, live at the foot of His Cross, and share His sufferings, soothing by my love the pain of His wounds and pierced Heart. I will give myself to Him without reserve, and consent, if such be His will, to be, in my turn, stretched upon the cross; I will accept suffering of body and soul, uniting it with His suffering; and I will sanctify my death beforehand by associating it with His death, deriving from His heart strength and sweetness.

I will serve Christ crucified by means of prayer, adoring Him, and interceding for the souls He loves and wishes to save, and for the salvation or welfare of which He calls me to labor with Him. I will serve Him by means of *penance*, by accepting suffering or voluntary mortifications; by penance that prays and penance that makes reparation. I will serve Him by means of charity, giving myself to souls with truly apostolic zeal.

I will bear in mind that love of Christ crucified is the mark of chosen souls; that everything done for me by God constitutes a sort of vocation to works of charity and reparation.

I will show to those around me my love of our crucified Savior, by displaying more true kindness and gentleness, and more intelligent sympathy with the needs, joys, and sorrows of my neighbor. I will not forget that the manifestations of my interior life would be worthless in God's sight if they did not afterward find expression in toil, good works, and sacrifices.

⚜

Seventh Month: Detachment of soul

This somewhat odd heading occurred to me this morning, while I was reading a chapter of the Imitation.

The soul created by God is united by Him with a body, and this body clings to the soul by bonds more or less strong, according to our will and divine grace. The chief of these bonds, with which no human being has any right to tamper, will be loosened by Divine Providence at the hour appointed by the eternal will. But there are many other bonds, formed either by evil or our own frailty, which are not in conformity with God's design, and render the soul the slave of the body. I desire to devote myself particularly to the task of setting my soul free, a task that, by divine grace, I have already begun.

It behooves me, therefore, to bring my body more and more into subjection to my soul, and my soul more and more into subjection to God. By means of unflinching and persevering effort, I must day by day break these numerous fetters which bind my soul too closely to my body.

Freedom must be restored to my soul, and my body forced to resume its position as servant — a position which will gradually become easy and even pleasant.

Of course, I ought to treat my body with consideration and even with respect, because it is destined to live again and share in the eternal happiness promised to me; nevertheless, in this world it is only an instrument of which my soul ought to make use freely, just as my soul itself is only an instrument in God's hands. It is necessary for the soul to escape as far as possible from the trammels of the body, and to control and govern it, however great may be the body's weakness or weariness, and however much it may rebel.

It goes without saying that there must be nothing here that savors of false spirituality. I am not a pure spirit, and I am bound to accept in all humility this companion, which is so often burdensome to me. Here there is an opportunity for very wholesome and sanctifying mortifications. These penances, accepted and offered up in silence, will be hidden under outward smiles and a gentle manner. Austerity must be within, attractiveness without.

O God, how far I am from all this! Help me, Lord, and in spite of my frequent faults and many imperfections, make use of me in dealing with the souls that Thou lovest. May others see enough of my frailty to render me humble, and enough of the graces that Thou hast bestowed on me to be led to glorify Thee and marvel at Thy great and amazing goodness.

⚘

Eighth Month: Obedience

Obedience to God. Obedience on the part of my soul, which should be closely in union with God's will, and cling to it amid difficulties, in spite of suffering, discouragement, and spiritual dryness; lovingly and without any consolation, welcoming the accomplishment of God's designs in or through me, precisely as He makes them known to me. Such obedience is a complete, generous, and joyful gift of the soul to Him who is our Father, Friend, and Master.

Obedience on the part of my body, which must be made altogether subject to my soul, and become a willing servant, an instrument for my soul to use, just as my soul is an instrument for God to use.

Obedience to superiors. To spiritual superiors: the Holy Father, bishops, and priests, insofar as I am dependent upon them; complete, humble, joyful, and ready obedience to my spiritual director. To temporal superiors: my husband, my mother, and all toward whom I owe respect, submission, and consideration. In everything that is not a matter of conscience, I must allow their interests, wishes, and pleasures to take precedence of my own, and treat them with that tender consideration which is the outward manifestation of my earnest affection for them. I must be careful to show them little attentions, and to display my love, seeking to make myself pleasant.

Obedience to the special resolutions that I have formed, to what is strictly my vocation, that is, God's call to me. Not to neglect the smallest things, the most trifling duties of religion or of my state in life. To observe strictly my rule for the arrangement and employment of my days, but to do this in a quiet, broad-minded way, following the example of the Sacred Heart of our Savior and the love of God. I must redouble my personal austerities, my outward kindness, gentleness, and courtesy. I must not seek for myself any sensible consolation, but try to lavish on others happiness and spiritual light. I must give a great deal, and continue, until I receive further orders, to take nothing except from God. This means a great deal — in fact, everything!

Ninth Month: Poverty of spirit

Our divine Lord loved poverty: it was His companion from the manger to the Cross. He was Himself poor and lived among the poor, and ever since, many souls, chosen by Him, have followed His example and made poverty the foundation of their life, having adopted it permanently. This is not my vocation, but still I must not forget the very special graces given me by God, nor the consecration of my soul and my life to Him. He has, to some extent, set me apart, and my most earnest desire is that He will deign to make use of me for His own glory and the good of souls. How, then, can I, without disregarding the duties of my state in life, practice the poverty which my Savior has blessed?

By means of spiritual poverty.

Poverty of *spirit* means detachment from all that is purely human; making oneself small before God, our Creator and Master; practicing humility; seeking in nothing one's own gratification, and waging war upon the least traces of pride or self-love.

Poverty of *heart* means cutting oneself off from every attachment that cannot last in eternity, ridding oneself of every human burden, and retaining only the love of God, and the deep and holy affections that He can bless, and that will develop more fully in Heaven. A heart devoid of all earthly desires and regrets attracts

God's notice, and is chosen as His dwelling place. I must not cling to money, position, the esteem of others, or the comforts of life, but be prepared to see all these things disappear and still be happy.

As far as is compatible with my duties in life, I will practice a little poverty. In matters affecting myself alone, I will avoid luxury and self-gratification in dress and occupations. Occasionally I will undertake lowly or somewhat humiliating tasks which I am not strictly bound to perform. I will aim at simplicity in my food, and choose in church and elsewhere a place among the poor, sometimes deliberately setting aside whatever might flatter my vanity. I will efface myself in favor of others, and lead them to forget the advantages of birth or fortune that Providence has bestowed upon me. Even when engaged in good works, I will not put myself forward, but strive everywhere and with all men to be in some small degree one of Christ's poor.

⚭

Tenth Month: Prayer

Prayer seems to be, according to God's will, the basis of my spiritual vocation.

Action is often impossible for me, but prayer is a field always open to apostolic zeal. It is the safest mode of action and does not endanger humility. It keeps the soul in close and constant union with God. It effects much good in ourselves and others. It never breaks the deep silence that ought to prevail in the soul. It passes unnoticed by all, and this is seldom possible in the case of action.

I must therefore pray — the wholly *interior prayer* of the soul, proceeding from its innermost depths; without words, offering God my most ardent desires and love, and giving myself to Him. Prayer for myself, for the souls dear to me, for all souls, for the Church. Such prayer is an inward movement of my heart toward Christ, and a consecration of myself to Him, my Master and Friend.

My *vocal prayer* must be very regular; I will never allow myself the least license in my exercises of piety, my morning and night prayers, daily meditation, liturgical prayers, frequent communions, Rosary (at least one decade), the gift of all the indulgences gained during the day to the souls in Purgatory, and the offering of the day's works and sufferings for particular intentions, for the welfare of souls or of the Church. I must bring to bear upon my exercises of piety all the attention, recollection, and fervor that my spiritual weakness and bad health allow.

I must pray in the spirit of *humility* for myself, weak and sinful as I am, for I have many sins to expiate and stand in need of much help.

I must pray in the spirit of charity for my neighbors, for the souls dear to me, for those whom I cherish with ardent affection through and for Jesus Christ, for the most sinful, most distant, and most abandoned souls, and also for the Church, whose loving and devoted daughter I am.

I must pray in the spirit of *reparation*, for myself, because I have much to make good, for those whom I love, for sinners, for those who forsake and betray our Lord and His Church, for those who know them not, and for those who have no regard for Him who is alone love and truth.

❧

Eleventh Month: The spirit of penance

We are all bound to do penance; none of us has a right to dispense himself from it, for none of us is without sin or without great need of expiation. For a soul, however, that is called to walk in the way of Christ's counsels, penance and prayer are the most important works, the most efficacious means of salvation for the soul itself and for others, the most useful instruments in the task of reparation to which chosen souls are called.

It is necessary first to possess the spirit of penance, and I must obtain it by means of renunciation, humility, and the complete union of my will with that of God. I will ask God to show me more and more how insignificant I am, and all that He has done for me. I will examine my conscience with merciless severity regarding even the smallest defects.

I will practice penance under its twofold form of suffering and mortification.

Suffering. I must accept all the sufferings that God sends me, not merely bearing them — as I do sometimes, with cowardly acquiescence, or yielding to inward despondency — but welcoming them with a glad heart and cheerful face, remembering that each of them is a fragment of my Savior's Cross, and offering them up for the welfare of souls and the glory of God, on behalf of those dear to me and to make reparation.

Mortification. I must accept all the mortifications, spiritual or corporal, which it is God's will that I should undergo. Further, I must seek out the mortifications of heart and mind which abound in daily life — if only we know how to find them — and also bodily mortifications arising from my state of health or from food and other outward things. I should never do anything imprudent which might injure my health or go against the wishes of others regarding myself, but there are many bodily mortifications that would do me more good than harm, and that would tend to making my body entirely subject to my soul, that would punish it a little without hurting it, and would greatly benefit my soul. I must often practice mortification as a prayer, or in the spirit of reparation.

I must accept or seek sufferings and penances in secret, doing nothing that would attract attention, but, on the contrary, showing more kindness and friendliness than usual.

⚬

Twelfth Month: Abandonment to God

To ascertain God's will ought to be the object of my soul, the aim of my existence. I ought to offer myself to God, so that He may dispose of me as a poor, clumsy, sluggish instrument, and use me in His service and for His glory. I ought to strip myself of everything and put myself in His hands, desiring one thing only — namely, what He Himself desires for me. In seasons of good health, I will thank Him and work; in times of sickness, I will accept it and offer it up joyfully; in sorrow or happiness, sadness or prosperity, I will gather up everything, give everything, and make everything serve for the good of souls, for a work of reparation.

I will put most absolute and loving trust in Him who is at once my Master and my Friend, and serve Him with a generous soul and joyful heart, quietly and with all my might.

In times of trouble and spiritual darkness, I will increase my prayers and mortifications, and force myself to act with greater energy. My life being so uncertain, I must pray a great deal, and offer up my trials and sacrifices for the good of souls and in a spirit of reparation. Whenever I am able, I must bestir myself, without haste or excitement, but not become absorbed in active work that does not seem to be especially designed for me by God. Prayer, the practice of humility, and renunciation ought to take precedence of everything else.

I will put my works, sacrifices, and prayers in our Savior's hands, leaving Him to dispose of them, although I will continue to offer Him each morning the acts or sufferings of the day for particular intentions, those whom I love, the souls in Purgatory, or the Church.

I will always bear in mind the needs or spiritual wants of souls, especially of certain souls, that I may lay them before God, and beg of Him great graces for these souls.

I will make myself all things to all men,[124] increasing my kindliness and devotion, avoiding all harshness and exaggeration in speech, and not putting forward my own ideas and opinions. I

[124] 1 Cor. 9:22.

must remember that spiritual food is too strong for many souls, and that it must be offered cautiously, and in some way diluted. I must be content not to go more quickly than God, and know how, in dealing with certain souls, to go at a walking pace or even more slowly still. Once more, let me repeat that the hour and the means are in God's hands, and that my business is, as a humble worker, to pray, suffer, and act, in full reliance on Him, and with absolute humility.

❧

Resolutions

I resolve to hide my spiritual life and, to a great extent, my sufferings, interests, and material or personal occupations under a veil of *silence*.

I resolve to build up my spiritual life on four solid foundations: humility, renunciation, obedience, and poverty of spirit, for these underlie all interior life and Christian perfection.

I resolve to build up my spiritual life and fill up my existence by practicing prayer, penance, and charity.

Prayer with great confidence in God.

Penance of heart and mortifications.

Charity under two forms: love of Christ crucified and love of souls.

I resolve to detach my soul from my body, making the latter subservient to the former, and my soul subservient to God.

I resolve to make these meditations each year, developing or varying the thoughts that they contain.

✂

Prayer to the Sacred Heart

Divine Heart of Jesus,
I adore Thee, I love Thee,
I believe that Thou lovest me tenderly,
and because I believe in the
infinite tenderness of Thy Heart,
I ask great favors of it.

Grant me Thy love;
enable me to aim steadfastly
at perfection according to my state
in life, and to prove my love by trusting
Thee so that nothing can destroy or
check my confidence.

O most kind and gentle Jesus,
grant me also (*mention the favor
especially desired*).

I expect all this of Thine infinite
goodness, and doubt not
that I shall receive it.

I rely upon the Heart of my God,
whose power is infinite; upon the Heart
of my Father, whose loving kindness fills
my heart with peace and happiness.

I am so sure of being heard that
even now I call upon the angels and saints
to praise Thee, O my God, and Thy
goodness toward so poor a creature.

To prove my gratitude to Thee,
I desire to live in peace of mind, resting
with love on the tenderness of Thy Heart,
which is so good, so lovable, and so generous.

And do Thou, O Immaculate Virgin, my
Mother, help me to praise and thank the
Heart of my Savior. In union with thee,
making use of thy words and intention,
I say, "*Magnificat.*"

❦

*Preface
to the Little Treatises
on Hope and Peace*

⚜

My dear little Marie,

I am copying out for you two little treatises composed for your godmother, at her request, in order that you may keep them in memory of her and me.[125] They are of no particular value, but are just the outpouring of my heart under the influence of an affection such as does not often exist in this world, and under the inspiration of faith which God has rendered day by day more deep and reasoned.

One of the blessed memories of my life is of the moment when I placed these few pages in Juliette's hands, and we read them together, once more with our souls united and our tears flowing.

Now I give them to you in your turn, for you are the second child of my heart[126] and someday you will be a friend, provided that God thinks there is something for me to do in this world for a few years longer.

Now, my beloved child, I understand, at least as far as my weakness allows, the deep reason underlying the trials of my life, the

[125] These treatises, composed in 1904 or 1905, were written for Elisabeth's niece, Marie. Elisabeth's sister Juliette was Marie's godmother.

[126] Elisabeth had almost a mother's love for her sister Juliette. In a letter addressed to a friend, a few days after her sister's death, she wrote, "For years I have looked upon her almost as my own child." She expressed the same feeling frequently.

deprivation of certain pleasures, and my long spiritual struggle, the phases of which are known to God and myself alone, although it has altered my whole life. When a poor wayfarer is climbing up a steep and difficult path, he sees only what is immediately before him, and the means of overcoming or avoiding each obstacle as it occurs; he forgets the road already traversed and thinks of nothing but the stones which bruise him and the brambles which tear his hands. But when he is higher up and able to halt, he turns around and looks back upon the way that he has come, and perceives that, in spite of his doubts, blunders, and weariness, he has advanced by unknown paths toward a goal determined beforehand, and that the sun, with its life-giving heat, is rising above the horizon.

By God's grace, I have reached this point, dearest; the road has been traversed, and, as I look back, I see again the various stages through which my soul has passed, and I recognize, in the guidance of my life, a will that is steadfast, unchanging, and harmonious, and a love so fatherly that I am able to believe in Divine Providence after seeing it, so to speak, at work in my life and heart. The great, true sun has risen above the horizon of my soul, and all the clouds of suffering fail to obscure its brightness, while it has tinged them with its divine radiance. My wish is to live and die in its light, veiled now so that our poor mortal eyes may endure it; but I look forward to the full glory of that light in eternity, when I shall be reunited with those whom we have loved so dearly and shall love forever.

But since my journey is not yet ended, and the region of clouds and darkness is not yet passed, ask God to give me grace to walk bravely, as a Christian should walk, and to do a little good in this world, following the example of Christ, our only model. Pray that I may not be a bad steward of the many graces granted to me, and that, because I love, I, together with all those dear to me, may one day find admission to the embrace of Him who is infinite love, and to life everlasting.

The Little Treatise
on Hope

꒰

Hope is not a human virtue.

In childhood and youth, and sometimes even later, man, if left to himself, by means of a natural instinct, feels a kind of joyful anticipation, which makes him look forward to, desire, or pursue what he believes to be happiness. But sometimes early, sometimes later in the course of his life, he sees his illusions perish one by one, and his pleasant anticipations are seldom realized. To many lives, each day brings some regret, sorrow, or disappointment; many hearts retain nothing of their dreams but a kind of faint perfume, such as a bottle retains after its contents have evaporated.

In the case of those who have no faith and do not pray, who have never gathered up all the faculties of their souls in an act of fervent adoration, the anticipations of yesterday are apt to become painful realities today.

Who can comfort them and speak to their broken hearts words of encouragement and consolation? Human speech, when devoid of divine inspiration, is an empty sound that dies away and leaves no trace behind. Our poor words derive all their efficacy from the Eternal Word.

Hope alone can accomplish this task, but it must be supernatural hope. Human hope is only a state, not a virtue, a passive condition of the mind, influenced by circumstances apart from itself. But a virtue, as the word implies, is a force. In the case of a natural virtue, it is a force acquired by personal effort; in the case of a supernatural virtue, it is a force bestowed by a special grace. Under present circumstances, however great our efforts may be, we shall never succeed in hoping when everything goes against us, when trials crush us, and agony of body and soul lays hold upon and overwhelms us. No, sooner or later even the most persistent and selfish optimism breaks down, and the most desperate persons are often those who expected much from life, and upon whom fortune long seemed to smile.

What most people call "hope" is nothing but pleasant anticipation, which has as its reverse disappointment. It is here that the teaching of Christ again reveals its sublime and consoling features, more plainly perhaps than elsewhere. It is the great source of faith, and "no man cometh to the Father" but by Him,[127] that is, Jesus Christ. Through charity, it gives us all our energy for good, and that peculiarly passionate love which is implied by the very word *charity*.

Here, then, we have two theological virtues, which are not natural virtues, not the result of our experience or the product of our unaided exertions, but a force proceeding directly from God, a grace given by Him alone of His own free will, of which our free will can then make use. This force is something outside our souls, but takes possession of them by freely given, indescribable mercy.

Hope is also a theological virtue, a divine gift, although many Christians seem to forget this fact. Of ourselves we cannot acquire it, but we can ask for it in fervent, humble prayer, which obtains everything. We can and ought to ask for God's grace to impart to our souls that strength and serenity which will be a light to our lives, and will completely transform our souls, the world, and life itself in our own sight.

We must, of course, prepare the soul for this grace, as for every virtue, by continually exerting ourselves, taking care to avoid all preoccupations and anxieties likely to disturb God's action within

[127] John 14:6.

us. But, when this is done, it remains for God to bestow upon us supernatural hope and the life that it imparts to our souls.

When God has done this, and has revealed to us Christian hope, and our souls have, in some degree, assimilated this virtue so as to live upon it; when we have allowed God to work within us; and when, perceiving the perfection of His work, living beforehand on the eternal truths and seeking light and sustenance in His sacraments, we find out how much harmony we can, with His help, bring into our lives, then, however great may be our sorrows and disappointments due to people or things, however keen our regrets for the past and our fears for the future, all will disappear, or rather, will be transformed.

Man becomes stronger than what kills him, as Pascal says, and whether we live or die, in joy or in sorrow, in active life or on a sickbed, we can utter St. Paul's words, of which the Church reminds us continually in Her beautiful Liturgy, and serve God with joy and gladness, with Jesus Christ dwelling in us. We know that nothing is lost, either in the material or spiritual world, and that the lowliest of our actions, the most secret of our prayers, has immeasurable force, for it echoes on through time and space, and it may be that, ages hence, some human heart may be brought into mysterious contact with us.

Is not this a reason for being active? Does not this explain suffering? Does this not give us an object for our efforts and life? The human race may well be pitied for cherishing hopes that are indestructible, while it fails to base them on what is eternal.

Let us sum up these thoughts:

Hope is supernatural, a force given by God. It throws light upon life and makes us understand it, as well as suffering, death (which is only a continuation of life), and all the truths that concern life after death. It puts us into closer union with God, and extends our view into that wonderful region of souls which faith first opens to us, and which charity allows us to penetrate fully. It is a region never entered by those who live on the surface of things, and yet it is free to every Christian.

Lacordaire[128] used to say that sooner or later, one lived for nothing but souls. Let us seek them, understand them, and love them, from the soul of the maidservant in our house, and those that are shrouded sometimes under a ridiculous or gloomy exterior, to those distant and unknown souls that can nevertheless be affected by our prayers and sufferings, although it is only in eternity that they will learn how our passing sorrows or our humble sacrifices have won for them life everlasting.

Let us place all our desires, affection, and human anticipations under the protection of supernatural hope, and let us ask for it daily for ourselves, for those whom we love, and for souls, that our lives may be more fruitful to all men, our souls more calm and sweet, and our death useful and happy. And may this hope abide with us until we reach the threshold of eternity, where, in the living unity, charity alone will remain radiant and divine. Other virtues will pass away, but charity will last forever.[129]

☙

Prayer to Ask of God the Virtue of Hope

My God, who hast allowed us human hopes,
but who alone bestowest Christian and supernatural hope,
grant, I beseech Thee, by Thy grace, this virtue to my soul,
to the souls of all I love, and to all Christian souls.
Let it enlighten and transform our lives, our suffering,
and even our death, and let it uphold in us, through the
disappointment and sadness of each day, an
inner strength and unalterable serenity.

---

[128] Henri Dominique Lacordaire (1802-1861), Dominican preacher.
[129] Cf. 1 Cor. 13:8.

*The Little Treatise
on Peace*

❧

On the eve of His Passion, after keeping the Pasch with His disciples, and for the first time celebrating the mystery of love which has come down to us, and on which souls will live as long as the world exists, our divine Lord uttered that beautiful discourse preserved by St. John, in which occur the words: "Peace I leave with you; my peace I give unto you."[130]

Did those around Him understand the profound meaning of these words? Did they know that, by transforming the hearts of men, this saying would affect the whole world? We may doubt it, for their eyes were still blinded, and the light of Pentecost had not yet shone upon the ignorant men to whom their Master said: "You know not of what spirit you are."

Peace! Not an uncertain peace, proceeding from without, desired and sought all through our short life without our ever succeeding in obtaining it, or in keeping it if we have once secured it; but peace, inviolable peace, bestowed upon us by supreme goodness, a force surpassing our strength, is one of the many gifts of Christianity. The lowliest Christian can and ought to know this peace, if he is imbued with the true spirit of the gospel, and really possesses faith — that is to say, does not merely hold certain opinions that have been presented to his mind with no effort on his part, but feels an absolute certainty, which is so closely assimilated

[130] John 14:27.

to his own being as to form its life and spiritual substance, and be in a sense the leaven that raises and transforms our poor, heavy human nature.

It is interesting to notice how often joy is mentioned in Holy Scripture, and this seems almost paradoxical when we remember how much stress both the Jewish law and the Church lay upon human suffering, the uncertainty of life, and the fleeting character of happiness, pointing out emphatically the permanence and various kinds of pain. The Catholic Liturgy is the work of ages, and consists of the aspirations, sufferings, and petitions of every generation enlightened by the Holy Spirit. It has preserved for us in phrases full of vigor this call to inward joy and eagerness for peace. In the Old Testament, we read words such as the following, inspired by the thought of Him who was to come, with a foreknowledge of the peace that He alone could bring: "In Him our heart shall rejoice."[131] "Thou wilt turn, O God, and bring us to life, and Thy people shall rejoice in Thee."[132] "Rejoice greatly, O daughter of Sion; shout for joy, O daughter of Jerusalem."[133] "Take courage, and be strong; fear not, and be not dismayed."[134]

Holy Scripture tells us regarding him who possesses divine wisdom that it "shall give joy and gladness."[135]

In the Liturgy for Christmas Day, after calling us in the words of St. Leo to enter into holy joy, the Church proclaims that true peace has today come down to us from Heaven. It would take too long to examine all the passages in the New Testament that contain allusion to Christian joy. The abyss between God and His humiliated and suffering creatures was bridged when He who is

---

[131] Ps. 32:21 (RSV = Ps. 33:21).

[132] Ps. 84:7 (RSV = Ps. 85:6).

[133] Zeph. 3:14.

[134] Cf. 1 Paralip. 28:20 (RSV = 1 Chron. 28:20).

[135] Cf. Wisd. 8:16; Ecclus. 15:6.

called "the author of all peace" appeared on earth. Unknown to almost all, He accomplished His task and the work of redemption. From the source of love, He brought to mankind that supernatural and living love that sheds its radiance on all without exception, and knows neither Jew nor Gentile, neither bond nor free, neither male nor female, for all are one in Christ Jesus.[136] He planted in the human race the little grain of mustard seed, which was destined to grow and to shelter all generations[137] — namely, the Church, which continues always Her slow and painful growth, and will last until the end of the world.

The peace revealed by Christ is to a Christian not only a precious grace, but the foundation of all his spiritual life. Without it, his interior life would break down at the smallest attack; without it, there would be no strength, no living unity in the Church; without it, no one could ever exert a real and lasting influence on his neighbors or on the souls with whom, in the course of his existence, his own soul comes in contact.

"Blessed are the meek," said our divine Lord, "for they shall inherit the earth."[138] Does this not mean that the meek shall possess power over souls and control them by their very gentleness, which, far from being passive, consists of strength, self-possession, and unchangeable serenity? One who is assailed by the sufferings and trials of life, and never flinches; who, by God's grace, has learned how to hide the depths of his own soul under a veil which allows the soul's light to shine on others without permitting its central point to be reached by agitation or trouble from without, is strong by God's own strength, and can say with St. Paul, "I live, now not I, but Christ liveth in me,"[139] and giveth me His peace.

[136] Gal. 3:28.
[137] Matt. 13:31-32; Mark 4:31-32.
[138] Matt. 5:4.
[139] Gal. 2:20.

We have all met persons of this sort. They are rare, no doubt, but there flows from them such an intensity of inner life, such calm strength, such true beauty that merely to come into contact with them soothes and comforts us. After all, this is only natural. Our outer life is the reproduction of our inner life, and the visible part of us reflects what is unseen; we radiate our souls, so to say, and, when they are centers of light and warmth, other souls need only to be brought into contact with them in order to be warmed and enlightened. We give out, often unknown to ourselves, what we carry within us; let us strive to increase daily this reserve store of faith and quiet charity.

Too often a Christian does not know how much he can affect his brethren by the influence he exerts. This influence is obtained, however, only at the cost of constant vigilance and complete self-control. Nothing is more delicate, nothing more finely shaded than a soul; nothing can be more easily rebuffed, chilled, or estranged. If we desire no single soul ever to turn away discouraged from us, because our cares, needless agitation, and lack of peace have hidden the means of access to our souls, we must make every soul realize that we are firmly established in God, close to that soul, quick to understand it by means of that wonderful grasp of spiritual things which they alone possess who pray, meditate, and profoundly feel their own weakness and God's grace.

It may be that the whole moral life of one of our brethren depends upon the words uttered then; in any case, uneasy spirits, who doubt and seek in the darkness a spark of light from above, will soon perceive that, although we belong to the world as they do, we nevertheless bear within us something not of this world, and, at the hour appointed by God, they will, perhaps, come, sure of being understood, to seek of us the secret of our strength and calm.

God alone is the author of all peace, and therefore it is of Him that we must ask for peace day by day. If we relied upon ourselves to obtain peace, we would soon be disappointed. Each day is made up of little complications, little annoyances and trifling duties, and unless we bring order into this confusion, we shall soon be overwhelmed and lose our moral balance. This is particularly the case in times of distress or sickness. In every trial, physical or moral, unless it is rendered supernatural, there is an indescribably crushing force. It breaks down our energy, depresses our mind, embitters our disposition, and robs external objects and daily occurrences of all beauty and charm. It is solely human suffering, and the burden is too heavy for our shoulders; we endure our pain and misfortunes either in a rebellious spirit or with dull submission. Gradually our moral qualities fail, we become absorbed in the contemplation of our own troubles, and the trial passes over us, having done us no good, and leaving us weaker and farther from God than before.

What ought we to do, in order to preserve, in spite of pain, that peace which is productive of all good? In the first place, we ought to pray, and ask God every day to keep us in peace and give us the joy that nothing can destroy. We ought to seek grace in the Holy Eucharist, the sacrament in which He bestows it so freely. We should set our occupations, our soul, and our life in order, and never let the annoyances and evil suggestions from without or the little troubles of life disturb the soul so as to injure its spiritual realities. It is our duty to fill our souls with those things which alone are worthy of them, to live in close union with God, near to the Heart of Christ, in the full light of the Holy Spirit, so that our outward existence may be transformed thereby, and our words, actions, and outlook on life may express our own innermost convictions and our spiritual life. Finally, suffering must be rendered fruitful by being accepted willingly, and offered up for the welfare of others; and it will acquire in this way power to vivify and redeem.

We must keep near to the souls God puts in our way, and try to understand and love them. Here we have discovered, by God's grace, the sources of peace and the means of possessing it fully.

When we are established in this peace, and our soul, to use Bossuet's[140] expression, "is mistress of the body which it animates," then we shall be true disciples of Him who was gentle and peaceable. We shall have the hearts of apostles, and like the rough fishermen of Galilee, who, under the influence of the Holy Spirit, became fishers of men,[141] we, too, shall catch in our nets many poor souls, souls whom Christ loves, for whom He suffered, and on whose behalf He calls upon us to pray and suffer in our turn.

Thus we shall accomplish what is here below the task of every Christian, before he possesses the living peace that is eternal. This task is to extend the kingdom of God, to bring Christ to the world at large and to the souls of individuals, and to sow in tears and with painful exertion the seed that will bring forth at last a supernatural harvest.

[140] Jacques Bénigne Bossuet (1627-1704), Bishop of Meaux.
[141] Matt. 4:19; Mark 1:17.

❦

The Faithful Servant of Christ

Blessed are they
who keep judgment and
do justice at all times.

Psalm 105:3
(RSV = Psalm 106:3)

⚘

*To my dear godson, the child of my heart, I offer a little
of the soul that will ever be ready to welcome him.*[142]

My dear child,

Last May, we passed together through a period that we can
never forget. You, a little child, still full of imperfections, received
for the first time a visit from God, and we were happy in joining
you in this great act of Communion, which brings with it such incomparable blessings.

I am sure that you were not alone at the altar. Our Lady was
there, blessing your childish heart; your guardian angel was there,
praying for you; and with them was a blessed soul, happy in the joy
that can never be taken from her, and she went with you to the tabernacle. While you were making your thanksgiving, one of those
prayers which God never fails to hear was uttered close beside you,
on your behalf, by her who loved you so dearly and who loves you
now more than ever.

Perhaps — and here we touch upon the great mystery of the
other life, the mighty Communion of Saints — perhaps at the
very hour when the profound life of the soul was really beginning
for you, your dear aunt Juliette, reminding God of some of her

[142] Elisabeth wrote this treatise for her nephew André shortly after his First Communion, which took place on May 17, 1906.

sufferings that are over now, but will bear fruit forever, begged of Him in return to give you grace to be always true to Christ and, better still, to be an apostle. You will understand later that souls like that of your dear little aunt, through their trials, sow the seed of sanctity in others. When you are a man, a Christian, you will perceive that whatever good you do is like a flower growing on a fertile soil that has been watered by the tears and cultivated by the painful toil of another. Although my offering is not worth as much as Juliette's, may God grant that some of the sorrows of my life, sweetened as they have been by so much affection, may also fall upon you in the form of interior graces, peace, and salvation, and that my constant prayers may obtain for you divine light and the fullness of supernatural life.

When I have gone to wait for you at our last happy meeting place, I want to leave you something to remind you of the blessed day of your First Communion, and of your godmother, whose love for you you do not yet fully realize. That is why I am adding to the little book containing the notes of your retreat[143] a few pages that I beg you to keep and read over in times of joy or sorrow, and especially in hours of doubt or temptation.

∽

Pray and work

My dear child, the words *Orare et laborare* ("pray and work") should be the motto of your life. If you can understand and practice these two things and make your existence one of work and prayer, you need fear nothing; your life will be useful and your death blessed, and your influence for good will remain active for ages to come.

[143] Elisabeth went with her nephew to the instructions given at the retreat before his First Communion, and took notes, which she wrote out for him in the book mentioned above.

When we pray, we believe in and worship God; we acknowledge that our existence has a supernatural aim, and that we have not only a bodily, but also a spiritual, life; we put God before men, other people before ourselves, and ourselves before the things of this world, before all that perishes and does not equal our immortal souls in value.

When we pray, we remain in a union with God that is strong, quiet, and lasting; we look at everything from God's point of view, and are so peacefully anchored on eternity that annoyances, unavoidable struggles, and continual activity have no power to disturb our souls or to drag them down.

Do not think that, when I speak in this way to you about living beforehand in eternity, I forget that, although you are a future citizen of Heaven, you are at the present time a little citizen of earth. I am far from urging you to neglect your human duties.

When life is established on a solid foundation of faith, and we are aided daily by grace, we can dwell on earth and do our part in building up society. And, at the same time, we can enjoy the happiness and affection that come in our way, to a degree almost unknown to those who do not bring a little of eternity to bear upon their love and pleasure. Nothing human is foreign to us, and we possess the priceless privilege of being at the same time members of the human race and sons of earth, and also members of the heavenly race and sons of God.

The second half of what is to be your motto is the necessary complement of the first. Prayer calls for action, just as action needs to be inspired and directed by prayer. *Orare!* Yes, indeed, let us pray a great deal. *Laborare!* Let us work always with courage for ourselves, our brethren, and God.

I want to explain to you in a few words how prayer and work ought to stand side by side in your life and never be separated, and also what piety and work united ought to be for you during the three chief stages of your career.

⤸

Arm your heart against temptation

Just now and for some time to come, according to circumstances, you will look at life from the Christian point of view, being still irradiated by your First Communion. Make the most of this period; you will be equipping not your intellect, but your heart, for warfare, and the preparation that you make now will enable you perhaps to pass unscathed through the difficult periods that you must expect in the future; I say this with sorrow, but with full assurance. Store up reserves of piety, of humble, trusting faith, of intense charity and kindness. Someday you will see that I have not misled you, and that you must have plenty of good corn stored up in your heart, if you are not to die of hunger during a season of want.

We need not dwell upon this period of your life; you will look back upon it later with pleasure, and will recall with emotion the days when the valiant Christian you will then be was only an innocent, pious child.

How long will this period of your existence last? I cannot tell. A year or two, or perhaps a little longer, but certainly not much more. The time of moral transformation and of individual existence, the time of struggle and temptation, will begin too soon to please your dear mother and all of us. What is the use of denying it or of trying to hide it from you? You will experience temptation under many forms, as varied as the forms of evil itself. And, if you desire to overcome it, you will undergo a stern struggle from which you will come forth strengthened, ready for the task assigned you by God, which is, in the precise sense of the word, your vocation. This is a thought that I wish to impress upon your mind: there is for every young man and every young follower of Christ a time that is absolutely decisive with regard to his physical and moral being, his future here and in eternity. One who aims solely at saving his soul, and has no higher ambition, can always trust in God's mercy, and even those who have wasted the gifts of nature and grace may hope to become laborers at the eleventh hour,[144] provided they are not called away before this hour strikes.

But you, the son and grandson of Christian women, for whom your dear aunt Juliette suffered and on whose behalf she desired something more than strictly personal salvation: you may possess holy ambition. You ought not to be a laggard in the Christian army, but one of those stout-hearted leaders of men who encourage others and plant their standard — the cross — more or less everywhere in the world and in the souls of men.

Therefore when the crisis comes of which I am speaking, you must remember that it is a serious time, and that your own future, and that of many others through you, depends upon your exertions and the decisions made then.

This crisis may take two different forms; it may be exterior, due to human temptations, or interior, affecting your mind and faith. I think I may venture to tell you that, apart from a very rare and special grace, temptation will assail you under both these forms.

You will have to struggle, in the first place, against the world, evil suggestions, bad companions, and a terrible thing that few withstand: sarcasm. To be able to stand firm in spite of a disdainful smile is a token of perfect moral strength. For you, dear child, I dread a companion who makes fun of you, more than one who makes a brutal attack upon you; the latter will disgust you, but the former will disturb your peace of mind, and this disturbance is often the first sign of weakening.

Later on, if God allows, I shall deal with this delicate topic at greater length, for the sake of my dear nephews; but at the present moment, I only want to tell you that every thought and deed that you would not like your mother to know may be regarded by you as evil. This is the great criterion. At the same time, I wish to advise

---

[144] Cf. Matt. 20:6.

you never to be afraid to reveal to your mother everything that might disturb or surprise you. She will understand everything, share and explain your difficulties; she will always be ready to do this, and this affectionate confidence will certainly safeguard you against many faults and failures.

⚭

Beware temptations to renounce your Faith

Let us turn now to the other form that your moral crisis may assume: the intellectual. There will come a time when you will encounter, more or less unexpectedly, the shock of hearing our doctrines denied. Even if the shock is not violent, you will nevertheless be aware of the influence of our modern intellectual atmosphere. And perhaps unconsciously you will breathe in the air that surrounds young men of the present day, and in time you will be surprised to find that it has intoxicated you, and that you feel uncomfortable in the atmosphere of faith. You will notice that an outwardly religious life does not correspond with the state of your soul, and, in your surprise and discouragement, you will be tempted to cast aside what will seem to you burdensome and a hindrance to the free development of your intellect.

Few people, and especially few young men, escape this crisis in their faith, and perhaps we should not regret it, were it not that many poor souls are rendered incurably gloomy by their distress of mind. Those who, by God's assistance and by the means of which I am about to speak, pass safely through this dangerous period, possess thenceforth manliness of spirit and know what faith really is. They have what St. Teresa used to call "experimental knowledge" of the supernatural; they understand what the sphere of faith is and how it differs from that of knowledge, which it may be said to extend, since it possesses methods and experiences peculiar to itself. Young men of this type attain to that firmness of faith, accurate insight, and vigorous charity that God alone bestows, when we have earned them by our previous efforts and humble good will. Men such as these have strong, apostolic minds; one of them alone can influence all around him, the members of his own family and of society and also the hearts of men.

I am sure you will be one of these brave men, not a coward or a weakling, as are, unhappily, only too many of those who call themselves Christians. But before you can attain to this end, you must face the struggle, and it behooves us to consider the means that must be used if you are to pass unscathed through the crisis that will render your faith complete and reasonable.

In the first place, never forget that you have a mother to whom you can always unburden your heart; do not hesitate to tell her about the ideas that come into your mind, the doubts that may arise, the difficulties that you may have to encounter, and all that affects your moral and spiritual life.

Do not forget that I, too, place at your disposal the results of my experience, the fruits of long, interior efforts, and the holy work wrought in me by God with no merit on my part. He refused me a son like you, but I think He intended me to be the spiritual mother of your precious soul and perhaps of other souls, too. He prepared me for this task by giving me experience of spiritual things, and bringing me into contact with people of all sorts, who either deny the Faith or are hostile or indifferent to it. By His grace, the world within and the world without have made my faith too strong for it ever to be shaken; I say this humbly but confidently, since God is never the first to withdraw from us, and I can no longer live without Him, now that I know the reality of His presence and the happiness that He brings to us.

I beg you, therefore, to come to me whenever intellect and faith appear to you to be at variance. You have no idea how easy it sometimes is to disperse the clouds overshadowing the mind. It is quite possible for a beautiful harmony to exist among all the powers of our being, when we have carried our human knowledge (at least, such as each of us can acquire) to its farthest limit; and then we pass beyond this barrier, which is, after all, not far off, and enter the sphere of the supernatural and infinite. Nothing in the world is so beautiful as this union of human reason and faith, of earthly and divine knowledge, of an intense supernatural life and a very active outward existence, entirely devoted to what is good.

A man who has attained to this exquisite unity of all his being is truly a strong man; he exercises over others an influence whose scope we cannot calculate. He exerts it by merely coming into contact with others and by his example. Without any premeditation perhaps, in the surroundings in which God has placed him, and under the circumstances designed by Providence, he acts as an apostle, in the fullest dignity, beauty, and meaning of the word.

❧

Make use of prayer and work

In order that you may, in a few years' time, pass unscathed through this critical period of physical, spiritual, and intellectual change, you must make use of the two means at your disposal; there are no others, either from the human or the supernatural point of view, but the first is all-powerful, and the second, which derives the chief part of its efficacy from the first, will also be most useful to you. These two means are prayer and work.

When you are a prey to temptation, doubt, or cowardice, you must not argue or hesitate, or give any foothold to the enemy, but fling yourself headlong into God's arms. We who are baptized and confirmed in the Faith and are the children of light must call upon the Spirit of love and life, who never refuses to illumine those who turn to Him in fervent prayer. I have already told you that the life of reason and the supernatural life have not the same methods and are not sustained by the same food. The soul lives by prayer, just as the intellect absorbs intellectual nourishment and the body material substances; the soul perishes when it lacks divine warmth, just as the body dies for want of food and the mind for want of education. Someone has well said that prayer is the breath of the soul in God. Let us never lose this breath by giving up that inward prayer which brings down grace upon us and makes us live.

Work, serious work, preceded and sustained by prayer, will help you to pass happily through those early years which are, as I have said, absolutely decisive. Begin to prepare for your future career by careful study; it matters little whether you achieve brilliant success, for this is often due to the possession of great abilities and does not always involve continuous efforts and energy. Work conscientiously, doing what you do, as used to be said of old. Be convinced that this is your absolute duty, for Christianity requires men of solid worth as its representatives. In the world, few people are capable of forming a personal opinion regarding a doctrine; they look at it through its representatives, and the best way to make men appreciate and love Catholicism is, perhaps, to show simply by one's example what a Catholic is.

❦
Work to bring Christ to others

You will prove once more that a man may be learned and highly cultured without ceasing to be a humble, fervent Christian. The strength of your convictions coupled with a delicate regard for the feelings of others will, perhaps, contribute to overthrowing the absurd prejudice existing against us, and you will show triumphantly that all the human lights collectively cannot obscure the pure light of God, but gain, on the contrary, additional radiance from it.

When I speak of work, dear child, I include all that your age and occupations allow you to undertake. Every person of good will has spare moments that may become means of saving others. I know no more touching sight than that of the young men — students, pupils at the public schools, and artisans — who devote their hours of leisure and their Sundays to visiting poor families, looking after young apprentices, or organizing popular lectures and meetings that will bring them into personal contact with their less fortunate brethren. These young men promote social peace and true charity, and work slowly and patiently at the necessary reconstructions of which Joseph de Maistre[145] used to speak. These are no fanciful political reconstructions, for history teaches us that forms once abolished hardly ever reappear, and God does not require any set forms in order to direct mankind toward their future destiny; but they are real reconstructions, built upon the cornerstone, which is Christ, and fostered with motherly care by the Church, which is unchanging and yet ever new, and which our Savior said that He would be with to the end of time.[146]

You will be surrounded by affection which will screen you from evil. You will be sustained by prayer and by the divine grace that it obtains and that the Sacraments, too, convey to you. You will be hindered from frequenting bad places of amusement and harmful acquaintances by serious occupations and the good works to which you will devote part of your leisure time. Consequently I hope that you will pass happily through this period of your youth and reach the age when your active life begins, not without having encountered evil (for you must learn to know what it is), but without its ever making you swerve from your path, and without your bestowing on it anything but a glance of pity, while you reserve your strength for the task that lies before you, which will be your lifework.

Seek and follow your vocation

When you reach this full development of your youth and are about to enter upon manhood, it will be of the utmost importance for you to perceive and follow your vocation.

[145] Joseph de Maistre (1753-1821), French writer.
[146] Cf. Matt. 28:20.

The word *vocation* means "calling": it is God's secret call to the conscience to walk in the path that He has traced. According to the design of Providence, each of us is intended to do some special work and has a task assigned to him that is determined before-hand. Human society would be beautiful and harmonious if each man in his appointed place accomplished all the work set before him by the Master of the household, and if we, laborers of the first hour, tried to discover His will at every stage of our lives. This can-not be, because, from the beginning, evil entered into the world, but we can at least take up our stand among those who desire to carry out God's designs in and around themselves, among those faithful servants who bring a heavy sheaf of corn to their Father's house and patiently prepare the soil for future seed-times and su-pernatural harvests.

Seek, therefore, when the time comes, to find out God's will with regard to yourself. In order to do so, you must pray, fortify yourself with the wise and loving advice of your parents and of others in whom you recognize a moral worth entitling them to be consulted, and especially of the priest who is the friend and guide of your soul. Withdraw into yourself alone with God; face the thought of death, which throws light upon so many things, and then consider your tastes and aspirations, and try to find out what career and what kind of life will be productive of most good to yourself and others; strive to see clearly where you will be able to do most good while freely developing your faculties. Devote to this patient investigation as much time as is necessary; the aim in view is worth all the exertion and thought that may help you to reach it; it is better to spend a long time in looking for the right road than to risk going astray or choosing a rough and difficult path. Ask God to give you light; He will not withhold it, but will show you the way.

Then set to work with courage, always trying to keep your real task in sight and to perceive the utmost amount of good that you can do, telling yourself that, whatever your calling may be, there are everywhere sufferers in mind or body to be comforted, angry feelings to be soothed, and stricken hearts to be healed. Look at the souls of those whom you meet on your way through life, and do your best to influence these souls for good by your example. During all this active period of your existence, let your motto be always *Orare et laborare*.

Be faithful to your morning and night prayers, and to that honest examination of conscience which strengthens and controls the moral life. However absorbing your occupations may be, reserve each day a few minutes for recollection and vigorous meditation, which will renew your energy for the combat.

⚭

Nourish your soul with Holy Communion

Above all, go often to Holy Communion in a spirit of simple love and confidence, approaching our Savior without disturbance or uneasiness of mind as being the Friend able to understand and sympathize with everything, to whom you can speak of your joys and sorrows, the temptations encountered, even the doubts that He can remove, and your human interests and supernatural hopes.

Do not fancy, as some people do, that, before going to Holy Communion, you must be worthy of our Lord's visit. Such an idea is the result of a misconception of the aim and action of the Holy Eucharist. When our bodies are weak, we have recourse to the bread that restores us and the food that gives us life; let us do the same with regard to our souls. If we were saints, the same gulf would exist between God and ourselves; but since He fills it up with His love, let us go to Him as friends whom His majesty does not alarm and whom His goodness attracts.

Above all, never give up Holy Communion on account of feeling no pleasure in it. Sometimes we are delightfully aware of our

Savior's real presence, and are tempted to believe that this sweet sensation ought to recur at each Communion. This is a mistake, for if it were so, Communion would be Heaven itself, whereas it is intended only to be the way to there. The far-reaching effects of the sacrament and the life that it imparts to the soul exist even when all sensible consolation is absent. Just as food acts upon the body, so does God act upon us without our perceiving it, and our interior life grows stronger the more frequently He comes to replenish our inward store of grace, which He alone can give to nourish our souls.

Let your manhood, both in its earlier and later years, be full of strenuous work and sanctified by prayer.

Orare et laborare: once more, let me beg you to make this your motto throughout life, and especially during those years of mental and physical vigor when so much can be done to further God's interest. When these years have been wasted, it may be possible later to make good the loss, but they cannot be given back, and privileged people like you will have to render a strict account of them.

I think with emotion, my dear child, of the noble use that you will be able to make of the gifts which you have received. You are beginning life under the following circumstances: God has bestowed upon you good health and intelligence; you are well born and belong to a united family; you have an excellent father and a Christian mother; you have received very great gifts in the supernatural order: Baptism, Confirmation, and the Holy Eucharist, and also again and again various proofs of the special love of our heavenly Father for you.

Hitherto you have been able to offer Him nothing in return except a little love and good will; but now you should think seriously about what you will soon be able to do for Him, and by means of what brave exertions, good works, and sturdy piety you will become a real, true soldier of Christ, in the sense in which the words *Miles Christi* ("soldier of Christ") are inscribed on Montalembert's[147] tomb.

⤸

Your Christian life will prepare you for old age

When all the years of your childhood, youth, and manhood have been spent in accomplishing the task assigned to you by Providence; when, in accordance with your vocation, you have done God's will; when, both at home and in your professional and civil life, you have generously and scrupulously fulfilled the duties that fall to your lot; and when you have bravely practiced that self-denial without which nothing great can be effected in this world; then you will be able to enter fearlessly upon the last period of life, the darkness of old age, on which faith can cast its light and beyond which dawns eternity.

This last stage of your life will, like the other stages, need to be transformed by prayer. Your human activity will be over, or rather, will assume another form, and you will set a noble example to others, letting them benefit by your advice and by that kindly influence that an aged Christian can exert in a most effectual manner. You will pray for all men, especially for the souls for whom you are responsible to God, and in a spirit of recollection, you will prepare for your last great journey. You will sanctify your death beforehand and make this last act of life a supernatural work of salvation for yourself and others.

I cannot at this moment discuss these serious subjects at greater length; we have cast a hasty glance together over the life of a Christian. May this little book be like a signpost at the corner of a road, pointing out to travelers the right way which will not lead them astray.

---

[147] Charles René Forbes Montalembert (1810-1870), Catholic historian.

✣

May Jesus guide you always

As to the paths that will make your journey safer and more direct, I ask God to reveal them to you, and to give you our Lord Jesus Christ as your Guide, Master, and Friend on this difficult way, for without Him, we cannot overcome the obstacles that beset us. May He be near you in your struggles, temptations, and labors; may He be with you in your joys and sorrows; may He rest in your soul frequently through Holy Communion.

May He stand by you when you have to fight and suffer for His sake and resist evil in and around yourself; when you strive to be strong in the midst of degradation, chaste in an atmosphere of impurity, and good in spite of scorn and antagonism.

May He be with you during all the important stages of your life: during youth, to keep it pure and holy; during manhood, to make it fertile in good works; and during old age, to shed upon it the light that comes from Him.

Whatever your age may be, when you withdraw into yourself to examine your conscience and survey the road that you have traversed, may you be able to bear testimony before God that you have been a man of prayer and of action, that you have "fought the good fight,"[148] and struggled, toiled, and striven for the sake of God and man, and have shown yourself a good soldier of Christ.

Miles Christi: this is the prayer of one who is your spiritual mother through your baptism and in affection, who loves and blesses you as she writes the last of these pages, in which God will supply, for the welfare of your dear soul, all that she would have liked to express, although she has failed to do so.

---

[148] 2 Tim. 4:7.

※

Christian Womanhood

A good tree cannot bring forth evil fruit;
neither can an evil tree bring forth good fruit.
Every tree that bringeth not forth good fruit
shall be cut down and shall be cast into the fire.

Matthew 7:18, 19

*To my beloved only niece, my godchild by a precious and
sacred bequest, and my adopted daughter, I offer this
token of my deep and Christian affection.*[149]

My beloved child,

For a long time I intended — and the very intention was a joy
to me — to dedicate to you in a special manner the months preceding your First Communion; and to give you on that day — the
happiest and most important in your spiritual life — a little of
what God's grace has bestowed on me; and to show you what a
treasure every Christian soul bears within itself, a treasure that is
increased by our personal experiences, our sufferings, and the daily
more intimate contact with Him who is Himself the truth and the
life.

I did not form this delightful intention by myself; it was shared
by another soul, fairer and loftier than my own. Your dear godmother looked forward eagerly to this day and hoped for a complete union of our souls, when you should receive our divine Lord
for the first time.

---

[149] Elisabeth composed this treatise for her niece, Marie, at the
time of her First Communion. Juliette, before her death (five
weeks before Marie's First Communion), had asked Elisabeth
to take her place and act as godmother to the child, whom she
loved dearly.

If we are really Christians, can we say that her hopes have been disappointed, and that Providence did not grant her earnest desire?

If only we know how to withdraw for a space into the depths of our souls, where God dwells, and how to contemplate the eternal realities, as far as our weakness allows, we shall realize how much love and fulfillment of our desires is hidden in our great sorrow, which seems at first sight all the more painful because it has come upon us just before your eagerly awaited First Communion.

No, dearest, none of us will really be absent from our family gathering. What would have occurred if your godmother had been far away, stretched on a bed of sickness, will not take place now. In the fullness of her faith and love, she longed for your soul and hers to be united in God. This union will now be more complete than it could have been were she still alive. In this world, many things keep souls apart, but those who live in the one true Light are indeed near to us; they know and understand us as they never could here below, where the best and truest part of ourselves remains always hidden in the secret recesses of our being, and some profound truths cannot be expressed in human language.

As it is, during our whole lives, we shall be in touch with our dear one, whose influence will guide our consciences, strengthen our wills, and obtain for us peace and strength to do our work in the world and perform the special task assigned to each of us. Your godmother will do more for you now than if she were alive; she is, and will continue to be, your protectress, and her love for you is greater than ever in the Infinite Love in which she lives.

As for me, darling, I do not deserve the happiness that she enjoys; my life and heart have been devoted to her for months, and I have not been able to think about you. But now I want to talk to you and pass on to you some of my most precious thoughts and deepest convictions, which, by God's grace and at His instigation, are the fruit of the efforts, meditations, prayers, and work of many years. All that is good in me I owe to God alone, whose fatherly action is continuous and is so plainly visible in my life that, in spite of great trials and this recent sorrow — the greatest of all — I can still offer Him fervent thanks and must try in future to transform my soul and life to His service.

I will talk to you about your First Communion, and especially about your life as a Christian, which will follow it. I will talk about what you can and ought to do to make your character really strong, to render your existence fruitful in good works, and to hand on to others, in accordance with the great law of Christian solidarity, the gifts that you have received.

God calls us to bear good fruit in the world

In speaking of our divine Savior, St. Peter says that He went about doing good.[150] Happy are those who, at the hour when all ends and all begins, are conscious of having done a little toward diffusing light and love among their brethren and, to use an expression that your godmother liked, of having raised the level of the human race by lifting themselves to a higher point.

You are reaching the age when, in a degree that each successive year will increase, you are able to do good. You are coming to the turning point when you will make your life one of two things: either, as many people do, a vague, aimless existence, without any strong moral discipline, useless and consequently harmful (for neutrality is impossible where what is good is concerned); or else beautiful, harmonious, and purposeful, sowing good seed on the earth and preparing a rich harvest for eternity. Every human being is an incalculable force, bearing within him something of the future. To the end of time, our daily words and actions will bear fruit, either good or bad; nothing that we have once given of ourselves will perish, but our words and works, handed on from one to

[150] Acts 10:38.

another, will continue to do good or harm to remote generations. This is why life is a sacred thing, and we ought not to pass through it thoughtlessly, but to appreciate its value and use it so that, when we are gone, the sum total of good in the world may be greater.

Your First Communion is your first step on this path of well-doing, and I do not intend to say much to you about it, for others will tell you better than I could, and you will soon see for yourself what the mysterious union is between the soul and Jesus Christ. Nothing can be compared to it, and later on you will experience still more fully all the strength and joy imparted by this contact with our Lord. You will understand that all our human happiness, sorrow, and repentance are transformed in the heart of Him who alone gives pardon, consolation, and peace. Communion is, strictly speaking, a communication of life by God Himself; you will come to realize this personally, and nothing that I could say about it would be worth as much as your own experience. I will only tell you that if I have been able, without sinking under the burden, to bear the sufferings of the last few months, culminating as they have done in this agonizing loss, it is because I have derived strength from its fountainhead — namely, the Holy Eucharist and union with Jesus Christ.

After your First Communion, and when you have received the Sacrament of Confirmation, which will convey to you the light and gifts of the Holy Spirit, you will really begin life, and I want, as far as my weakness allows, to tell you what I wish this life may be to you. I hope and pray constantly that, in its human aspect, your life may be happy, and that you may enjoy all its sweetness. I hope that you will someday be a wife and mother, that you will have a husband worthy of you, as good a man as your dear father or your Uncle Felix, and that you will pass on to your grandchildren the good example and teaching that you have received. I hope you will have good health, and trust that the sufferings of your dear godmother and her prayers will obtain this precious gift for you. I hope you will live to a great age, and that, in the words of the marriage service, you will see your children's children to the fourth generation.

But I have no desire to dwell upon this purely human aspect of your life; I want to speak of the higher life of the soul, and of the effect that this inner life will have upon your own actions and those around you.

⚜

The light of faith illumines our lives

In the first place, a Christian is a human being like everyone else. Every individual is a thinking, reasoning being, illumined by that natural light which is the first degree of the divine intelligible, as you will learn later from St. Augustine.[151] This is the light that St. John says "enlighteneth every man that cometh into the world."[152] Those who know no other will be judged by God according to this light. We, too, possess it, and it leads us to the point where the light of faith begins, where, as Pascal says, "the last step taken by reason is to perceive that there are innumerable things beyond its reach." This light of faith proceeds directly from God, and forms the supernatural existence, bestowing on our actions, although they apparently resemble those of other people, an aim that others have not, and an incomparable value to ourselves and souls. As beings possessed of sense and reason, we live lives that differ in no respect from that of the other members of the human race, but there is something beyond, which is not, as too many people suppose, antagonistic to this life. There is a higher life, which sheds its radiance upon our whole individuality, transforming it, giving it motives for action, supernatural like itself, and

[151] St. Augustine (354-430), Bishop of Hippo and Doctor of the Church.
[152] John 1:9.

fashioning our outward life after the likeness of our inward existence, so as to produce a harmonious whole.

This supernatural light never casts a shadow over the human mind and intellect. It throws its rays upon them and illumines them, but at the same time, it is superior and, as it were, exterior to them. It irradiates humble as well as powerful minds, reaching their souls within them and bestowing upon them a principle of life and action, and a comprehension of suffering and death, while it reveals also the beauty and usefulness of our activity in this world, and its supernatural results.

There is no peculiarly Christian kind of learning. Learning is the same for all, whether they are believers or not; but there are Christian scholars who, using methods common to all in the sphere of science, advance beyond the sphere of sense and, by quite another method, well adapted to its object, reach those mysterious realities that constitute man in his entirety, and that he seeks to discover behind the veil hiding them from his view until the day when he will at last behold in eternity the one light of Truth.

A Christian is, therefore, in one sense complete, for his field of thought and action may be as wide as that of the greatest scholar — depending on his intellectual faculties — and at the same time, the sphere of the infinite and eternal lies open to him, revealing not merely the world of sense, the knowledge of the changes and events that take place, but also the infinitely greater and unchanging world of God and the human soul.

This is the life of faith, understood not as a passive acquiescence on the part of the mind, but as an active acceptance, a lively assimilation of truths beyond our comprehension, which constant experience, sustained and directed by grace, impresses upon us. You will possess this life, and it is now about to begin in you.

What others have received and passed on to you, as it was passed on to them, will become real and living to you. You will be a link in the long chain that Christian tradition is slowly forming and that will last to the end of time. And you will, in a greater or lesser degree, enrich the collective consciousness of Christianity by your efforts, energy, and sacrifices. Henceforward you ought to prepare yourself for this great task that is required of each of us, or at least of those who are inspired by faith. You are a Christian, and from a purely Christian point of view, your duty will present itself to you under various aspects, when you take into account the state of Christianity at the present time. Every Christian has the same aim and ideal, in every age, whichever race he belongs to, and whatever may befall him, but circumstances force him to vary his mode of action and the form of his apostolate. Just now a Christian's duty appears under a threefold aspect: intellectual, domestic, and social. I do not add its religious aspect, because the other three are only different forms of the religious duty incumbent on us all.

Dedicate yourself to truth and learning

In the society in which you will live, you will have an intellectual duty to perform, and this is more important now than ever. You ought to be a woman of real worth, well educated and with your mind open to every argument from without. You ought to know how to discover amid incoherent and varying ideas and systems what is true or useful in each. The Fathers of the Church said that each of these systems contained the soul of truth, which must never be allowed to perish.

Never be afraid of words, and always go beyond externals. In this patient search after truth, and this spirit of fairness that we ought to possess toward men and theories, we need uprightness of mind, clear judgment, and solid learning. You will gradually acquire these things, and you will do so more readily when your convictions become more based on reason.

Consequently you need a serious education; there should be nothing superficial or mean, not only in your literary and scientific studies, but also in the intellectual knowledge that you ought to have of Christ's teaching and Christianity. I am sometimes horrified to see how absolutely ignorant most women are of the religion that they profess. Its very spirit is totally unknown to them; its living and imperishable dogmas are to them a dead weight that they drag about with them; and their appalling narrowness in matters of doctrine shows how completely they fail to recognize the heart of Christ beating for them under the veil of rites and symbols. They have even lost all appreciation of our wonderful Catholic Liturgy, which forms part of our life from the cradle to the grave, and is made up of all the most beautiful utterances of humanity in every age, inspired by the Holy Spirit. They are that dreadful thing, that body devoid of a soul, which is what people call a woman who only outwardly practices her religion, but they do not possess that nobility of spirit, that interior beauty and activity of soul which every Christian woman ought to display.

Do not fancy that, when I say this, I have any desire to condemn religious practices. Nothing is farther from my intention; but pious practices ought never to be anything but the manifestation of what lies in the depths of the soul. We must first be convinced of the truth that such practices help to quicken within us; we must realize the harmony in the Church as a whole, the vitality and power of Christian dogma, and the moral and social value of Catholic doctrine. I trust, my dearest, that from the intellectual point of view, you will be a thoughtful Christian, and that you will know the reasons underlying your Faith and the grounds that you have for hope and worship. Then, when you have risen gradually to the level of all the great thoughts presented to us by Catholicism, you will bring real loftiness of mind to bear upon the outward manifestations of your piety, and you will reject all that might lead others who have no faith to suppose Christians to be queer, narrow-minded beings. St. Vincent de Paul[153] makes the following exquisite remark: "Evangelical practices ought to be no more burdensome to a Christian than wings are to a bird: both alike are means of leaving the earth and rising to Heaven."

You will do your best to increase your store of human learning; I would like you to be very well educated, or even learned. The word *learned* does not alarm me, in spite of Molière,[154] whose learned women are nothing but foolish pedants. In our generation, a learned woman can do a great deal of good.

A woman has duties toward her mind, and ought to increase the sum of her knowledge and enlarge her intellectual horizon, so as to be capable someday of playing her part as mother, and, at the same time, of taking her place in the society in which she lives, for it stands in need of light from us all, faint though it may be. When we labor for no trivial gratification, but in order to strengthen our mental powers and to let others benefit by our work, we may be sure that it will be fruitful and that God will bless it. One day, sooner or later, it will bear fruit such as we never expected. Once more, let me remind you that none of our disinterested or generous efforts is ever lost.

⚜

Devote yourself to family life

The second duty that you will have to discharge is toward your family; it is certainly not new, but so great and important that I want to speak about it again. With the Church, I believe that the whole structure of our moral, national, and social life is based on the family. And I am convinced that everything done for the sake of the family adds to the greatness and strength of nations and

---

[153] St. Vincent de Paul (c. 1580-1660), Founder of the Lazarist Fathers and the Sisters of Charity.

[154] Jean-Baptiste Poquelin Molière (1622-1673), playwright.

society, whereas, they are irretrievably destroyed as soon as family life, the cornerstone of the structure, is attacked.

You will therefore do your utmost to uphold, in every way, respect and regard for family life. Later on, when you have a family of your own, you will make your home a glowing center of influence, and will be yourself the conscience of those who live in the light that you diffuse. To your husband you will be a friend and companion, and to your children, a guide and the personification of moral strength. You will possess that precious treasure that your dear godmother and I have so often discussed, and that she preserved amid all her sufferings — namely, calm and peace of mind, which nothing can destroy, neither trials nor losses, since it is of divine origin; and God bestows it sometimes in proportion to our sufferings, giving us one of those mysterious compensations of which mankind knows nothing, and of which He alone holds the secret.

Then, and even now, in the midst of your relatives, you will make an effort daily by the help of God's grace to "possess your soul in peace,"[155] to be quiet and unruffled in your attitude toward events, people, and life itself. Sometimes to be able to smile requires true heroism; may your smile, whether thoughtful or merry, always do good. You will meet many human beings on your way, but go by preference to the weakest, the most embittered and most abandoned, and whatever may be your trials and sorrows, you should know how to rejoice with those who rejoice, and to share in the happiness of others.

⚹

Love all souls

There is also a duty toward society which every Christian woman has to discharge. And as your education will give you real

---

[155] Cf. Luke 21:19.

worth, you ought to exert yourself to the utmost in order to improve the material and moral condition of others, and especially of the masses which, although robbed of their birthright and often led astray, are nevertheless still sound at heart, and are the reserve force of the nation and of the Church.

You see, we must never forget the tender words uttered one day by our divine Lord on seeing the crowd assembled around Him: "I have pity on the multitude."[156] Like Him, let us have pity, and love these people who are deprived of so many material advantages and, above all, of the Supreme Good which alone could make their sacrifices and hard daily work meritorious — namely, the knowledge and love of God and of the things of eternity. Let us go to them as brethren, not as superiors or benefactors, and show them that real equality is found only in the doctrines of Christianity, which recognizes in all men souls of similar nature, assigns to them the same end, and promises them the same happiness. Let us prove that the Church alone carries out the ideal of fraternity and imposes it as a law upon Her children, and that She alone, in accordance with our Savior's words, secures for us true liberty: "You shall know the truth, and the truth will make you free."[157]

In a greater degree later on, but soon, to the extent that your parents think advisable, you will be able to share in the social activity that is being shown in all directions, choosing always such works as are the outcome of the highest and most practical aims. In working with others, you should display plenty of adaptability, devotion, and energy, a sense of the need of discipline, and very little self-assertiveness. Never be one of those who desire to take the lead and not to be members of the rank and file, who would like to devise good works for themselves alone, and never acknowledge as good anything that is not done in their particular

[156] Cf. Matt. 15:32; Mark 8:2.
[157] John 8:32.

way and according to their own methods. Here, as elsewhere, you should have a broad mind and generous heart; put up with the contradictions and difficulties that are the price of success; toil day by day without being too eager to see results, but sure that God will make something of your efforts.

Remember, however, that if you are to concern yourself profitably with the important questions of the present day, during the period of transition through which we are passing, if you are to labor to bring about a new order of Christian society, you must prepare yourself by making a serious study of these direct problems, and you must bring to bear upon any attempt at their solution very great prudence, together with the courage that befits a Christian. Catholics are not afraid of democracy; they know that the Church baptized, transformed, and civilized barbarous nations, and that the masses of our people still retain a rudimentary germ of Christianity, capable of growing and developing into a tree with spreading branches. Catholics love these souls, and long to make them Christian. Even if they should render themselves liable to be regarded as socialists or revolutionaries by their embittered opponents, they would continue their work of social progress, saying to themselves that, after all, they may be satisfied to be socialists in the company of St. Thomas Aquinas, or revolutionaries with the Fathers of the Church, and that people who do nothing at all are the only ones who can hope to avoid having unpleasant epithets attached to their names. At this cost, what Catholic worthy of the name would be anxious to avoid them?

⚘

Face suffering and death with courage

You and I are at this moment casting a very rapid glance over Christian life as a whole. Our survey would be altogether incomplete were I not to mention two solemn and holy things, which it would be painful to contemplate if a gleam of divine light did not illumine them. I mean suffering and death: one is the path leading to a higher life; the other is the gate giving admission to the only true life.

I assure you that, in the case of a true Christian soul, the anticipation of suffering and the thought of death will never cast too deep a shadow upon life. The bravest people, who, with stout hearts, face struggles, losses, and trials; who can meet death with a smile, and make it for themselves and others a supreme offering — they are those who once for all have grasped the fact that suffering is closely intermingled with life, is part of God's law and productive of redemption and sanctification, while death destroys nothing but pain. They rest in the belief that God alone is beauty, truth, and love, and that death is the road leading to Him and, in Him, to fullness of happiness and life. They know, too, that in Him we shall meet, never to lose them again, those dear ones whom He has called away before us.

Like everyone else in the world, a Christian suffers, but he does not suffer like others "who have no hope."[158] Our hopes are great and glorious, my darling, and, over and above the happiness which our trials prepare for us, we have the Catholic dogma of the Communion of Saints that helps us to bear them.

About this dogma I will only tell you what I told you about the Holy Eucharist: that you will not understand it until you have, so to say, experienced it in life. It brings about a sweet communion and mysterious interchange of prayers and merits among all God's children: those who have already received their reward, those who are still undergoing purification, and those who are fighting here below. Our sacrifices, actions, and efforts, when they have a supernatural aim, possess a purifying and sanctifying force that we can use for the good of our brethren, living and dead. It is indescribably sweet and consoling to feel that, when we weep, our tears may

[158] 1 Thess. 4:12.

be bringing peace or conversion to some beloved or distant soul, and that we are not suffering or acting for ourselves alone; for this, as your godmother used to say, would not be enough. She suffered a great deal, and offered up many of her sufferings for you. Only in eternity, when all secrets are made known, shall we learn all that she thus obtained for you, and by what trials faith, a Christian life, and perhaps also those human joys that she never tasted, were won for you.

We shall all die, but, as you are a Christian, you will not fear death, and you will remember that the best way to prepare for it is to live and act in the manner befitting a Christian. Tell yourself that death is the child's return to his Father, the creature's return to its God, and that only through death shall we ever possess the happiness and enjoy the realities of the world to come, for the affection and joy of this life only foreshadow what shall be hereafter.

Turn to these words for inspiration and consolation
Circumstances force me to cut short this little treatise, and at the present time, you will understand very little of it. When it has once been read aloud to you, you will put it aside and make haste to forget it. With your soul transformed by our Savior's first visit, you will go back to your work and play, and your daily occupations, and my poor little manuscript will lie forgotten in some corner. But as the years pass and you grow up, and also later in life, in times of joy or sorrow, or when you need some special inspiration, you will, I hope, take up my poor little book again. It has no outward merit, but you will find in it the trace and reflection, as it were, of a heart that loves you. You will feel yourself encircled by my affection, and, if God allows it, a little of what my soul contains will pass into yours.

Then, if you feel consoled and strengthened; if, after reading this book, you have greater love for your human brethren and can make a more earnest act of faith and love, then, whether I am still in this world or in everlasting bliss (provided that I attain to it), I shall be able to raise a song of thanksgiving and say with boundless gratitude: "O Lord, Thou hast tried me by suffering; Thou hast withheld or withdrawn from me many of the joys of earth, but Thou hast compensated me a hundredfold, inasmuch as Thou hast revealed to me, in addition to Thy love, the sweetness of human affections, and hast allowed me to do a little good to the child whom I loved so much, and whom our Juliette had, in a way, entrusted to my care before returning to Thee."

�֍

Biographical Note

❦

Elisabeth Leseur
(1866-1914)
Felix Leseur
(1861-1950)

Elisabeth Arrighi was born in Paris in 1866 to an affluent family of successful lawyers and civil servants who were representative of the French *haute-bourgeoisie* of the time. Elisabeth was educated privately into her late teens, receiving excellent training in languages, literature, and the fine arts, interests that would remain with her throughout her life. Her religious formation was typical of the conventional Catholic practice of her social class.

At the age of twenty, Elisabeth made the acquaintance of Felix Leseur, a wealthy twenty-five-year-old from Rheims, who was completing his medical studies in Paris in the hope that it would enable him to enter the civil service in one of France's colonies in Africa or Indochina.

After a two-year courtship, Elisabeth and Felix were married in Paris in July 1889. Despite Elisabeth's delicate health (due to an intestinal abscess that never fully healed), the young couple kept up a lively schedule of travel, entertaining, and cultural activities in the glittering French capital. Until 1894, Felix worked as a journalist with a special interest in political and colonial affairs.

Afterward, when it became clear that Elisabeth's health could not withstand the rigors of foreign climates, Felix became a director at a large insurance company.

The early years of Felix and Elisabeth's marriage were very happy. By the mid-1890s, however, their religious differences began to create tension between the young husband and wife. Like Elisabeth, Felix had been brought up and educated as a Catholic, but he had lost his faith during his medical studies.

When they married, Felix had agreed to respect Elisabeth's desire to continue her practice of Catholicism. Before long, however, he began to try to erode and even destroy her faith. He teased her constantly about her piety, made her read anti-Catholic literature, and created all manner of petty obstacles to her practice of her religion, even going so far as to insist that they serve guests meat on Fridays in violation of the fast laws then observed.

Worn down by Felix's continued efforts and the worldly secular circles in which they then socialized, Elisabeth abandoned her practice of Catholicism by 1898. In the summer of that year, however, reading the heretical *Life of Jesus* by Ernest Renan triggered in Elisabeth a profound conversion. She returned to the Faith and immersed herself in the Bible and other Christian literature, adopting a regular program of prayer, meditation, and sacramental participation to which she remained faithful for the rest of her life. Elisabeth's *Journal* (originally published as *Journal et pensées de chaque jour*) is the record of her interior life in the years following her return to the Faith.

Despite her spiritual alienation from Felix, which caused her tremendous pain, Elisabeth strove to fulfill her duties as a wife and never ceased to pray and offer sacrifices for Felix's conversion. In the years following 1898, Felix and Elisabeth continued to travel widely; they built a summer home in the French countryside and participated fully in the joys and sorrows of their large extended family, which included parents, siblings, a niece, and several nephews. One terrible loss experienced during these years was the death of Elisabeth's younger sister Juliette in 1905 from tuberculosis at the age of only thirty-two.

Between 1907 and 1908, Elisabeth's health began to decline. Liver trouble, perhaps related to the unhealed intestinal abscess, began to plague her more and more, requiring her to give up travel and spend long hours resting in bed. Nevertheless, Elisabeth continued to write short treatises and letters on the interior life, and to give spiritual direction to the many different sorts of people who came to her for advice and consolation.

In April 1911, Elisabeth was operated on to remove a malignant growth on one of her breasts. After surgery and radiation treatment, she was well for a few years, but the cancer recurred in the late winter of 1913 and spread throughout her body. Elisabeth Leseur died in the arms of her beloved husband, Felix, on May 3, 1914.

Felix's hostility to Catholicism had softened in the last years of Elisabeth's life, when he saw how much comfort and strength it brought her in her suffering. After her death, Felix found her journal, read it, and learned that Elisabeth had offered all of her many trials for his salvation.

Inspired by her example and moved by her prayers for him, Felix returned to the Faith in 1915, and shortly thereafter decided to enter religious life, as Elisabeth had predicted some years before her death. Felix entered the Dominican order in 1919, and was ordained to the priesthood in 1923.

Encouraged by all to whom he showed it, Felix published Elisabeth's spiritual diary in 1917. By 1930, it had sold 100,000 copies and had been translated into every major European language. From 1924 until the early 1940s, Felix traveled all over Europe speaking to audiences eager to learn about Elisabeth's apostolate of prayer and accepted suffering. He published three other collections of Elisabeth's writings — *The Letters on Suffering, The Letters to Unbelievers*, and *The Spiritual Life*, whose contents are included in *The Secret Diary of Elisabeth Leseur* — and a full-length biography of Elisabeth. Those convinced of Elisabeth's sanctity and intercessory power convinced Felix by 1934 to open the process for her beatification; this process occupied him until his health began to fail in 1942.

Felix Leseur died in February 1950. Elisabeth's cause for beatification, which had been halted by Felix's poor health and by the disruptions of World War II, was reopened in Rome in 1990.